Sermons Forged In

The Fire

For Busy Pastors

By

Terry Sisney

Terry Sisney

Table Of Contents

Chapter

About The Author

Other Books By Author

Terry Sisney

Sermons Forged In The Fire
For Busy Pastors

Copyright © 2019 Terry Sisney

Purchase books through: Amazon

Publication date: December 1 2019

Language: English

Kindle Direct Publishing

Independent Publishing Platform

Printed In The United States of America

ISBN-9781713325635

Sermons Forged In The Fire

For Busy Pastors

1
I Shall Not Be Moved

Psalm 1:1-3 KJV "Blessed is the man that walketh not in the counsel of the ungodly, nor standeth in the way of sinners, nor sitteth in the seat of the scornful. But his delight is in the law of the Lord; and in his law doth he meditate day and night. And he shall be like a tree planted by the rivers of water, that bringeth forth his fruit in his season; his leaf also shall not wither; and whatsoever he doeth shall prosper."

Psalm 16:8 KJV "I have set the Lord always before me: because he is at my right hand, I shall not be moved."

Psalm 62:5-6 KJV "My soul, wait thou only upon God; for my expectation is from him. He only is my rock and my salvation: he is my defense; I shall not be moved."

Proverbs 12:3 KJV "A man shall not be established by wickedness: but the root of the righteous shall not be moved."

Psalm 92:12-14 KJV "The righteous shall flourish like the palm tree: he shall grow like a cedar in Lebanon. Those that be planted in the house of the Lord shall flourish in the courts of our God. They shall still bring forth fruit in old age; they shall be fat and flourishing;"

It has long been a sort of a long standing joke within the church to talk about people who are stuck, stuck in the past, stuck in their traditions, stuck in the old ways of doing things. And we often joke about it and make fun of them and criticize them, and we apply the song to them... I shall not be moved.

And the truth is there are a lot of people that are stuck, and refuse to be moved. And the problem comes in when a person is planted in their own way of doing things, or the old way of doing things, and they reject the new and the better, and the greater, to hold on to the old.

This is the person who is satisfied with themselves and with everything around them, and they have no desire, and no motivation for change or for progress.

These people usually are not only satisfied to stay like they are, where they are, but they also fight the possibility and opportunity for change and progress to come to anyone around them.

They are like an old house in the middle of a construction zone for a freeway. "They demand that the freeway not come at all, or if it does come, it must go around them."

I've known a good many of those people in over thirty-five years of ministry. But if the truth be told, I know that to some degree, more or less, I have been that person.

I have resisted change just like so many others. But the truth is... there is no growth without change, there is no progress without change.

But all change is not good change. Change is not our incentive and motivation. Our incentive and motivation for change is progress... advancement, greater influence, more of the glory and the power of God, and to be a truer representation of Jesus.

So what am I saying? I am saying that while we're joking about those who stubbornly resist change, and dig in their heels against all progress...

There is a flip side to that. These scriptures I have shared with you today speak of being planted... rooted, grounded, established.

● Trees don't have wheels, because they need to be planted, they need to be able to put down roots in good soil, and get the stability and the nutrients from the soil they're planted in.

"A tree that is not planted will not grow right."

● Trees belong in an established place. Trees become established by being in an established place.

If I weren't pastoring, I would immediately search to find the soil I need to be in, and plant myself under a pastor and begin to support that pastor and that body with my presence, my tithes, and my prayers.

- A true church is not built on its entertainment value; it's built on its ability to grow people up in God.

I'm going back to our first scripture; I want us to see from the Bible what a planted man or woman of God looks like.

Psalm 1:1-3 KJV "Blessed is the man that ...

1. Doesn't walk in the counsel of the ungodly.
2. Doesn't stand in the way of sinners.
3. Doesn't sit in the seat of the scornful.
4. His delight is in the law of the Lord.
5. In his law doth he meditate day and night.

And the result is...

He shall be like a tree planted by the rivers of water,

- He will bring forth his fruit in his season.
- His leaf also shall not wither.
- Whatsoever he doeth shall prosper.

This is what David was talking about when he said, "I shall not be moved."

➤ I am persuaded
➤ I am established
➤ I have a root system
➤ I am connected
➤ I have a connection with the soil
➤ I am a producer.
➤ I bear fruit.

And then it means... Because I am planted, and because I have roots that run deep. I am not shaken. I am not fearful and fretful. I am not blown around anywhere and everywhere. I know what I believe. I live by what I believe. I am persuaded, I shall not be moved.

Let's declare this together, I shall not be moved.

Just recently we had a very well known minister who publicly renounced something he had been preaching and teaching for many years.

It was shocking. He said the Holy Spirit convicted him.

But I thought, that's ok, everybody has to be persuaded in their own heart and mind about what they believe and why.

But here is what bothered me. He didn't just renounce his own beliefs and practices; he criticized any one who continues to live according to what he had been teaching and preaching for 40 years or more. Well this is the way I see it...

It's ok if you get more light on a subject than me, but don't criticize me because I haven't got there yet. If you really have more light than me, walk in it and show me how much better it is, so I'll be willing to let go of the lesser for the greater.

This is why I'm sharing this word with you today. Every single member of the body of Christ needs to be planted, and established, not just in a church, but in their faith.

You must believe what you believe because you found it for yourself. You must have roots that are wrapped around the Word of God. You must be <u>persuaded.</u>

Persuaded means convince, win over, to believe and have faith in., and to rely on by inward certainty.

I love this man of God, and he has had a great impact on my life, but I am not casting away my confidence in the principles of Gods Word that I have found through my personal study.

I am planted, my roots go down deep, I am persuaded, I shall not be moved.

"Let every man be fully persuaded in his own mind" Ro 14:5b

➤ If you don't believe in speaking in other tongues, that's fine, that's up to you, but don't attack me because I do.

➤ If you don't believe in miracles, that's fine too, but don't attack me because I do.

➤ If you don't believe in sowing your seed to get a desired harvest, that's fine, that's up to you, but don't attack me because I do.

➤ If you don't believe that God can deliver the demon possessed and oppressed, that's up to you, but don't attack me because I do believe it.

Pastor why are you saying these things? My friends, the reason I'm saying these things is because the winds of adversity and opposition, and criticism are blowing strong in this nation, and you are going to have to be planted.

Every kind of false doctrine is blowing through the land today, and multitudes of people are being swept away by them.

You need your roots to go down deep and take hold of the pure unadulterated word of God. You need to know what you believe, and you need to be fully persuaded, fully convinced, or you will be deceived.

Eph 4:14 KJV "That we henceforth be no more children, tossed to and fro, and carried about with every wind of doctrine, by the sleight of men, and cunning craftiness, whereby they lie in wait to deceive."

Precious friends, Whatever this man of God's reasons are for his change of position concerning the Word of God are, it tells me something very important...

It is saying to me... If this man who has been preaching the gospel for 40 years could feel like he was missing it, and misrepresenting the gospel, then...

1. We need to be planted more than ever before.
2. We need to be sure of the soil we're planted in.
3. We need to be faithful to the place God has planted us.

I want to be like Paul the Apostle who said...

2 Timothy 1:12 KJV "For the which cause I also suffer these things: nevertheless I am not ashamed: for I know whom I have believed, and am persuaded that he is able to keep that which I have committed unto him against that day."

I am not criticizing today, I know that we can be distracted and we can get off track, and get distracted from the main thing, and sometimes we have to get recalibrated by the Word of God.

But what I feel stirred about today is this, how many people will readjust their belief system because of one mans words?

Dear friends, my responsibility as a pastor is to lead you to faith in Christ, not faith in my faith.

Precious friends,
- I cannot be your Bible.
- I cannot be your conscience.
- I cannot be the conviction of the Holy Spirit in your life.

Do you pray?
Do you read your Bible?
Do you spend time worshipping God?
Do you study so you can have your own foundation for your faith?
This is going to sound a little gross but to expect me as a pastor, or anyone else to supply all your spiritual food and nourishment, is like ordering a big thick steak and expecting me to chew it up for you.
You're supposed to grow your own teeth.
"I shall not be moved, why?"
Because I have put down roots.
Because I am planted.
Because I have an established place.
Because I have a connection with the soil, I shall not be moved.

Colossians 2:6-8 TLB "And now just as you trusted Christ to save you, trust him, too, for each day's problems; live in vital union with him. Let your roots grow down into him and draw up nourishment from him. See that you go on growing in the Lord, and become strong and vigorous in the truth you were taught. Let your lives overflow with joy and thanksgiving for all he has done. Don't let others spoil your faith and joy with their philosophies, their wrong and shallow answers built on men's thoughts and ideas, instead of on what Christ has said."
Let me close with this one last portion of scripture.
Psalm 46:1-5 God is our refuge and strength, a very present help in trouble. Therefore will not we fear, though the earth be removed, and though the mountains be carried into the midst of the sea; Though the waters thereof roar and be troubled, though the mountains shake with the swelling thereof. Selah. There is a

river, the streams whereof shall make glad the city of God, the holy place of the tabernacles of the most High. [5] God is in the midst of her; <u>she shall not be moved</u>: God shall help her, and that right early.

2
The Light Shineth

I have a word today and I really believe that it's from God, I felt like the Holy Spirit is wanting to confirm and reaffirm to our hearts today, that no matter what it looks like, sounds like, or feels like, he is at work in the earth.
God is still moving.
God is still saving.
God is still healing.
God is still delivering.
God is still working miracles, signs and wonders.

Now I know l would be foolish to act and talk, and pretend like everything is wonderful, and that it's a beautiful day in the neighborhood, and that we have no problems, and that our country is doing fine.
That would be ridiculous, because the truth is, our country is in a mess. The truth is, there is a great darkness that is coming upon the land.

The truth is, people are becoming increasingly more evil and wicked.
But that shouldn't be a big shock to us if we read our Bibles.
The Bible says...

"Arise shine, for thy light is come, and the glory of the Lord is risen upon thee. For behold the darkness shall cover the earth, and gross darkness the people: but the Lord shall arise upon thee, and his glory shall be seen upon thee. And the Gentiles shall come to the thy light, and kings to the brightness of thy rising." Isaiah 60:1-3

So the Bible is very clear that two things are happening at the same time, "there is darkness and there is light."

But that has always been true, that's not anything new.

The portion of Scripture the Holy Spirit brought to my heart was this...

"In the beginning was the word, and the Word was with God, and the Word was God. The same was in the beginning with God. All things were made by him; and without him was not anything made that was made. In him was life; and the life was the light of men. And the light shineth in darkness; and the darkness comprehended it not."John 1:1-3

Verse five says; and the light shineth in darkness and the darkness comprehended it not.

So let me zero in there for a minute,

"The light shineth" that word shineth, is in the present tense: that means it is happening now.

That means it happened then, it's happening now, and it's going to continue to happen. It is an action word.

"The light shineth"

The light shone.

The light is shining.

The light will continue to shine.

I feel this is what the Holy Spirit wants to bring to our attention today, because it is so easy to become engrossed, overwhelmed and discouraged by the darkness.

*The Bible does not say darkness is not present. *The Bible does not say that darkness does not exist. *The Bible does not say that evil is not present, or that evil is not active in the earth.

As a matter of fact the Bible is very clear on the fact that we have an adversary. Be sober, be vigilant for your adversary the devil goes about like a roaring lion, seeking whom he may devour.

The Apostle Paul tells us that we are at war with principalities and powers, rulers of darkness, and spiritual wickedness in high places.

And Jesus tells us that the thief comes to steal, kill, and to destroy.

The battle is real, our enemy is real.

The Bible does not try to minimize the fact that there is darkness.
The Bible does not teach us to ignore the darkness and it will have no affect on us.

The truth is, the Bible teaches us that there is darkness and the darkness is very active, and the darkness is very heavy and oppressive.

In Isaiah 60, the prophet said, darkness shall cover the earth, and gross darkness the people.

The word gross can be defined as thick and dense, and unseemly, shameful, heavy, oppressive, and degenerate.

How many know that, that Scripture is being fulfilled right now.
Darkness is covering the earth, and Gross darkness is covering the people.

The prophet Isaiah said...

"Woe unto them that call evil good, and good evil; that put darkness for light, and light for darkness; that put bitter for sweet, and sweet for bitter!" Isaiah 5:20

Isaiah said there is a people who will pull their sin along with a rope like a cart.

"Woe unto them that draw iniquity with cords of vanity, and sin as it were with a cart rope:" Isaiah 5:18

I really don't take any pleasure at all in talking about the darkness, the evil and the perverseness that is rampant in the world today, but the Bible says it.

*The Bible says it so we will not be deceived.
*The Bible says it so that we will be alert and aware of the presence of darkness and evil.

*The Bible says it, so that we will recognize the contrast between darkness and light, between good and evil.

1. Arise
2. Shine
3. Thy light is come
4. The glory of the Lord is risen upon thee.

Yes there is darkness, but it's no big deal. The big deal is, your light is come, and the glory of the Lord will be seen upon thee.

Literally, there will be such radiance about you that the lost, the Gentiles, and even the kings of the Gentiles, will come to the brightness of thy rising.

"We are saved to shine, not whimper and whine."

I think it is very easy for us to become overwhelmed by the darkness, but when I read Isaiah chapter 60 only one verse even speaks about darkness, that is verse two.

Verse one, and from verse three on, is speaking about the glory of God, and the effect, and the influence, and the impact of the glory of God through the children of God.

I read this chapter over and over, before it hit me... this is not about darkness, this is about light, and the glory of God.

The word the Holy Spirit spoke to my heart for you today was just three words. The light shineth.

The light shineth.

The light shineth.

Praise God, if I didn't say anything else in the rest of this book that would be enough to drive away depression and discouragement, and hopelessness.

The light shineth.

Who is the light? Well of course, first of all the light is Jesus.

John said that Jesus is the light of the world.

John said Jesus came to the world as a light into the darkness.

You see, darkness was present when Jesus got here. Jesus came into the darkness.

(Jesus invaded the darkness)

Darkness represents everything that is evil, and perverse, and deceptive, and destructive.

Darkness represents everything that we typically try to avoid.

The only people that really like <u>darkness</u> are the people whose deeds are evil.

The Bible says,

"And this is the condemnation, that light is come into the world, <u>and men loved darkness</u> rather than light, because their deeds were evil." John 3:19

*Jesus came to a dark world.

*He came to a hostile environment.

He came to a planet that was under the dominion, and oppression of the kingdom of darkness that was holding the entire human race in the captivity of darkness. The devil was abusing and oppressing the whole human race.

So here we see this picture of a world in darkness. For   400 years there had been no word, no voice of God.

It was as though God said: Ok I see your self-will and rebellion.

I see that you don't want to hear my voice, so I'll quit talking.

So he did.

For 400 years God didn't say anything to anybody.

"No prophets were speaking."

The world became a very dark place.

Can you imagine what condition our country and our world would be in if God stopped talking for even 50 years?

For 400 years Prophets had lockjaw, they had nothing to say because God wasn't talking.

Then John says this: "The Light" not a light, not a reflection, but "The Light" shineth in darkness.

Let me say it this way,

The Light, penetrated, and invaded the darkness.

The light didn't come to mingle with the darkness, or co-exist together. The light   came to displace, replace, and obliterate the darkness.

As I said... Darkness symbolizes everything evil, and wicked, and perverse, and destructive.
Every sickness.
Every disease.
Every mental disorder.
Every emotional disorder.
Every thief.
Every liar.
Every fornicator.
Every pedophile, and every child molester.

Every evil, rebellious action falls under the category of darkness. And the Bible says, the light shineth in darkness and the darkness comprehended it not.
One definition of the word "comprehend" means, to understand.
But another definition comes from the greek word "katallambano" and means to seize, and to lay hold of, to over-come, to capture, to overtake.
So John is saying, yes there was darkness, there is darkness, but the darkness never-has and never will be able to take hold of or capture, or overtake the light.
I don't care what that darkness is today... I have been instructed to declare to you; "the light shineth."
The light shineth... and the darkness never has and never will, comprehend, or apprehend, or overtake the light.
Yes, first of all we are speaking of Jesus, but now the narrative shifts, and now it's Jesus talking,
And Jesus is talking about us, and he says...
*Ye are the salt of the earth.
*Ye are the light of the world; a city that is set on a hill cannot be hid.
Now I want to take you back to Isaiah chapter 60.
Yes there is darkness, and gross darkness has fallen upon the people. But listen to these words...
This is the passion translation; it says in verses 2-7

Look carefully! Darkness blankets the earth, and thick gloom covers the nations, but Yahweh arises upon you and the brightness of his glory appears over you! [3] Nations will be attracted to your radiant light and kings to the sunrise-glory of your new day. [4] Lift up your eyes higher! Look all around you and believe, for your sons are returning from far away and your daughters are being tenderly carried home. Watch as they all gather together, eager to come back to you! [5] "Then you will understand and be radiant. Your heart will be thrilled and swell with joy. The fullness of the sea will flow to you and the wealth of the nations will be transferred to you! [6] Caravans of camels will cover your land, young camels loaded with goods from Midian and Ephah. All the wealthy merchants from Sheba will come, bearing gold and frankincense and singing the praises of Yahweh! [7] All the flocks of Kedar will be gathered to you, and the rams of Nebaioth will be yours as acceptable sacrifices on my altar, and I will adorn with more glory my glorious temple.

That's what the Holy Spirit said to prophesy to you today...

Because the light shineth, and because you have not com-promised, and because you have not let cultural

relativity, or desire for popularity or position taint your   message, and you have not put your light under a bushel.

The Holy Spirit says, get ready, get ready, get ready. You say … what for? For verses 3-7 to start manifesting in your lives.

These verses are a prophecy to any people who refuse to compro-mise and will let the light shine.

"The light shineth" Precious friends, I declare to you, the light is always shining somewhere, (no not everywhere, there are dark places on this earth,) but anywhere the light shineth, the darkness leaveth.

While Jesus was in the world, he was the light of the world, now it is our responsibility to let the light shine and drive out the darkness.

Finally, let me show you something that is happening at the same time darkness is coming upon the earth.

(God is blessing his people)
Look at verse 17, "For brass I will bring gold, and for iron I will bring silver, and for wood brass, and for stones iron: I will also make thy officers peace, and thine exactors righteousness."

Note that whatever level you are on there is upgrade. There is increase. There's higher, there's better. From glory to glory.
Now prophesy over yourself… I'm ready for an upgrade. I'm being upgraded.
Now prophesy upgrade, increase, (new level,) and greater glory.
New level of anointing.
New level of influence.
New level of prosperity.
New level of authority.
New level of power.
New level of peace.
New level of joy.
I feel it right now. The anointing of upgrade is flowing; receive it now in Jesus name.
So in conclusion dear reader, while most of the Christian community is distracted by the darkness, (The light shineth).
And wherever this light shines, the glory of God is revealed.

3
Back To Bethel

I'm not going to take the time to read it here, but for your own personal benefit you can read these scriptures, they will help you to really grasp what I'm going to share with you. Genesis 28:10-22

As I was praying waiting on the Lord I heard a word come up in my spirit.

The word is this "Back to Bethel."

Of course I have preached on this before so I knew what he was talking about.

All this week I've had my ear tuned to heaven to hear what the Holy Spirit has to say to his people.

Many times it seems that he speaks to me in relation to what's happening in the world, current affairs etc. So I was really listening to see if he had something to say to us about the deception, hate, and corruption that is happening in our world, and in particular, the United States of America.

In actual fact I was a little surprised when I heard him speak 3 words. "Back To Bethel."

I heard the Holy Spirit say to me, it's time to go back to Bethel.

I knew the Holy Spirit was speaking to me about the place where Jacob had his open heaven encounter with God.

But I think we need to ask some questions about Bethel.

What is the significance of Bethel?

What does Bethel mean to me?

Why do I need to go back to Bethel?

What happened at Bethel?

First of all, Bethel is where Jacob spent the night when he was running for his life, after cheating his brother out of his birthright.

- As I said, Bethel is where Jacob had his open heaven encounter with God.
- Bethel is where Jacob vowed to serve God and honor him with his tithes.
- Bethel was the place where Jacob landed when he was running from his brother Esau.
- Bethel was a place of weakness. In other words it was a place where Jacob's weakness was exposed.
- Bethel is the place where Jacob made a pillar of stones and poured oil on it and declared the place to be the gate of heaven.
- Bethel is where Jacob had a personal experience and encounter with God.

I know this word today won't speak to everybody right now because some of you hopefully are really walking closer to God than ever in your whole life right?

But here is the reality of it today…

It doesn't matter who you are, or how close you have walked with God, or how anointed you are or have been.

- We have a tendency to begin to pick up stuff as we go along.
- We have a tendency to get lazy, to get sloppy.
- We have a tendency to become halfhearted about our relationship with God.
- We have a tendency to become independent and self-sufficient.
- We have a tendency to drift off course.
- We have a tendency to think we don't need to pray like we used to, and we don't need to read and study the Bible like we used to.

It happens to us all… That's why from time to time, the Holy Spirit will speak to us, if we will listen, and he will say, it's time to go back to Bethel.

Yes we are always talking about going forward; the DNA of God is forward. But sometimes to go forward you have to go back.

In other words you have to go back...

- ➢ Back to your first love.
- ➢ Back to the place where you needed God.
- ➢ Back to the place where you had a personal experience with God.
- ➢ Back to the place where you were hungry for God.
- ➢ Back to the place and time where the most important thing in your life was your relationship with God.
- ◆ Bethel is a place of stripping off all the excess.
- ◆ Bethel is a place of returning to our first love.
- ◆ Bethel is a place of getting rid of all the useless junk that we have accumulated.
- ◆ Bethel is the place where we lay aside every weight and the sin that doth so easily beset us and run with patience the race that is set before us.

Jacob came to Bethel the first time as he was running from his brother Esau. Jacob was running in fear.

Jacob was running away.

At this time, Jacob basically had nothing but the clothes on his back. But years later as Jacob trusted God and followed God, God blessed and God prospered Jacob.

- ➢ Jacob had increased
- ➢ Jacob had grown wealthy.
- ➢ Jacob is not alone anymore.
- ➢ Jacob had a large family.
- ➢ Jacob had many descendants.
- ➢ Jacob had herds and flocks.
- ➢ Jacob had servants.

But true to human nature, even though God had blessed and prospered him, Jacob had drifted off course.

Not only had Jacob drifted off course, but everyone in his family, and every one of his descendants had drifted off course too. What I mean is, they had began to accumulate the world's junk.

They had begun to mingle with the spirit and with the culture of the world.

They had become comfortable with other gods.

25

Their hearts had grown cold and indifferent toward God.
But aren't you glad for the love and mercy of God?
He could have just let them fall right off the Cliff.
He could have let them self-destruct.
But He didn't, and He doesn't, He sends us warnings. He puts up roadblocks.
One of the most powerful messages I ever heard was titled, 7 roadblocks on the road to hell.
In other words, God makes it very hard for someone to go to hell.
If you go to hell you will have to climb over these 7 Roadblocks.

- The Word Of God.
- The mercy of God.
- The blood of Jesus.
- The witness of the saints.
- The conviction of the Holy Spirit.
- Your mother's prayers, the prayers of the saints.
- The preachers messages.

God saw Jacob getting off course and he sent him a message... Go back to Bethel.
Genesis 35:1-7
And God said unto Jacob, arise, go up to Bethel, and dwell there: and make there an altar unto God, that appeared unto thee when thou fleddest from the face of Esau thy brother. Then Jacob said unto his household, and to all that were with him, put away the strange gods that are among you, and be clean, and change your garments. And let us arise and go up to Bethel, and I will make there an altar unto God, who answered me in the day of <u>my distress</u>, and was with me in the way which I went. And they gave unto Jacob all the strange gods which were in their hands, and all their earrings which were in their ears, and Jacob hid them under the oak which is by Shechem. And they journeyed, and the terror of God was upon the cities that were around about them, and they did not pursue after the sons of Jacob. So Jacob came to Luz, which is in the land of Canaan, that is, Bethel, he and all the people that were with him. And he built there an altar, and called

the place El Bethel, because there God appeared unto him, when he fled from the face of his brother.

- This is what I felt the Holy Spirit saying to me. While it is definitely important what is happening to our country, his primary focus, and his primary concern is not the Whitehouse, it's his house.

In other words, it's not the politicians that the Holy Spirit is concentrating on right now, it's the Christians.

Primarily and most critically, it's the Christians who have drifted away from God. You can go to church every Sunday, pay your tithes, sing in the choir, and still be far from God.

I feel in my spirit today that I am feeling the heart of God. I believe that many are being distracted from their relationship with God, and they are drifting off course.

Notice that these were Jacob's family, Jacob's descendents, and Jacob's servants... Jacob the man who had an open heaven encounter with God.

Jacob the man who had wrestled with an angel and had his name changed.

Jacob had drifted from God. Jacob's godly influence had faded away till now his family and his servants were worshipping other Gods.

It seems almost impossible. How can it be possible that this great man of God who had experienced such a powerful supernatural divine encounter, could drift so far from God.

It tells me... the same thing can happen to anyone of us. If you and I do not stay in pursuit of God, we can grow cold and before you know it, you have let your heart be captured by other Gods.

Your children become more important than God.

Your Job becomes more important.

Your reputation becomes more important.

Your comfort and your complacency becomes more important than God.

What do you do? You follow the same path that Jacob took, you make your way back to Bethel.

Today, this book can be a Bethel for you. It can be the very instrument that God is using to bring you home. To bring you back to a right relationship with Him.

I know this word is for me. I know God is calling me back to Bethel.

I know it's not an easy trip back to Bethel. But I know, it will be worth it.

4
We've Got This

I've lived long enough to know that life isn't always fair. And I've lived long enough to see that bad things happen to good people, and that sometimes you can get beat up and beat down by life.

You can be going along one day and everything is amazing, then all of a sudden the bottom falls out and you're in the worst storm of your life.

But I have a word for you today, "We've got this." Whether you're on the highest mountain, or in the deepest darkest valley, we've got this.

Whether you've just killed the biggest giant of your life, or you're walking through the greatest fire of your life. "We've got this."

Somebody needs to hear this word today.

No not everybody is going through the fire today, not everybody is fighting a giant of sickness and disease. Not everybody is spending sleepless nights interceding for your prodigals.

Not everybody is struggling under a heavy load of debt, or fighting a spirit of depression. But somebody is.

And the Lord told me to say this to you, "We've got this."

It doesn't mean that everything is going to be easy and we won't have to fight, but ... we've got this.

You are not alone. You have help. You have friends in high places

Ok, let's look at these two very powerful verses here in Joshua, chapter 10, and verses 24-25

And it came to pass when they brought out those kings unto Joshua, that Joshua called for all the men of Israel, and said unto the captains of the men of war, which went with him, come near, put your feet upon the necks of these kings. And they came near, and put their feet upon the necks of them. And Joshua said unto them, fear not, nor be dismayed, be strong and of good courage:

for thus shall the Lord do to <u>all</u> your enemies <u>against whom ye fight</u>. [Joshua 10:24-25]

Beloved, is the devil beating up your family? Is he messing with your money? Is he attacking your body? Is he mocking you? Are you fed up with his mess? The next question is, what are you going to do about it?

God said to tell you that today the tables are turning; If you'll hear the Word of God, you're never going to see yourself the same way again, today is a day of transformation.

Joshua called for all the men of Israel, and said unto the captains of the men of war, which went with him, come near, put your feet upon the necks of these kings. And they came near, and put their feet upon the necks of them.

Now look at verse 25... *And Joshua said unto them, fear not, nor be dismayed, be strong and of good courage: for thus shall the LORD do to all your enemies against whom ye fight.*

Here's another powerful verse that goes right along with that one.

Deut 2:24 Rise ye up, take your journey, and pass over the river Arnon: behold, I have given into thine hand Sihon the Amorite, king of Heshbon, and his land: (begin to possess it, and <u>contend with him in battle</u>).

That's the King James Version, but I like this same verse in the basic Bible English translation.

Deut 2:24 Get up now, and go on your journey, crossing over the valley of the Arnon: see, I have given into your hands Sihon, the Amorite, king of Heshbon, and all his land: (<u>go forward to make it yours, and make war on him</u>).

Do you see the context of these verses? You have to engage the enemy and make war on him.

Behold, I give unto you power to <u>tread</u> on serpents and scorpions, and over all the power of the enemy: and nothing shall by any means hurt you. [Lu 10:19]

These verses tell us something.

You have to go after it; you have to engage the enemy in battle.

Sometimes we Christians act like the devil is bigger and more powerful than God. You say, no way pastor we don't believe that. Well ask yourself these questions...

Who do you talk about the most?

Who's actions and activities do you talk about the most?

What do you do most of the time, Praise or complain?

Sometimes the adversary and the problems can look so big in our lives that they get all of our attention.

First of all, we need to remember that God never promised you a life without battles, he promised you the advantage, and the victory, if you fight.

Everybody shout, I've got the advantage!

Dear reader, I have really been feeling this word growing in my spirit all this week.

It's easy to look at the darkness and the evil in the world today and get overwhelmed. That is one of the devils most effective tactics... to present such seemingly impossible overwhelming odds to our sight, that we forget that we have the advantage.

This has always been a strategy of the enemy, because he wants to make it seem like it is a lost cause before you even get in the fight.

That is what he did to the 10 negative spies and all the first generation children of Israel, and it worked.

They were totally defeated and the enemy never even had to draw their swords.

The enemy tried that tactic again on a man named Elisha. But it backfired. It backfired because Elisha already knew he had the advantage. It didn't matter what level of opposition the enemy presented, Elisha already knew he had the advantage.

Here's the story...

The setting of the story is in 2 Kings 6:8-17

Let me paraphrase for you.

The king of Syria was at war with Israel, and he planned to ambush the king of Israel, but God revealed to Elisha their plans and he told them to the king of Israel so they avoided the ambush.

This happened over and over and over. The king of Syria asked, who is the traitor here? Then one of his servants answered, we are all for you king. But there is a prophet in Israel named Elisha and he tells the King of Israel the words you speak in your bedchamber.

So the king of Syria finds out that Elisha is in Dothan and he sends horses and chariots and a great host to get Elisha.

Verses 14 -15 say... *And they came by night, and <u>compassed the city about</u>. And when the servant of the man of God was risen early and gone forth, behold, <u>an host compassed the city both with horses and chariots.</u> And his servant said unto him Alas my master! how shall we do?*

Friends, there is no reference or record whatsoever that Elisha poked his head out of the door or even looked out the window.

Elisha just said to his servant... fear not: and the servant is probably thinking... (Why not?) Then Elisha says, for they that **be** with us, notice he said **be with us,** not will be, but are with us right now. They are more than they that be with them.

In other words, Elisha is saying... We've got this. He is saying... "Don't worry about it, we have the advantage"

Hallelujah! I'm starting to feel something in my spirit right now. I'm feeling some faith rising up.

Dear reader, Child of God, Woman of God, Man of God… You have the advantage. I have the advantage. We have the advantage. We've got this.

Advantage means, a condition or circumstance that puts one in a favorable or superior position.

Here a few more words that describe the advantage.

The upper hand.
The edge.
The trump card.
The mastery.
The sway.
The authority.
The power.

You remember when Solomon's brother Adonijah, decided he was going to be king, so he called all the people together and the priests to anoint him, and he had a big party and made a big show of it.

1 Kings 1:5 Then *Adonijah the son of Haggith exalted himself, saying, I will be king: and he prepared him chariots and horsemen, and fifty men to run before him.*

Then look at verse 19... *And he hath slain oxen and fat cattle and sheep in abundance, and hath called all the sons of the king, and Abiathar the priest, and Joab the captain of the host: but Solomon thy servant hath he not called.*

How did it turn out?

We find it here in 1 Kings 1:33-35,

The king also said unto them, Take with you the servants of your lord, and cause Solomon my son to ride upon mine own mule, and bring him down to Gihon: And let Zadok the priest and Nathan the prophet anoint him there king over Israel: and blow ye with the trumpet, and say, God save king Solomon. Then ye shall come up after him, that he may come and sit upon my throne; for he shall be king in my stead: and I have appointed him to be ruler over Israel and over Judah.

What am I saying? I'm saying that Adnonijah had a lot of noise and fanfare and popularity. But Solomon had the advantage. He had the word of the King and he was riding on his mule.

All I'm trying to say today is this... It's time to get our eyes of all the hype, the fanfare, the crowds, the haters, the manipulators, and the intimidators.

Its time get our eyes off the giants and off the mountains, and get our eyes back on Jesus and remember, we have the advantage.

Jesus said... *upon this Rock I will build my church and the gates of hell shall not prevail against it.* (Mt 16:18)

So Elisha without so much as a nervous twitch or a quiver in his voice prays this simple prayer... 2 Kings 6:17 *Lord, I pray thee, open his eyes, that he may see. And the Lord opened the eyes of* *the young man; and he saw: and, behold, the mountain was full of horses and chariots of fire <u>round about Elisha</u>.*

That's what I'm talking about, Hallelujah! The enemy compassed the city, but the host of the lord compassed the enemy.

That's the advantage. Are you starting to get this today? It doesn't matter what the enemy is presenting to your physical senses... <u>they that are with us are more than they that are with them</u>.

We've got this!

In the Bible we are told that we have weapons of warfare that are mighty given to us by God, and with these weapons we can pull down strong holds, we can cast down imaginations, and high arguments, and theories that exalt themselves above the knowledge of God, and we can bring every thought into captivity to the obedience of Christ. [See 2 Co 10:3-5]

In our text Joshua said to his captains who were representative of the whole nation of Israel: you see these kings under your feet, God will give us this kind of victory over every enemy that we fight against.

Again we see that God has promised the victory but it is dependent upon the action on our part.

I'm reminded of the great walls that surrounded the city of Jericho, (Joshua ch 6) God promised Joshua and the children of Israel that he would give them the city, but they had to march around the city for six days without saying a word, then on the seventh day and the seventh time around they were to blow their trumpets and shout the victory shout.

I believe one of the greatest problems we have in the church today, is many of Gods people are not properly trained and equipped to engage the enemy in battle.

They just don't want to fight.

They are unwilling to embrace the mindset and the attitude of a warrior.

The Bible says... *From the days of John the Baptist until now, the kingdom of heaven suffereth violence and the violent take it by force. (Mt 11:12)*

And then it says... And these signs shall follow them that believe; In my name shall they cast out devils; they shall speak with new tongues;18 They shall take up serpents; and if they drink any deadly thing, it shall not hurt them; they shall lay hands on the sick, and they shall recover. [Mk 16:17-18]

Yes, we have the advantage, but we still have to fight.

We must do as the Apostle Paul said in Ephesians chapter 6. Put on the whole armor of God that you may be able to stand against the wiles of the devil.

We understand from scripture that the child of God is not supposed to lose in life.

2Co 2:14 Now thanks be unto God, which (always) causeth us to triumph in Christ, and maketh manifest the savour of his knowledge by us in every place.

But this fact stands absolutely upon the premise that you and I are going to fight.

I want you to realize that you are the righteousness of God in Christ Jesus, and that you are seated with him in heaven places and the devil is under your feet.

I want you to realize that in the mind of God you are the winner, you have the advantage."

Advantage means...

A condition or circumstance that puts one in a favorable, or superior position.

A factor or circumstance of benefit to its possessors.

Hallelujah, that's me, and that's you my brother and sister in Christ.

We hold all the cards. We have the upper hand. We have received the factor that is of benefit to its possessors.

Friends, I hope you're getting this; I'm about to shout right now. You have the Word of God, and you have The Power of The Holy Ghost. You are anointed!

Now say it to yourself: I am anointed.

Now tell the devil: I am anointed.

I'm anointed: The same spirit that raised Christ from the dead dwells in me. The same anointing that was upon Jesus is upon me. *[Acts 10:38] How God anointed Jesus of Nazareth with the Holy Ghost and with power: who went about doing good, and healing all that were oppressed of the devil; for God was with him.*

[1Jo 2:20] But ye have (an unction) from the Holy One, and ye know all things.

[2Co 1:21] Now he, which stablisheth us with you in Christ, and hath (anointed us,) is God;

You can sit around complaining about how bad everything is, and about what the devils doing, and about what you don't like, and how you wish things were different.

But I'm going to ask you this question one more time…

What are you going to do about it?

You have the ADVANTAGE NOW!

You are called.

You are chosen.

You are anointed.

You have the name of Jesus.

You have the word of God.

You have the power of the blood of Jesus.

You are the righteousness of God in Christ.

You are the light of the world and the salt of the earth.

You are heirs of God and joint heirs with Jesus Christ.

The greater one lives in you.

We've got this!!!

How long will you let the devil kick you around? How long will you let the devil harass your family before you say, I've had it and make the decision to put your armor on and take your sword and take your authority as a Son and a Daughter of God and take that devil out?

You have the Advantage.

You have been raised up and seated together with Christ in a heavenly place.

You have the Advantage.

The Bible says... when the servants eyes were opened he saw the mountains were filled with horses and chariots <u>round about Elisha.</u>

Friends, we are not alone, we have the advantage, we have divine assistance.

We've got this!

5
Dropped But Lifted

And Jonathan, Saul's son, had a son that was lame of his feet. He was five years old when the tidings came of Saul and Jonathan out of Jezreel, and his nurse took him up, and fled: and it came to pass, as she made haste to flee, that he fell, and became lame. And his name was Mephibosheth. 2 Samuel 4:4

Let's talk for just a minute about Mephibosheth. His name translated from the Hebrew means, dispeller of shame, or one who removes shame. That was his destiny. He was to be a person who removed shame.

What a great destiny. Called and anointed by God to be one who dispels and destroys shame.

Ok, I know this is a book but I have to admit, I feel a little bit preachy right here. As a matter of fact I feel like prophesying to someone reading this book right now. You are not reading these words by accident. Almighty God has brought us together through the pages of this book so I can prophesy and speak over your life your divine destiny.

Just like Mephibosheth, you also my friend are called by God to be a dispeller of shame. You are called by God to be an instrument of his power... to be his hand extended reaching out to those who have been dropped in life. There is an anointing coming upon you now to lift the heavy burden of guilt and shame off the shoulders of those who have fallen down or been knocked down by life.

My precious friend, just lift your hands right now and receive this burden removing, guilt busting, yoke destroying anointing in Jesus name.

Ok let's move on with our story. Mephibosheth had a destiny over his life to deliver people from shame... But something happened

to Mephibosheth that derailed him. Something knocked him off track. He was dropped.
But let me quickly interject here that even though he was dropped, he didn't die.
He was dropped but not destroyed
Dropped but not dead
Dropped but not helpless
Dropped but not defeated
Dropped but not done
Pastor Terry, what do you mean by Dropped? Well I'm glad you asked me that.
What I mean is, things didn't work out like you were hoping for.
Your dream marriage turned into a nightmare.
You weren't treated right. Somebody was abusive to you verbally, physically or emotionally.
Or maybe you just weren't handled right.
Somebody was ignorant of your worth and your value, and they took you for granted, and they were careless with your heart.
You were overlooked, underestimated and ignored.
Dropped means, to fall or move to a position that is lower, farther back or inferior.
Here are some more definitions:
*Bungled
*Fumbled
*Flattened
*Floored
I think if we would be honest about it, based on these definitions, we have all been dropped at some point in life, at least in some measure.
Some to a greater and some to a lesser degree.
Dropped...
Damaged but not destroyed.
Broken but not useless.
Fumbled but not forgotten.
Flattened but not forsaken.

The wonderful thing is this; God does his best work with broken people.

Remember these awesome verses?...

1 Corinthians 1:26-29 For ye see your calling, brethren, how that not many wise men after the flesh, not many mighty, not many noble, are called: But God hath chosen the foolish things of the world to confound the wise; and God hath chosen the weak things of the world to confound the things which are mighty; And base things of the world, and things which are despised, hath God chosen, yea and things which are not, to bring to nought things that are: That no flesh should glory in his presence.

I have to tell you, I know what it's like to be dropped.

I know what it feels like to be flattened and floored.

I know what it feels like to see your dreams vanish into thin air.

I know what it feels like... to feel like you are damaged goods and no one will want you.

I know what it feels like... to feel like you're invalidated and that the rest of your life you will be less than.

Less than what you should be, less than the best you could be.

I'm sure that Mephibosheth felt those exact same feelings.

No not the very day he was dropped. On that day all he felt was pain as his legs or ankles were broken.

But as he grew, as time went on, he felt the lasting effects of being dropped.

- He felt the pain of being less than other boys his age.
- He felt the emotional pain of being inferior to others.
- He couldn't run. He couldn't jump. He couldn't kick a ball or climb a tree.

Then add to that the fact that he was displaced from a position of honor and wealth and influence, and had to live his life on the run hiding out.

Now when we read about Mephibosheth we have a little better insight into his life. He had been dropped... not Just physically, but life itself had dropped him. He had been dealt a bad hand.

So when we look at Mephibosheth, we are looking at a disappointed, disenfranchised, depressed, and discouraged man. This is the condition he is in when David finds him.

Many years prior to this day, before the day Mephibosheth was dropped, his Daddy Jonathon and David entered into a Covenant; that when David was king he would show favor to his house.

Now that David is established as King, David's heart is yearning to find some one of the house of Saul and of Jonathan so he can fulfill his Covenant promise and show them favor and mercy.

2 Sam 9:7-8 And David said unto him, Fear not: for I will surely shew thee kindness for Jonathan thy father's sake, and will restore thee all the land of Saul thy father; and thou shalt eat bread at my table continually. And he bowed himself, and said, What is thy servant, that thou shouldest look upon such a dead dog as I am?

When David finds Mephibosheth, he is living in the land of Lode-bar The word Lode-bar means, pasture-less. in other words, dry, and desolate.

It was very much a reflection of the heart and the self-image Mephibosheth had of himself.

How do I know this?

Because when Mephibosheth came before David this is what he said about himself... What is thy servant that thou shouldest look upon such a dead dog as I am?

● Mephibosheth was not only crippled physically, he was crippled mentally, and emotionally.

His words reflected his self Image and his estimation of his self worth.

◆ He said, I am Dead = useless, helpless, non-productive.
◆ He said, I am a Dog = Contemptible, to be despised.

Mephibosheth had let his circumstances and his environment define him. He had let what had happened to him decide what happened in him.

In other words, he let a bad experience set the course for his life.

41

Listen my friends; there is not one of you reading the words of this book who has not had a bad experience in life.

But there comes a time when you have to make a choice.

➢ Who do I want to be?
➢ Who am I going to be?
➢ Which one am I going to believe?

Am I going to believe what my circumstances have said about me? Or Am I going to believe what God has said about me?

I want to share a revelation with you; this came to me as I was preparing this word.

Here it is...

● David didn't make Mephibosheth something that he wasn't already.

What do you mean pastor Terry?

◆ He was already royalty
◆ He was already kingly seed
◆ He was already the Grandson of King Saul

Most likely if the Kingdom had not been given to David, Mephibosheth would have ultimately became king.

The point is: David didn't make Mephibosheth something he wasn't already.

But what David did was pick him back up.

● He lifted him back up.
● He spoke to the king in him.
● He spoke to the potential and to all the possibilities that were in him.
● He spoke to the greatness in him.
● He spoke to the anointing in him.
● He spoke to his destiny.
➢ David didn't focus on his lameness, he focused on his greatness.
➢ David didn't focus on his weaknesses, he focused on his strengths.
➢ David didn't put him in a back room eating with the servants... David put him right at the kings table.

2 Samuel 9:13 So Mephibosheth dwelt in Jerusalem, for he did eat continuously at the Kings table: and was lame on both his feet.

The point of this Verse is this...
- It didn't matter where Mephibosheth came from.
- It didn't matter his lameness.
- It didn't matter that he had been dropped.
- It didn't matter all the things he had missed.
- It didn't matter that for years and years he lived like a beggar.

I wished you would say those words with me... It doesn't matter.
It doesn't matter where you came from, or what you came out of, or what happened to you.
It really doesn't even matter if you were dropped, or if you fell down, or if you jumped. What matters is...
What are you doing now?
What decisions are you making now?
Which direction are you going now?
Ok you were dropped.
Ok you fell down, you slipped, and you made a mistake.
Ok well, you weren't dropped, and you didn't slip, you actually with forethought and intent ran and jumped right in the middle of it. Well, so did David, and so did Moses. But God still used them. And God will still use you.
There's room at the table for you.
- In the presence of the King everything changes.
- In The presence of the King it doesn't matter that you were dropped.
- At the Kings table we're all the same.
- At the Kings table no one talks about all our fallings and our failings.
- At the Kings table, the focus is not on our failings but on our fellowship, and our future.

Yes, I was dropped, but I've been lifted.

6
When Uzziah Died

When Uzziah died, Isaiah saw the Lord, as he always was, but Isaiah's vision had been blurred.

It's interesting to me that it says in the year. Not month, or week, or day, but in the year, that Uzziah died.

That tells me that Isaiah was just like me; sometimes I struggle with priorities in my life. I should say proper priorities, or God ordered priorities.

*Isaiah was a prophet, but Isaiah had misplaced priorities.

Uzziah, was holding Isaiah's attention.

Uzziah can be anything that you allow to take your attention and your affection away from God.

I'm going to say something here. You might need to buckle up for this. It's a dangerous thing to give someone or something, the place that belongs to God.

Notice as soon as Uzziah is removed from the equation, Isaiah's vision is corrected.

*You can't have two kings at the same time. You can't serve two masters.

As soon as the earthly king is dead, and it took him a year to die, or we could say it took Isaiah a year to let him go.

Anyway as soon as the natural king is gone, Isaiah sees the Lord on the throne high and lifted up.

Now, divine priorities are being established, or I should say re-established.

*The sovereign King of the universe comes into view.

He is on a throne, high, and lifted up. He has always been on the throne-lifted up. But Isaiah's vision had been obscured.

Now the Bible says, his train, his presence and glory, filled the temple.

My friend God is ready to fill his temple today. But he will not compete for your heart and for my heart.

I want us to note that it wasn't sin that was holding back the presence and the glory of God; it was the presence of another king.

Uzziah means, my strength is Jehovah.

*Uzziah started out trusting in God, and God was with him and God helped him.

But the Bible says in 2nd Chronicles 26:15- 21, He was marvelously helped till he was strong. But when he was strong, his heart was lifted up to his destruction. For he transgressed against the Lord his God.

That's why Uzziah had to die, that's why the glory wasn't filling the temple.

*Uzziah represents pride, self-effort, good works, self-sufficiency, and dead religion.

I believe that this is the very battle that we are fighting in the church today. I believe this is the very reason we are not seeing the presence, the glory, and the power of God like we need to see.

*There was a time when we knew that we were weak, and we knew that we couldn't do it by ourselves, and we knew that without God we were nothing.

There was a time when we believed that prayer was indispensable.

But like Uzziah, something started happening. We started thinking that we are somebody; we began to think we don't need to pray every day. We began to think, we don't need to read the Bible every day, we don't need to study the Bible. We started thinking... I don't have to go to church like I used to, I'm strong now.

Yes, I used to need to go to church every service, I used to need to hear the preaching and the teaching of the word. I used to need to join together with my brothers and sisters in the faith and worship God together.

45

But I'm strong now. I'm mature. Once a week, or two or three times a month is plenty church for anybody.

Listen to this; the last act of Uzziahs life was pride-fully trying to act in the office of the priest.

In other words, by his actions he was saying to God, I'll serve you the way I want. It happens all the time.

Then what happens? Uzziah is smitten with leprosy. Uzziah died as a leper.

Leprosy is a type of sin, like sin, it is incurable.

If God doesn't heal the physical leper, they will die of leprosy. And the same is true concerning Sin; if God does not cure it, it will destroy your soul.

This leprosy that came upon King Uzziah was produced through pride.

The pride that opened the door to leprosy is the thing that grieved the Holy Spirit.

Uzziah is still grieving the Holy Spirit. The spirit of religion, pride, and self-sufficiency, and ultimately rebellion, is resisting the glory of God.

God will not cohabitate in his temple with pride, self-sufficiency, arrogancy and rebellion.

There can only be one king in this temple.

Your body is the temple of the Holy Ghost and there can only be one king on the throne of your heart.

If we want to see the glory and the power of God in his temple, Uzziah must die.

It took a whole year for Uzziah to die from Isaiah's heart. In other words, it took a whole year to get Uzziah off the throne in the temple.

But as soon as Uzziah died, the glory of God filled the temple.

Dear reader let me ask you a question, where do you see Uzziah in your life today?

Where is Uzziah saying, I'll do it my way, I have decided how I'm going to serve the Lord.

Isaiah had a glorious encounter with the glory and the power of God, after Uzziah died.

The difference for you and me is this. Uzziah is not going to die out of your life. You have to crucify him. You have to dethrone him. Uzziah will never leave, he must be evicted.

I guess you can see that in Isaiah's life King Uzziah represented double mindedness, indecision, and instability.

The same is true for you and I. To become a Man or Woman of God that is settled, rooted, grounded, and established, Uzziah must die.

Remember these words? If any of you lack wisdom, let him ask of God, that giveth to all men liberally, and upbraideth not and it shall be given him. Then it says... But let him ask in faith, nothing wavering. For he that wavereth is like a wave of the sea driven with the wind and tossed. For let not that man think that he shall receive anything of the Lord.

Why? Because a double minded man is unstable in all his ways. (See James 1:5-8)

A double mind means, indecision, wishy washy, instability.

Dear reader, God wants to establish you and plant you in an unshakeable place of confidence and stability, but you must let Uzziah die.

7
You've Got To Make It

Mark 4:35 and the same day when the even was come he saith unto them, let's pass over unto the other side. Then look at chapter 5:1 And they came over to the other side of the sea
for somebody today that's your word that's your Rhema word, that's what you need to hear right now.
I'm talking to somebody who has a word from God:
*Maybe God told you he was going to save your children.
*Maybe he told you your ministry was going to another level of influence and effectiveness.
*Maybe he told you that you were going to meet that husband or wife you've been believing for.
*Maybe he told you he was going to bless and prosper you financially, and that you're going to get out of debt.

*You've got a word from God.
Just say that with me… I've got a word!

But now here's the problem, your word is being challenged.

Is there anybody who knows your word is being challenged?

Between your word and the other side or the manifestation of your word, you're going to have to fight the good fight of faith.
I want to help somebody today:
I want to tell you that the devil has enough power to challenge your word, but he doesn't have enough power to change your word!
Jesus said, let us go. I love that, because that means we are in this together.
His Divine presence is guaranteed.

There's something about his presence that makes the difference. He doesn't promise us exemption from problems. But he promises Divine presence in the midst of our problems.

David said, yeah though I walk through the valley of the shadow of death I will fear no evil, why David could you say that? And he answers, for thou art with me.

Moses was so dependent upon the presence of God that he said, if your presence does not go with us, don't take us from this place.

The Bible says, Strength and honor are in his presence. Here is the exact wording... 1 Chronicles 16:27 Glory and honor are in his presence; strength and gladness are in his place.

Psalms 16:11 in his presence is fullness of joy.
Heb 13:5b ... For he hath said, I will never leave thee nor forsake thee.

Let's be honest about it, there are people who start out with you and they say you can always count on me; I'll be there for you. But when things get bad you look around and they're either gone or have become invisible.

When you've got money you've got friends, but a real friend is one who is still there when the money is gone.

If you've got one real friend in life you are rich.

Jesus said: I'll be that friend that sticketh closer than a brother. He was there before you had any money, before your position, before you had a beautiful house, before the new car, before you were all dressed up.

He was there when you were in the projects, and you were walking to work, or riding the bus, and you had to buy your clothes from the Goodwill store.

Somebody knows what I'm talking about. Like the time when you were trying to decide should I pay my electric bill or should I get some groceries? Yeah, He was there then.

He promised no matter what comes your way in life I will be there with you and for you.

Why don't you just go ahead and say that for your own personal edification: I've got a friend.

The Scripture verses we are looking at say: there arose a great storm. Notice those words... a great storm.

The Bible says, there arose: that means it came up out of nowhere, with no warning, no advance notice. Everything was going good, smooth sailing, then "bam" all of a sudden it's in your face.

- You're hearing the doctor's report saying I'm sorry there's nothing medical science can do for you.
- You're sitting across from that husband or wife and out of the clear blue sky they hit you with those words... I want a divorce.
- You went to work on the job you've had for 5 or 10 or 20 years, you thought you had job security, you had seniority, you had a nice little retirement building up. But they told you the economy is bad, the company is downsizing, and we have to let you go, and worst of all you lose all your benefits.

I know these words are hitting home for somebody. You saved and saved; doing without so you could get that car you always wanted. Then sickness hit you or you were injured on the job, you missed one month's payment and they came and got your car.

Yes my friend, in the real world storms come, and sometimes they come up with no warning. And let me say this about storms... there are storms of life, then there are what I call real storms, there is a difference.

Having lived for many years in a place called tornado alley, you learn the difference between a common everyday type storm, and a super cell storm. An every day type storm may have a little wind and rain, maybe some thunder and lightning, and maybe even some pea size hail.

But a super-cell can produce softball size hail, it can produce winds over 100 miles an hour, and it can spawn multiple tornadoes, and it's almost always filled with deadly lightning.

A super-cell is self-perpetuating, in other words, the longer it last the stronger it gets.

The Bible says: it was a great storm.

Those words, Great storm, means it is distinguished as more than just a run of the mill garden-variety type storm. It was a bad storm. It was what we might refer to as a super-cell.

I believe I'm talking to someone right now, who is in a storm, and it's not your everyday storm, it's not just a little wind and

rain and pea sized hail, it's a super-cell it's a bad one.

And judging by your circumstances it looks hopeless. The doctor says it's hopeless. The banker says it's hopeless. The lawyer says it's hopeless. The marriage counselor says it's hopeless. Your enemies say it's hopeless, and even your friends are starting to agree.

But I am so happy to tell you today, it's never hopeless. As long as there is a God in heaven there is hope.

Now we come to the place where the Bible says… their boat was now filled with water.

Beloved friend, the devil wants to drown you.

Drown you in debt, and drown you with sickness, drown you in fear and despair, drown you in depression and confusion.

But I have a word from the Lord for you, you are unsinkable.

Tell the devil: you can't drown me, I'm unsinkable.

Everything around me may go down but you can't drown me.

Friend, your word, your destiny makes you unsinkable

The destiny in you is greater than the storm you're in.

- What you do when you're in the middle of your storm?

You go back to your word

(Your word will get you through)

Say that with me… I've got a word.

Declare it now for yourself… I'm coming through on the Word.

The disciples said: Peter get back in this boat, you can't walk on water, have you lost your mind? But Peter said I've got a word.

Jesus said come and if I got a word (I'm unsinkable).

Dear reader, a word is all you need, it don't take the whole book, not even a chapter, not even a whole sentence, just one word, one word from God is all you need.

A word will do for you what money can't do.

A word will do for you what education can't do.

A word will do for you what friends can't do.

A word will open doors that were closed in your face.

A word will cause things to turn in your favor.

A word will hold you up when everything else is falling down.

Let us go over to the other side

Before I ever got in the storm: I got a word.

God is not a man that he should lie neither is he the son of man that he should repent, hath he said it, will he not do it hath he spoken it shall he not make it good? Numbers 23:19

I got a word: but God never said there wouldn't be any obstacles, he never said there wouldn't be any problems, he never said there wouldn't be things that rise up against me.

He never said there wouldn't be attacks on my marriage. He never said sickness wouldn't attack my body. He never said that I would never have to fight a financial battle. He never said your children would be the perfect angels, that they would never rebel or get on drugs or go to prison.

He never said people wouldn't lie on you, and stab you in the back, and steal from you. He never said you'd never have a broken heart, or there wouldn't be times when you cry yourself to sleep.
But what he said was let us go (let's go) we're together in this, you're not alone.
Let us go over to the other side <u>Over</u> "over this." You've got to get over it.

If you're going to get to the other side, there are some things you have to get over. Somebody lied on you: get over it.
Somebody cheated on you: get over it.
Somebody abused you: mentally, emotionally, sexually, physically, and you hate them you're holding unforgiveness in your heart towards that person or persons, you have to get over it.
Your destiny depends on it. To get to the other side you have to get over it.
Don't let what somebody did to you or didn't do stop your destiny, it's not worth it, they're not worth it.
No man or woman is worth your destiny.
No amount of money is worth your destiny.

Dear reader, it's time to get over it.

The Bible says the boat was now filled with water:
My precious friend… nothing from the outside can hurt you, in other words nothing from the outside can stop your destiny it's what you let in that has the potential to drag you down.

The boat was now filled with water.

I'm talking to somebody who has let bitterness and resentment and unforgiveness get into your boat. You let anger and jealousy and a critical spirit into your life.

And the only way to get to the other side is to get over it, get it out.

Your life depends on it. Your destiny depends on it.

Get it out before it kills you, get it out before it drags you down, get it out before it destroys your marriage, get it out before it kills your ministry, get it out before you say something or do something that you can't undo.

I don't know who I'm talking to but God said: you better get it out.

Verse 38 says: and he (Jesus) was in the hinder part of the ship asleep on the pillow.

Dear reader, how could Jesus be sleeping, be resting, be at peace, be calm, in the same storm; the same circumstances that were causing the disciples to freak out?

The answer is: he believed the word he spoke; he believed the words that came out of his own mouth.

He had declared: we are going over to the other side, and he believed that the word he spoke was more powerful than anything he had to go through to get there.

He was sleeping on the word.

He was resting on the word.

He was counting on the word.

You have to learn how to rest on the word.

But you also need to know how to fight with the word.

1Timothy 1:18 says... according to the prophecies that went before on thee, that thou by them mightest war a good warfare.

Dear reader, in my estimation one of the most powerful weapons you have is your prophetic word.

But let's be honest about it... that word doesn't do you any good buried in a dresser drawer.

It doesn't do you any good in a binder with 140 other prophecies.

You have to put that word in your mouth and declare it.
That's what the Bible means by this verse... thou shalt decree a thing and it shall be established unto thee. Job 22:28

I need to tell somebody today that you need to quit sitting around waiting for some prophet to come by and give you a word.
Of course I believe in prophecy and personal prophecy and sometimes I will give a personal prophesy over others.

But God wants you to know that you are the prophet of your own destiny.
Just like Ezekiel and the Valley of dry bones, nothing changed until he started prophesying.
I can prophesy over you till I'm blue in the face, but if you don't stir up your faith and open your mouth and prophesy to your own dry bone conditions... nothing is going to change.

So I say to you dear reader, wake up. You've got to wake up the prophet, that sleeping prophet in your own bosom.

Dear readers, please take these words to heart, and take them personally. You've got to make it. It's critical that you make it.
Why? Because there is somebody on the other side of your storm whose life depends on you making it over.
- There is somebody who is bound and you are the one who is going to set them free.
- Someone is sick, and you're going to lay hands on them and bring healing to them.
- Someone is suicidal and you're the one who is going to speak the word in season and restore hope to them and drive the darkness out of their lives.

- Somebody is going through the greatest storm of their lives and you're going to share how you made it through, and they're going to make it because you didn't quit. I've got to make it; you've got to make it.

I've got to make it not just for myself but also for my children, my grandchildren, and my brothers and sisters that are following behind.
The Bible says that there were other boats… little boats that were with them.

What is that saying to me? That is telling me that somebody is following you; somebody's watching you. You've got to make it, not just for yourself, but others also.
For somebody who is still in enemy territory under Satanic captivity.

Somebody's been praying and you're the answer to their prayer.
Somebody's waiting for you to show up and deliver them from their Devils.
You can't go under, you can't drown, you can't quit, and you can't give up.
Somebody needs you.
When Jesus got to the other side: immediately he was met by a man possessed by devils. That tells me that this man needed the disciples to make it to him. This man needed Jesus to make it, he needed the disciples to reach him so Jesus could set him free.
You've got to make it; somebody's life depends on it.
- Somebody's marriage depends on it.
- Somebody's ministry depends on it.
- Somebody's sanity depends on.

I know you're going through hell but you're going to make it, you're in the middle of the worst storm of your life but you're going to make it.
Everything you see and everything you feel and everything you hear is threatening to take you down but you're going to make it.

And when you get to the other side your testimony is going to be a lifeline to somebody who feels it's impossible, who feels their dream their vision their hope will never come to pass.

You've got to make it somebody's waiting on you.

Now before you close this book I want you to prophesy and declare Life over yourself. Declare to yourself… I'm going to make it, I've got to make it. I can't go down I can't go under. I've got to make it.

People are depending on me. Somebody needs me.

Dear reader, you're going to make it. That's why I wrote this book.

This is your personal prophecy. You're going to make it.

I won't let you quit, I won't let you give up, and I won't let go.

We're together in this.

You've got to make it.

8
A Miracle Is Coming Your Way

2 Kings 4:8-17
The Prophet symbolizes… The Word and the Power of God.
Elisha coming to Shunem is equivalent to the Word of God coming to your ears.

The day that you hear the Word of God is the most important day of your life.
The Word of God is the Power of God.
Your healing is in the Word.
Your deliverance is in the Word.
Your joy is in the Word.
Your prosperity is in the Word.
Your anointing is in the Word.
Your destiny is in the Word.

"In the beginning was the Word, the Word was with God and the Word was God, the same was in the beginning with God. All things were made by him (The Word) and without him (The Word) was not anything made that was made."   John 1:1-3
Everything begins with the Word.
You can shout dance, run, holler, talk in tongues and jump pews, but you haven't even got started until you get in the Word and the Word gets in you.
I don't know what your situation or condition or problem is, but I know what your answer and your solution is, it's the Word of God.

He sent his Word and healed them and delivered them from all their destructions.
Ps 107:20

Faith is the hand that reaches out and takes hold of the blessings of God, but it is the Word of God that quickens the hand of faith.

The Bible says... Elisha passed to Shunem where was a great woman.

The only Word the bible promises will bring life to you and health to your flesh is the word that you listen intently to, that you look at continuously and that you keep in the midst of your heart.

Let's see how she got her miracle:
First: She perceived the Word, she perceived the prophet as the spokesman for God.

You have got to recognize the Word as the very life force of God. You have to realize the Word is the creative power of God; it is not just another book.
It is alive with healing, salvation, deliverance, miracles, supernatural provision, direction, correction, and instruction.

Every promise is a miracle seed waiting to be planted in the soil of your heart.
When you truly perceive the power of the Word of God you will fall in love with it, you will eat it like a starving man, you will drink from it like a man dying of thirst.

Second :
She received the word, she took it in, and she made it personal. It's one thing to recognize the validity of the Word of God and the truth and the necessity of the Word of God, but it is another thing entirely to personalize it and make it the priority of your life.
She changed her house to accommodate the man of God, who symbolizes the Word of God.

Sadly today the attitude of many believers is to change the Word to accommodate their life style.

But the problem for them is this: there is no amended version; there are no amendments to the Ten Commandments.

The Word of God is non negotiable.

Forever O Lord thy Word is settled in the heavens. Ps 119:89

My covenant will I not break nor alter the thing that is gone out of my lips. Ps 89:34

To truly receive The Word means it has become the final authority in your life, it is the standard that you measure your life by and live by.

Look at these words again. In Shunem there was a great woman:

This woman had a reputation of being kind, and generous and hospitable, but what really made her great was her insight, her spiritual perception, and her ability to discern where God was at work.

Elisha had passed by many houses and they failed to identify the anointing and recognize the presence of God in his life.

In fact he had passed by her house also, and she had missed it.

Sometimes you have to miss it before you get it right.

Don't condemn yourself if you missed it. If you miss it once or twice that's sad, but if you miss it 5 or 6 times that's stupid.

Sometimes God hides his anointing in a shepherd boy. Sometimes in a Gideon hiding behind the wine press. Sometimes he takes a nobody from nowhere who nobody ever expected to do anything or go anywhere, and he puts his anointing down on the inside of them and uses them to change the world.

Sometimes we miss what God wants to do because we can't get past the wrapper, we're stuck on the packaging, because they don't fit our idea of what a man or a woman of God should look like.

Dear reader let me say this, there's more to me than what you see.
Don't judge me by my size, because I'm bigger than that.
Don't judge me because I was born on the wrong side of the tracks.
Don't judge me because I don't have a degree.
Don't judge me based on my car, or my house or my clothes.

If you're looking in the natural you're going to miss it.
If you judge me by the flesh you're going to miss it.

Henceforth know we no man after the flesh 2 Co 5:16

But we have this treasure in earthen vessels that the Excellency of the power may be of God and not of us
2 Co 4:7
One day this woman looked at her husband and said... I perceive (Now the eyes of my spirit are open).
I see something that was already there but I didn't know it.
Many times the reason we are not seeing with the eyes of our spirit is because our natural eyes are in control, our natural eyes are full of earthly matters and concerns, even good and legitimate things... our business or career, our spouses, our children, even our ministry. And God is passing by us and we are missing it because our spiritual eyes are closed.

Put your hand over your eyes and say:
Lord let me see it, open my spiritual eyes.

In between the passings of the prophet this woman got a revelation, she recognized the anointing of God in Elisha's life.
And basically she said to her husband, next time I'll be ready, next time I'll be watching, next time I'll be listening, next time I'm going to be looking with the eyes of my spirit.
Next time he passes by, I'm going to reach out and get a hold on him.

I can hear this woman say: I missed it the last time, but the last time was the last time.

I refuse to let him pass me by one more time. This time I'm going to make some room for him.
I'm going to clear the clutter out of my life and create an environment for the man of God, the Word of God, the anointing to be comfortable in.

Excuse all the commotion neighbor, but I've got to make some room. I've got to move some things around. I've got to get my priorities straightened out, there's some excesses in my life that have to go.
There's some movies I got to throw out, some music I got to get rid of, and there's some friends I've got to cut loose that are holding me back.

This woman was great because her spiritual eyes were opened and she recognized the authority of the Word of God and the presence of the anointing of God.
She was great because she created an environment for the Man of God, and because she pursued the anointing.

One of the greatest dangers we face as believers and as a church is that of becoming indifferent to the anointing, taking the presence of God and the Word of God for granted.
Every time we come to church we should be looking for where God is moving, pulling on the anointing pulling on The Word of God.
Constraining him, seeking him out.

This woman tapped into the miraculous because she perceived the anointing, and made room for the Word of God in her life.
And because she sowed into the anointing.

She sowed a room with a bed a stool and a table and candle, and she reaped a miracle harvest (a son).

Somebody needs a miracle harvest today:
It may be healing for your body, salvation for a loved one, or it may be a financial miracle that you need.
Or it could be for your ministry.
I don't know what your need is but I do know (your miracle is in your seed).

She named her seed, it was a son seed. Just as you would be specific when planting tomatoes. You wouldn't plant cucumbers and expect to reap tomatoes.
She was specific.
Your seed documents your faith.
Your seed tells heaven, I expect a miracle.
Just as the natural seed puts a demand on the soil, your seed puts a demand on the Power of God.
Something you have will create what you need.
Dear reader, all you need is a seed.
There is a miracle coming your way today.
You just need the ability to discern it, or I could say… recognize it.
Oral Roberts used to say; miracles are either coming toward you or going past you every day.
When your spiritual eyes are open you will be able to see the miracle and participate in it.
So how did this woman get her miracle?
1.She perceived the Word.
2.She received the Word.
3.She personalized the Word.
4.She brought her life into line with the Word.
5.She sowed a miracle seed.
There's a miracle coming your way today, are you ready for it?

9
Stir Up The Gift

Scripture: 2 Timothy 1:1-6

It doesn't matter how gifted you are, it profits you nothing if the gift is not activated.
Paul's exhortation to Timothy was to stir up, to agitate, and disturb, and wake up the gift that was in him.
This Gift is the Holy Ghost.
It is evident that Paul understood that it wasn't enough to receive this gift but the gift must stay active, the gift must be stirred, the gift must be activated.
It is also evident that Timothy was responsible for keeping the gift stirred and active.
We could say it another way: It was Timothy's responsibility to keep the fire burning.
(He was the Keeper of the Flame)
I want to say to every person reading this book. The most important thing that can happen in your life is to meet the Lord Jesus Christ, to be forgiven of your sins, to become a child of God. To be redeemed by the blood of the lamb and to have your name written down in the lambs book of life, and to know that Christ lives in your heart, and you are now a new creature in Christ Jesus.
That is the single most important thing that can happen to a human being.
I don't care how religious you are (you must be born again) I don't care how well you know the bible, or what church you belong to you, you must be born again.
I don't care how good or descent of a person you are (you must be born again)

Jesus said: Except ye be born again, you cannot see the Kingdom of God.

Then Jesus said: Except ye be born of the water and the Spirit, ye cannot enter the Kingdom of God.

(You must be born again).

But once you've been born again, once you've become that new creation in Christ Jesus. The next most important thing that can happen in your life is to be baptized with the Holy Ghost and Fire.

John said: I baptize you with water unto repentance, but there's one coming after me He will baptize you with the Holy Ghost and Fire.

Jesus believed the Baptism of the Holy Ghost to be so important that he commanded his disciples not to leave Jerusalem until they had received this Holy Ghost and Fire baptism.

Jesus said: Ye shall receive Power after that the Holy Ghost is come upon you and you shall be witnesses unto me both in Jerusalem and Judea and Samaria and unto the uttermost parts of the earth.

Then we find in Acts 2: When the day of Pentecost was fully come, they were all in one place with one accord when suddenly there came a sound from heaven as a mighty rushing wind and cloven tongues like as of fire sat upon each of them and they were all filled with the Holy Ghost and began to speak with other tongues as the spirit gave them utterance.

Why is this Holy Ghost and Fire so important?

Because the Holy Ghost is the supernatural power of God filling the human vessel in order to establish and advance the Kingdom of God in the earth.

The Holy Ghost is the supernatural equipment to fulfill the great commission, to carry on the ministry of Jesus.

What was the ministry of Jesus?

1. He came to seek and to save that which was lost.
2. He came to establish the Kingdom of God in the earth.
3. He came to destroy the works of the devil.

Acts 10:38 How God anointed Jesus of Nazareth with the Holy Ghost and with Power who went about doing good, healing all that were oppressed of the devil for God was with him.

1 Jn 3:8 For this purpose the Son of God was manifested, that he might destroy the works of the devil

Hebrews 13:8 Jesus Christ is the same yesterday and today and forever.

Jesus ministry has never changed: Now we are continuators, we are commissioned and anointed to continue his ministry in the earth.

1Jn 4:17 because as he is, so are we in this world.

The book of Acts is the diary and the record of the New Testament church in her infancy, (It is the record of the operation of the Holy Ghost through yielded vessels.)

The book of Acts is the pattern for the New Testament church.

Signs, wonders, miracles, and gifts of the Holy Ghost are the defining characteristics of the New Testament church.

In other words to say it another way, The New Testament church acted just like Jesus. They healed the sick, they cast out devils, and they performed signs and wonders and miracles and raised the dead and manifested the gifts of the Spirit. All by the Power of the Holy Spirit.

If there is one thing we need in our churches and in our lives individually today, it is a fresh anointing of the Holy Ghost.

We Need a Holy Ghost invasion.

We need God to crash our services.

We need a divine interruption.

We need the Holy Ghost to show up like he did in the upper room… suddenly, supernaturally, undeniably and indisputably, like he did in Act 4:29-31

They prayed: Behold their threatening and grant thy servants boldness that we may speak thy word, as we ought by stretching forth your hand to heal and that signs and wonders may be done by the name of thy Holy Child Jesus.

And when they had prayed: The place was shaken and they were all filled with the Holy Ghost, and they spoke the word of God with boldness.

It was a Holy Ghost invasion!

Just like when Peter was preaching at Cornelius house: The Bible says the Holy Ghost fell on all them that heard the word. (Not at the altar call) it was in the middle of Peters preaching. The Holy Ghost interrupted him.

That's what we need: Something that originates from heaven!

Something that will shake us up.

Something that will wake us up.

Something that will stir us up.

Something that will set us on fire.

We need God to interrupt our saying by his doing.

While Peter yet spake the words, the Holy Ghost fell on all them that heard the word. The Holy Ghost did not wait on Peter to finish his sermon, he just fell on them.

I would rather have 10 minutes of Holy Ghost doing than 10 months of saying.

You don't have to wait for me to finish to receive from God.

You can be healed right now, you can be saved right now, you can be delivered right now, you can receive the baptism of the Holy Ghost right now, and you can get your miracle, or your breakthrough right now.

Everything you need is in the Holy Ghost.

I started this chapter with Paul's words to Timothy, but he might as well have been speaking to us.

If there's one thing we're missing in our churches and personal lives today, it's the energy, the life, the vitality, the fire, the power and the anointing of the Holy Ghost.

We can look at the world and we can cite the world as being our problem, we can blame the atmosphere around us.

But the truth is: We can't blame anyone.

(You are the keeper of your own flame).

On the day of Pentecost when the Mighty Holy Ghost came:
Every head got a Flame
(It was a personal Pentecost)
Every person is responsible to fan the flame of Pentecost, to keep the fire burning.
We must stir up the gift that is in us.
The first step to stirring the flame is to remove anything that is flame resistant.
That means: Get rid of anything that is offensive or resistant to the Holy Spirit
That means: Repent of allowing the accumulation of junk in your life.
That means: To seek the Lord with all your heart.
That means: To Pray.
That means: To spend time worshipping and adoring Jesus.
That means: To read his word, eat his word, meditate his word.
That means: To Pray in tongues, building up yourselves on your most holy faith, praying in the Holy Ghost.
We have to stir up the gift.
There is an anointing in you.
There is a fire in you.
It may be low, it may be just a flicker, it may even seem like it's gone out, but if you'll begin to stir the ashes the wind of the Spirit will begin to blow again and the fire will burn again.
We can't afford to let the fire go out.
We're too close to the end: The bridegroom is at hand.
People are falling asleep all around us: Many believers are asleep in the church.
They're still singing the same songs, still saying amen and hallelujah, but the fire has gone out
It's time for us to stir up the gift that is in us.
Wake up that calling.
Wake up that destiny.
Wake up that anointing.
Wake up that fire.

It doesn't matter how big or how high performance your engine is, if your battery is dead, you're dead in the water.

It doesn't matter how much destiny is in you, or how many gifts or callings are within you, unless they are activated by the Holy Spirit, they're dead.

I don't care how many God given dreams you have, or how many prophecies you have over your life, they are never going to come to pass without the activation of the Holy Ghost.

When you are activated, you can activate others.

When you are on fire you can release the fire to others.

When Samson set the 300 foxes on fire, they become dangerous to the enemy.

They carried the fire!

And they released the fire; they spread the fire everywhere they went.

Everything they touched caught on fire. They didn't really even have to touch it, they just ran by and the fire jumped off them.

You can have that same kind of fire, that same kind of anointing.

Peter carried that kind of fire. They laid the sick and the diseased and the demon possessed in the streets and as his shadow passed over them they were healed delivered, and set free.

I want to pray with you and stir up and activate that fire and that anointing in you so that wherever you go you will carry the fire and you will be a threat to hell.

Holy Spirit I ask you to come now, and fall upon every hungry thirsty, seeking soul. Fall upon them now, as you fell on the day of Pentecost. Fire of God fall now and consume them and set them on fire, in Jesus name.

10
Persuaded

In one of the most powerful verses in the Bible, Paul said: "For I know whom I have believed and am (persuaded) that he is able to keep that which I have committed unto him against that day" (2 Tim 1:12).

I am Persuaded means… to convince by argument. I am convinced. I agree. I am confident of. I believe. I trust.

This is what made Paul such a force for God and such a threat to hell: He was persuaded.

He was not on the fence, he was not (maybe yes maybe no) he was not a well we'll try it for a while and see how it works out kind of guy.

He was not up one day, down the next, hot today, cold tomorrow, wishy washy, wimpy, limp wristed, half hearted, lukewarm Christian.

No sir, no mamm, Paul was a man on fire. He was all in. He had a backbone of steal, and an iron will, that was set on God. He was not blown from pillar to post, and from one wind of doctrine to another, Paul was established.

And He was persuaded.

Then in the book of numbers we see two of the most persuaded people in the Bible. To see what persuaded looks like, all we have to do is look at Joshua and Caleb. These two men of God were the perfect picture of persuaded.

Then you may say: but they didn't persuade anyone else.

But you'd be wrong: the fact is they persuaded the next generation to come back and take possession of that which their forefathers forfeited.

Think of that… two men who believed Gods report were able to persuade an entire nation to believe the promises of God.

Look at these awesome verses

"And Joshua the son of Nun, and Caleb the son of Jephunneh, which were of them that searched the land, rent their clothes:7 And they spake unto all the company of the children of Israel, saying, The land, which we passed through to search it, is an exceeding good land. 8 If the LORD delight in us, then he will bring us into this land, and give it us; a land which floweth with milk and honey.9 Only rebel not ye against the LORD, neither fear ye the people of the land; for they are bread for us: their defense is departed from them, and the LORD is with us: fear them not" (Numbers 14: 6 -9).

Joshua and Caleb Were Persuaded

Now let's look at a New Testament Persuader.

"Be not thou therefore ashamed of the testimony of our Lord, nor of me his prisoner: but be thou partaker of the afflictions of the gospel according to the power of God; 9 Who hath saved us, and called us with an holy calling, not according to our works, but according to his own purpose and grace, which was given us in

Christ Jesus before the world began, 10 But is now made manifest by the appearing of our Savior Jesus Christ, who hath abolished death, and hath brought life and immortality to light through the gospel: 11 Whereunto I am appointed a preacher, and an apostle, and a teacher of the Gentiles. 12 For the which cause I also suffer these things: nevertheless I am not ashamed: for I know whom I have believed, (and am persuaded) that he is able to keep that which I have committed unto him against that day" (2 Tim 1:8-12).

Paul was persuaded

Persuaded means, to convince by argument, to rely by inward certainty, believe, have confidence, trust, and yield.

One of the greatest needs in the body of Christ today is for men and women who are persuaded.

I'm even going to go so far as to say: you are no force for God and certainly no threat to the devil until you're persuaded.

The sad fact is: Multitudes of Christians, believers do not really live the persuaded life.

They live the hope so life, the wishful life, the unstable, undecided, unsure, and unconvinced life.

The greatest threat to hell in the Church are men and women, who are Persuaded, whose faith goes down deep, who have their roots wrapped around the Word of God, and they cannot be shaken.

To be persuaded means: won over, convinced, settled, established.

This is essentially what faith is. Faith is arriving at the place where you are convinced and won over and established by the Word of God.

Until one is persuaded, there is a struggle, feelings, emotions, circumstances, and they all war against the mind.

Let me give you some examples: I hear the word "By his stripes ye were healed" but I feel the pain in my body.

I hear the word "My God shall supply all your needs" but my pockets are empty.

I hear the word, but then there's the doctors report.

I hear the word, but there's the lawyers report.

And there is a war being waged.

Isa 53:1 Who hath believed our report? and to whom is the arm of the LORD revealed?

This war is waged in the mind:

It is a war that is between the Word of God and the natural circumstances and conditions that contradict the Word of God.

The devil wars with sickness, pain, financial problems, negative reports, etc.

If you become persuaded by the circumstances and conditions that contradict Gods Word, you will actually begin to stand in direct opposition to the Word of God.

Example: The 10 spies who allowed the giants and other things that they saw to persuade them, and convince them that they were unable to take possession of their promised inheritance.

Literally what they were saying was: we are persuaded by what we have seen and heard that God lied.

I know that is strong medicine but that is exactly what happened— they let their natural senses over rule Gods promises to them.

On the other hand Joshua and Caleb saw the exact same things, and heard the exact same things, but they were persuaded by the Word of God that they were well able to take the land.

Nu 13:30 And Caleb stilled the people before Moses, and said, let us go up at once, and possess it; for we are well able to overcome it.

Nu 14:9 Only rebel not ye against the LORD, neither fear ye the people of the land; for (they are bread for us): their defense is departed from them, and the LORD is with us: fear them not.

Joshua and Caleb were persuaded by the Word of promise.

The Word of God had prevailed in their thinking over every possible enemy.

To Joshua and Caleb it would not have mattered how many giants there were, or how big they were, or how high the walls of their cities were— they were convinced, and they had been won over. They were persuaded.

I believe this is the great need in the church today— to be persuaded.

For somebody the struggle is coming to an end, the war is coming to an end. Those giants that have been staring you in the face are getting ready to become bread for you .

In other words, instead of those things devouring you, you are getting ready to devour them.

Jer 30:16 "Therefore all they that devour thee shall be devoured; and all thine adversaries, every one of them, shall go into captivity; and they that spoil thee shall be a spoil, and all that prey upon thee will I give for a prey."

Remember when Aaron threw down his rod before the magicians of Egypt and it became a serpent. Then the magicians threw down their rods and they also became serpents, but Aaron's serpent rod swallowed up the magicians serpents.

The point is; the devil has been trying to devour you with sickness and fear, with poverty, lack, and financial problems. Problems in your marriage, problems in your ministry.

Your children aren't acting right, the devils trying to steal your peace and your joy.

The devils been trying to persuade you that Gods Word is not true, and that those prophecies and promises of God are not true and they will never come to pass.

The devil's been trying to get you to take his side and believe his evidence and to speak against the Word of God.

He wants you to say: it's too hard, it's too bad, it's too late, and it's impossible.

The devil has unleashed numerous circumstances against your promises, it seems like you are surrounded by the serpents of fear and doubt and negative circumstances.

But God is getting ready to flip the script.

Your setback is just a set up for your come back.

God allowed you to go through some struggles and tests so he could draw the enemy out of hiding, just like he did to the Egyptian magicians. God drew those snakes out of hiding and then he devoured them.

The rod of Aaron represents the authority, and the power of the Word of God.

The Word of God will swallow up every serpent that has been loosed against your life.

The devils greatest fear is that you will become persuaded that Gods Word is true.

When you are persuaded: you can look at the dry bone conditions of your life and prophesy your own healing, and your own deliverance, and break through.

The woman with the issue of blood for 12 years prophesied her own deliverance, she said: if I can just touch his clothes I know I'll be whole.

Jairus prophesied his daughter's resurrection; if you will come and lay your hand on her she shall live.

The centurion <u>prophesied</u> his servants healing; speak the Word only and my servant shall be healed.

Let the Word of God persuade you today...

*You are well able to take the land.

*You are able to defeat sickness and disease.

*You are able to break Satans power over your loved ones.

*You are well able to fulfill that ministry that God has called you to.

1 Jo 5:4 For whatsoever is born of God overcometh the world: and this is the victory that overcometh the world, even our faith.

1 Jn 4:4 Ye are of God, little children, and have overcome them: because greater is he that is in you, than he that is in the world.

Faith is not a struggle, faith is a rest. Once you are persuaded concerning the promises of God for your life the struggle is over.

You may have to walk some things out, but internally there will be a peace and a rest that it shall be even as the Lord hath said.

These are the kind of people Satan fears.

Why?

Because persuaded people have the ability to persuade others.

See (Acts 19:26) "Moreover ye see and hear, that not alone at Ephesus, but almost throughout all Asia, (this Paul hath persuaded) and turned away much people, saying that they be no gods, which are made with hands."

Look at that again: Not alone at Ephesus, but almost throughout all Asia this Paul hath (persuaded) and turned away many people from worshipping Idols that are made by men's hands.

*When you are persuaded God heals: you can help persuade others concerning healing.

*When you are persuaded that God restores marriages and heals broken homes; you can persuade others to trust God for their marriages and their homes.

*When you are persuaded that God can break habits and addictions and deliver the captives and set them free; then you can be a powerful tool to bring deliverance and restoration to others.

Persuaded people persuade people

The people who are intimidated and manipulated by their circumstances are no threat to the devil. The people who put hell on high alert are those who are persuaded.

They are the ones who say: it doesn't matter what it looks like or feels like, if Gods Word says it, that settles it… I shall not be moved!

I Am Persuaded!

11
The Real Battle

Exodus 17:8-17:13

Have you ever felt like life is throwing at you everything but the kitchen sink, and then, pow here comes the kitchen sink?

It feels like your theme song is (when it rains it pours) or nobody knows the trouble I've seen?

Let me take it a step farther: Have you ever felt like there's a target on your back and like there must be a neon arrow pointing at you saying, He's over here, she's over here?

One more question: Have you ever felt like; this is more than just natural everyday life's problems, and like this is getting ridiculous, and this is not normal, and this is unusual, and weird?
 Well let me Introduce you to the spirit realm. You have just entered the battlefield where every battle is won or lost.

The truth is we are always in a battle, and the truth is (it is spiritual) and the truth is there are always demons that are at work trying to draw you away from God, trying to destroy your families, and steal your health, and your peace and your joy, and ultimately trying to kill you.

That's what John 10:10 Says, The thief cometh for no other reason but to steal to kill and to destroy.

The thing is that: He often gets by with it, and he is often effective in his work because he is an expert at getting you to focus your attention on the natural.

The devil knows if he can get you to expend all your energy on fighting and struggling and warring in the flesh, that you are already defeated.

Spiritual battles can never be won on natural grounds.

Spiritual battles can never be won on physical grounds with physical weapons.

Spiritual battles must be fought with spiritual weapons

Eph 6:12 For we wrestle not against flesh and blood, but against principalities, against powers, against the rulers of the darkness of this world, against spiritual wickedness in high places.

Our battle, and our warfare is spiritual.

Your enemy is not your neighbor, and not that person that makes your life miserable, and your enemy is not the I.R.S. or DMV, or the DHS or the Gov.

And your enemy is not drugs, alcohol, nicotine, and your enemy is not homosexuality or lesbianism, or fornication or adultery.

And your enemy is not sickness and disease, and poverty and lack, (*Yes all these things may be manifest against us but they are just masks the devil wears.*

Your real enemy and mine is the (d-e-v-i-l).

The good news is: We have been given Spiritual weapons to fight this battle.

2Co 10:3-5 For though we walk in the flesh, we do not war after the flesh:

4 For the weapons of our warfare are not carnal, but mighty through God to the pulling down of strong holds; 5 Casting down imaginations, and every high thing that exalteth itself against the knowledge of God, and bringing into captivity every thought to the obedience of Christ.

Moses tells Joshua. Go and fight with Amalek: Note that Joshua and the children of Israel are in a very real physical confrontation. The Amalekites are not imaginary, they we're a real enemy that hated the Children of God and wanted to destroy them. This symbolizes how the enemy uses the natural, the visible, and tangible things to war against us.

Let me give you an Illustration: No doctor will examine a person and diagnose them with Cancer or with Tuberculosis, or arthritis, or deafness and say to you (it's a demon) No because they can only see the natural.
But we know that disease may manifest itself in the natural but its roots are spiritual (That's why sickness is healed spiritually through faith in the stripes that Jesus bore, and by the power of the Holy Spirit.

Sickness and disease came with the fall
Sin and Sickness are the double curse

But the blood and the stripes are the double cure. The blood for our sins, and the stripes for our Sicknesses and diseases.

 Moses said: I will stand on top of the hill.
 The hill = prayer, It's called a hill for two reasons.
#1 Because real prayer is hard work.
#2 Because the mountain represents the Higher realm, higher than the natural, above the natural.
With the rod of God in my hand.
What is the significance of the rod of God?
 #1 It represents the Word of God. Prayer receives its intensity and power through the Word of God. To pray with power you must pray the Word.
#2 It represents the authority we have as the children of God.

When Moses hands were raised with the rod of God the children of Israel prevailed, but when his hands and the rod began to fall Amalek prevailed.

If you see that the enemy seems to be gaining ground in your life, the first thing you need to do is ask the questions
#1 How's my prayer life?
#2 How's my Word life?
I mean serious prayer, not just those now I lay me down to sleep prayers.
And I mean serious word: and not just reading a few verses before bedtime. I'm talking about a steady consistent flow of the word of God pouring out of your mouth.
Rev 12:11 And they overcame him by the blood of the lamb and the word of their testimony.
Jesus defeated the devil with it is written, and then he vocalized what was written.
It is not what is written that defeats the devil in your life: it's what is written that lives in your heart and fills your mouth that defeats the devil.
The sword of the spirit that defeats the devil is the word of God spoken with authority from a believing heart.

The church and (the cause of Christ universally) advances in the earth through prayer. As the ark was carried upon the shoulders of the priests, so also has God committed his presence and power to the shoulders of praying saints.

On praying ground everyone is equal. The greatest calling of God is not apostle or prophet evangelist, preacher or teacher but prayer warrior. It is prayer that makes the apostle or prophet.

It is through prayer that we put on and activate and hold in place every piece of the Christian Armour.

Ephesians 6:18 Praying always with all prayer and supplication in the Spirit, and watching there unto with all perseverance and supplication for all saints.

There is no such thing as a victorious Christian life without prayer: It is by and through prayer that we wage war. It is through prayer that we receive our provisions for the battle. And it is through prayer that we receive power for the battle.
It is in the closet of prayer that the Christian, is dressed for the battle, and for life. You are not dressed until you've prayed.

Before David defeated Goliath publicly he had already con-quered the lion and the bear privately. This is symbolic of the prayer battle.
All public victory owes its accomplishment to private prayer.

Jesus said, he that prayeth to his father secretly shall be re-warded openly.
Your Christian life can be easily diagnosed by your prayer life.
Your prayer life is the thermometer of your spiritual life.
                    Charles Spurgeon said of prayer…
Send to all the churches of Great Britain, first of all, the power of prayer, and then shall there come conversions of multitudes of souls through the outpoured energy of the Holy One of Israel!
The real battle is Spiritual and the greatest weapon in that battle is prayer:
But it is not just any prayer that secures the hope and the help of the almighty God
James 5:16
The effectual fervent prayer of a righteous man availeth much.
EFFECTUAL means: "powerful" full of power to achieve results.
FERVENT, means, to be hot, to boil" speaks of "fervency" of spirit,

It's a little old fashioned: But I'm not embarrassed to say, I still believe in Holiness. I still believe in purity in word, in deed, and thought, and mind, and I still believe that Holiness is as holiness does. That means that if your heart is holy your life will be too, you will walk holy, and talk holy and dress holy.

I shouldn't have to see your church affiliation to know you're a Christian, I should be able to tell it by the life you lead and the company you keep.

It's not any old prayer that secures the victory. It's the prayer of the righteous, and it's the prayer of the fervent.

A man of prayer once said: "As a painted fire is no fire, a dead man no man, so a cold prayer is no prayer. In a painted fire there is no heat, in a dead man there is no life; so in a cold prayer there is no omnipotence, no devotion, no blessing. Cold prayers are as arrows without heads, as swords without edges, as birds without wings; they pierce not, they cut not, they fly not up to heaven. Cold prayers do always freeze before they get to heaven.

E.M. Bounds said: God can, and does tolerate many things in the way of infirmity and error in His children. He can, and will pardon sin when the penitent prays, but two things are intolerable to Him - insincerity and lukewarmness. Lack of heart and lack of heat are two things He hates.

*God does nothing except in answer to prayer. Ask and ye shall receive, seek and ye shall find, knock and it shall be opened unto you.

You have not because you ask not.

When Moses hands dropped the enemy gained the advantage. When your hands drop, Satan gains the advantage, look at your own life, and ask yourself this question: Have I lost ground? If the answer is yes, then it is due to our weakness in prayer,

This is where the real battle is and this is where it is won or lost.
It has been said … He stands tallest who kneels the most.

I love this story in the bible because it shows us the power of prayer and the inner workings of prayer.

Note that when Moses hands dropped the enemy gained the advantage.

That tells me that no matter how powerful or how anointed a man or woman may be, we need help.

Moses hands got heavy: That means he grew <u>tired</u> under the burden, under the weight of the need. That means he felt the weight of the burden.

If you have ever been under a real prayer burden then you know exactly what that feels like.

There is such a thing as a prayer burden that weighs on you, and presses upon you.

Let me add, this is never a bad thing, the burden of the lord is a blessing, it's an honor to get under the load of prayer, but it can get heavy.

We were never meant to carry the load alone

Aaron and Hur became Moses helpers in Prayer:

If we are going to win the battles that we are fighting we can't do it alone: We are fellow laborers, and we are comrades, and we are partners, we are a team.

They took a stone and brought it for Moses to sit on: This represents two things:

#1 It represents stabilizing, supporting, establishing, strength.

#2 It represents (rest) even though you are in a battle you can <u>rest now</u> because you are not in it alone. No you can't quit fighting, but you don't have to carry the load all by yourself. You can breathe now.

Exe 17:12-13 But Moses' hands were heavy; and they took a stone, and put it under him, and <u>he sat thereon;</u> and *Aaron and*

Hur stayed up his hands, the one on the one side, and the other on the other side; and his hands were steady until the going down of the sun.

13   And Joshua discomfited Amalek and his people with the edge of the sword

And his hands were steady until the going down of the sun. His hands represents his strength, his spiritual power, his effect in the spiritual realm.

I believe today this is the message that God wanted me to bring to you today.

#1 We are in a Battle

#2 The Battle is not imaginary, the battle is real.

#3 The real Battle is Spiritual not physical

#4 We must fight it in the spirit with spiritual weapons

#5 We cannot win alone

We need each other

Every prayer prayed by every person is an integral part of the victory that we win.

I just feel today that there are some that have felt like you have been up on that mountain alone, and you've been trying to hold off the hordes of hell all alone.

I want to tell you… You are not alone

I feel like somebody reading these words needs to be reminded: You are important. We need you, we need your prayers. We need each other.

 I am not complete without you.

We are comrades.

We are Co-workers and fellow laborers.

Dear reader, I hope that you have seen that the life we are speaking about is not automatic. This is a life of growing in the knowledge, the grace, the wisdom, and the power of God. This life is progressive. It is a lifestyle of daily pressing forward, and daily seeking God.

Precious friend, if you or I, or anybody for that matter… wants to be established, wants to be steadfast and unmovable in Christ, then there is no other way; you must pray. I must pray. We must pray.

12
The Stability Factor

Dear reader, in a world that has gone topsy turvy, and lost all sense of balance there is a stabilizing factor than can bring us back into divine alignment with the will, the purpose and the power of God.

We're going to see it right here in the Word of God…

And wisdom and knowledge shall be the stability of thy times, and strength of salvation: the fear of the LORD is his treasure. Isa 33:6

Those of you who have followed this ministry know that I am not just a preacher and a writer, but I am also a prophetic voice to my generation and I have been hearing something in my spirit for the last days several days and it has been getting louder and louder.

As we look around us today it seems as though the whole worlds gone crazy, It seems as though there are no longer any reference points.

When the prodigal son in the scriptures came to himself in the pigpen after wasting his substance, and wasting his life on riotous, self-pleasing, desires, he remembered where he came from, he had a reference point.

He remembered his father's house, he remembered what was good and what was evil, he remembered what faithfulness and honesty and integrity and dignity looked like.

He remembered what it felt like to be loved not on the basis of what he could do or the money that he had, but just for who he was. (He remembered all of that).

But this society has gone crazy, it's as though we (this society this generation) have been sucked up into a tornado and we are spinning out of control.

Elijah the prophet went up to heaven in a whirlwind of fire, but this nation and this generation is going down to hell in a whirlwind of hells fire.

This is no longer just the society that sins and does wrong and does evil, No sir no mam this is now the society that runs with passion and zeal to find the most wicked and perverse things that they can do to pervert truth and rebel against God, to spit in his face and to make a mockery of the cross and the blood of Jesus.

We are quickly becoming a zombifide people.

A zombie is defined as: the body of a dead person given the semblance of life but mute and will less (No will) controlled by a supernatural force for some evil purpose.

That's what's happening in this nation. People are becoming zombifide. You see in order to become a zombie you have to surrender your will, and once you surrender your will to evil then evil controls you.

That's what we see happening not only in America but around the world, nations are being driven by evil powers as puppets on a string.

They are murderous; acting without any concern for human life. Their thirst for power and World dominance has made them mad. They're off their rockers, they've lost it. They've gone off the deep end.

There is not a shred of decency or human compassion left to stabilize their actions.

In video cameras today, and even in our smart phones, we have something built into them called a stabilizer.

Some how while you're filming it keeps the pictures steady even though the phone is moving and bouncing around.

Airplanes also have these stabilizing capabilities: An aircraft is considered stable when there is no rotation motion or tendency, and the aircraft is stable if it returns to its initial equilibrium flight conditions when it's perturbed or disturbed or experiences turbulence.

But if that initial equilibrium or point of balance and stability is lost it is impossible to bring it back into the state of Perpetual stability.

That is what is happening in America, the initial equilibrium that we had in this country that was established in our trust and faith in God and obedience to his righteous commandments has been lost, and we are a nation in free fall.

That means that there are no restraints, there are no efforts being made to pull back on the yoke or pull up, or bring us back to course.

All stabilizing factors, all common sense, all goodness and decency are being rejected on every hand.

Thank God for what our newly elected president and leaders are trying to do, but a president can't fix the soul of this nation.

It's not a color thing, it's not a political party thing, and it's not even a money thing. It's a soul thing. Satan is bidding for the soul of this nation, and we as a nation are in free fall and this country is spinning out of control.

As I said, to a large degree we have become zombifide and we're completely oblivious to what is happening in the world. Like the zombie nothing affects us, nothing makes us happy nothing makes us sad, nothing makes us cry, nothing makes us angry, nothing evokes joy in us. Its just going through the motions, and the sad part about is… this society wants it that way.

That way there is no conscience, they can perform every evil sexually perverse thing with no sense of wrong. They can commit murder, and mayhem with no consciousness of guilt or shame.

Just a few days ago in Michigan (United States of America) Not some deep dark Jungle in Africa, not a deep dark corner in India.

But right here in the good ole U.S. of A. a doctor was accused of mutilating the genitals of young girls. Her defense was; it is part of our religious practices.

This doctor was one of two who were both charged with conspiring to perform female genital mutilations on minor girls. Authorities believe they have done this to several other young girls between the ages of 6-9 years old.

In 2014 an Oklahoma City man went into a woman's work place and cut off her head.
Then in February 2016 it was reported that in 16 months Oklahoma had experienced four more decapitations.

Pastor this is gruesome, why are you telling us this?
Because this is the real world: This is what America is becoming.
And because too many preachers won't tell the truth, they want to keep their people medicated and sedated, and in a catatonic state, just following along in a zombifide state oblivious to the world around them.
They keep them drugged up on feel good messages that never deal with sin, or the consequences, and don't tell them how to have power over sin and the devil.
The bible commands those who watch over the souls of men to lift their voices like a trumpet and sound the alarm.
Isaiah said: Cry aloud and spare not, lift up thy voice like a trumpet and show my people their transgressions and the house of Jacob their sins.
America is in a free fall spiraling to destruction, and much of the church world is just sitting around singing cumbayah.
Sin is in the church: Homosexuality, lesbianism, drinking, gambling, fornication, adultery, pornography, sexual perversion, lust, pride, hypocrisy, false doctrine (telling everybody that it doesn't matter what they do or how they live, that its already covered, your already justified they say. There's no judgment with God, there's no consequences to your sin, go ahead and fornicate, go ahead and lust and commit adultery, go ahead and practice homosexuality and lesbianism. They say the blood of Jesus has it all covered, and by the way there's no such place as

hell anyway, that was just something invented by some angry condemning religious zealots.

No hell was not the invention of law preaching condemning religious zealots.

Mt 25:41 Then shall he say also unto them on the left hand, Depart from me, ye cursed, into everlasting fire, prepared for the devil and his angels:

And the bible says because of the pride and rebellion of man Hell has enlarged herself to receive them.

Isa 5:14 Therefore hell hath enlarged herself, and opened her mouth without measure: and their glory, and their multitude, and their pomp, and he that rejoiceth, shall descend into it.

Beloved I am a positive person and I love to encourage people and build them up, but you don't heal a cancer by putting a band-aid on it.

It either has to be burned out or cut out.

Our country including much of the church world today has been thrown off balance and they have lost their stability, they have lost their stabilizing factor.

For just a few minutes I want to present to you what can stabilize the church, what can stabilize America.

What can bring us back to true center and true north.

There is hope yet for America, and there is yet hope for the laodicean modern lukewarm church.

And there is hope for you and I, no matter how out of balance and out of control things are around us.

There is a stabilizing factor: But I'm not going to lie about it, it's not going to be easy and a lot of people even church people will not accept it.

But it is not in my power to make people live right, but it is in my power and it is my responsibility to show them how.

Mal 2:7 For the priest's lips should keep knowledge, and they should seek the law at his mouth: for he is the messenger of the Lord of hosts.

And again the bible says:

Ezekiel 22:26 Her priests have violated my law, and have profaned mine holy things: they have put no difference between the holy and profane, neither have they shewed difference between the unclean and the clean, and have hid their eyes from my Sabbaths, and I am profaned among them.

In our text it is as though God is looking right down into the 21st century and He is seeing all the confusion, and all the perversion and all the chaos, and in His everlasting mercy and goodness He is saying...

I can help you, there is hope, I can get you back on course, and I can bring stability back into your life.

Church if we've ever needed anything in this world today and in the church: It's a stabilizing factor.

This whole world is a ticking time bomb:

Many times I have been in Oklahoma before a big storm hit and even though it was a beautiful day, you could feel the instability in the atmosphere.

The atmosphere in this country, and the world is unstable, it's volatile, it's explosive.

It could go off any minute, only now it's not bullets, and canon balls, it's nuclear interballistic missiles that can take out a whole country.

Everybody is stretching their muscles trying to prove to each other how powerful they are.

Its not interballistic missiles that we need, and it's not missile interceptors, that we need, It's the presence the power and the glory of God that we need.

There is a path back to the glory and back to a place of protection and power (back to the place of stability).

It's right here in this verse.

Isa 33:6 And wisdom and knowledge shall be the stability of thy times, and strength of salvation: the fear of the LORD is his treasure.

Wisdom and Knowledge, not human intellectual wisdom or intelligence. Not nuclear wisdom and knowledge. Not political wisdom and knowledge.

Godly wisdom and knowledge: Divine God given Holy Spirit imparted wisdom.

Now lets get to the heart of the matter

What is Godly Holy Spirit Imparted Wisdom?

This is what the Bible says it looks like…

The fear of the LORD is the beginning of wisdom: and the knowledge of the holy is understanding.

The Fear of the Lord is where wisdom comes from: Wisdom springs from the source of the fear of the Lord.

That is why our country has gone crazy, that is why America is in a free fall. That is why we are spiraling into destruction.

That is why the church is to a large degree a laughing stock of the world today, just more material for some filthy sitcom to use to ridicule and criticize the church.

That's why the church (I use that term loosely because there is a remnant church) though few by contrast, they are the pure in heart and they are true to the Word of God and true to the leading of the Holy Spirit.

But this psuedo church, this lukewarm, church without a cross, without repentance without the blood, without the presence and the power and the glory of God… they have lost the fear of God.

Ro 3:18 says, There is no fear of God before their eyes.

Isa 29:13 says, Wherefore the Lord said, Forasmuch as this people draw near me with their mouth, and with their lips do honour me, but have removed their heart far from me, and their fear toward me is taught by the precept of men:

God says: Their fear toward me is taught by the precept of men. (In other words, God says they have no true fear of God anymore because they have been taught by the precept of man a false fear, an unbiblical fear, a deceptive fear, a diluted fear, a comfortable fear.

And the church has largely been the guilty party because for so long we preachers have tried to make people comfortable around God. Take the rough edges off, smooth him down, and make Christianity easy to take. We have tried to make it palatable easy to swallow.

And we have stripped the true fear of God out of the church and out of the hearts of the people.

Preachers have told their people that the fear of God is just a respect, just an attitude of honor and appreciation that doesn't want to hurt God.

Friend for just a couple more minutes I want to show you from Gods word what the fear of the Lord looks like.

Pr 8:13 The fear of the LORD is to hate evil: pride, and arrogancy, and the evil way, and the froward mouth, do I hate.
Pr 14:27 The fear of the LORD is a fountain of life, to depart from the snares of death.
2Co 7:1 Having therefore these promises, dearly beloved, let us cleanse ourselves from all filthiness of the flesh and spirit, perfecting holiness in the fear of God.

The problem we have is we haven't been taught the true fear of God:
We've forgotten the God of the bible:
The God of the Bible: The one who wiped out the human race except for Noah and his family in the ark.
The God of the Bible: The one who opened up the red sea and swallowed up the Egyptians, The one who opened up the earth and swallowed up the sons of Korah.
The God of the bible: The one who burned up the two sons of Aaron because they offered to him strange fire.

The God of the bible: The one who rained fire and brimstone from heaven and destroyed the cities of Sodom and Gomorrah.

The God of the bible: The one who sent poisonous serpents among the people and many of them died, because of their sin.

Oh but Pastor that was the Old God: He was angry in the old testament, our God is the new testament God, He's all grace and mercy. He's not angry anymore. He's calm; He's better adjusted now, He's on Prozac and valiums.

Somebody should have told Ananaias and Saphira about that: Because they didn't get the memo.

You know the story of a Man and his wife who tried to deceive the Holy Ghost

They lied about the price of the land they sold and how much they received for it.

Acts 5:5 And Ananias hearing these words fell down, and gave up the ghost: and great fear came on all them that heard these things.

Acts 5:7-10 And it was about the space of three hours after, when his wife, not knowing what was done, came in.

8 And Peter answered unto her, Tell me whether ye sold the land for so much? And she said, Yea, for so much.

9 Then Peter said unto her, How is it that ye have agreed together to tempt the Spirit of the Lord? behold, the feet of them which have buried thy husband are at the door, and shall carry thee out.

10 Then fell she down straightway at his feet, and yielded up the ghost: and the young men came in, and found her dead, and, carrying her forth, buried her by her husband.

What was the result of this?

Acts 5:11-12 And great fear came upon all the church, and upon as many as heard these things. 12 And by the hands of the apostles were many signs and wonders wrought among the people; and they were all with one accord in Solomon's porch.

Ac 9:31 Then had the churches rest throughout all Judaea and Galilee and Samaria, and were edified; and walking in the fear of the Lord, and in the comfort of the Holy Ghost, were multiplied.

I am prophesying to you today: that one of the marks of this last day outpouring is going to be a drastic and sudden return to the fear of God.

That's the only thing that can put the church back on track, and back in equilibrium. We must have a new vision and desire for the fear of God to take hold on the church and on our lives.

Pr 10:27 The fear of the LORD prolongeth days: but the years of the wicked shall be shortened.
Pr 14:26 In the fear of the LORD is strong confidence: and his children shall have a place of refuge.
Pr 14:27 The fear of the LORD is a fountain of life, to depart from the snares of death.

I don't know what all this means: I don't know what God is going to do, or the means He is going to use, but I do know this… we better get ready, because there is a major house cleaning coming to the church, and along with it is coming a healthy dose of the fear of God.

Let me share with you one last verse of scripture… Proverbs 19:3 The Bible says, The fear of the Lord tended to life: and he that hath it shall abide satisfied; he shall not be visited with evil.
That verse says that the person who lives in the fear of God will abide satisfied. But as we have seen from so many scriptures, not only will the fear of the Lord satisfy you, the fear of the Lord will stabilize you. And if there is anything you and I need in the hour we live in, it is stability.

And then we can sing this song together… I Shall Not Be Moved.

13
Power From On High

Praise the Lord, my precious friends I am so excited about this book, in this book I will share with you many of the things that I have learned about the anointing of the Holy Spirit. I will also share with you some of my personal experiences.

All I can say is get ready for the fire, get ready to be "anointed for the battle."

Dear reader, I am convinced, to deal with problems here below we need Power from on High.

Through this book there will be some overlapping, there will be some scriptures that are quoted 2 or 3 times, but I am certain that you will benefit from the repetition.

Now, I don't want to come off sounding critical or sarcastic but I want to say this before we get started… If you have an aversion to or a critical mindset to the Pentecostal experience, or the work of the Holy Spirit, then you may not even want to read this book. But if you have at least an open mind and a hungry heart, then please read on.

I have to say from the very beginning, I love the Holy Spirit. I hope through the pages of this book that I can help you to know him better for yourself. I truthfully cannot imagine a life without the Holy Spirit in it.

Hallelujah, are you ready? All right, let's start by looking at a couple of verses that are directly related to receiving the power of the Holy Spirit.

Jesus said: *"And, behold, I send the promise of my Father upon you: but tarry ye in the city of Jerusalem, until ye be endued with power from on high." Lu 24: 49*

Then look at this one, *Lu 3:16-17 "John answered, saying unto them all, I indeed baptize you with water; but one mightier than I cometh, the latchet of whose shoes I am not worthy to unloose: he shall baptize you with (the Holy Ghost and with fire:) 17 Whose fan is in his hand, and he will throughly purge his floor, and will gather the wheat into his garner; but the chaff he will burn with fire unquenchable."*

Jesus looked at his disciples his faithful students and he recognized that they had received his instructions, they had studied, they had passed the course, but he said they were not fully equipped to carry on his ministry, they must have power from on high (they must be baptized in the Holy Ghost and fire).

For Many years the Baptism of the Holy Ghost and the ministration thereof has been going through "a process of disintegration" certainly not from Gods perspective, but from mans perspective. In particular, full Gospel churches.

Disintegrate means, to break apart, dissolve, powderize, break up, and crumble.

We have reached the place where even within the full Gospel churches of America, the Baptism of the Holy Ghost has been reduced to a mere acknowledgment of an indwelling presence of Jesus experienced by all believers.

There is today within the full Gospel churches, not only a depreciation for speaking with other tongues as the spirit gives the utterance as the initial sign and evidence of being spirit filled, There is tremendous opposition against speaking in tongues period.

We are being told, even in full gospel, "Pentecostal churches" that it is unnecessary to speak in other tongues to be filled with the Holy Ghost.

I do not want to argue with these great theologians and bible scholars but I have learned over a period of time that our experience and our relationship with God is built upon the Word of God, and when I build it upon the Word of God I am going to be safe no matter what the trend of the day is.

I'm going to agree with Smith Wigglesworth, one of the most powerful men of God who ever lived, He was known as the

Apostle of Faith. He cast out devils, healed the sick and raised 19 people from the dead,

He said: The baptism will always be as at the beginning, it has not changed, if you want a real baptism expect it just the same way as they had it at the beginning.

Well then, how was it at the beginning? We find the answer right here in the second chapter of Acts..

(Acts 2:1-4) "¶ And when the day of Pentecost was fully come, they were all with one accord in one place. 2 And suddenly there came a sound from heaven as of a rushing mighty wind, and it filled all the house where they were sitting. 3 And there appeared unto them cloven tongues like as of fire, and it sat upon each of them. 4 And they were all filled with the Holy Ghost, and (began to speak with other tongues) as the Spirit gave the utterance."

Then when Paul encountered new believers in Christ, the first thing he wanted to know was... Have you received the Holy Ghost since you believed?

The Bible says:

"And when Paul had laid his hands upon them, the Holy Ghost came on them; and (they spake with tongues,) and prophesied." (Ac 19:6)

When the door of grace opened to the gentile nation, they received this same gift and spoke with other tongues.

And again…

(Ac 10:44-47) ¶ "While Peter yet spake these words, the Holy Ghost fell on all them which heard the word. 45 And they of the circumcision which believed were astonished, as many as came with Peter, because that on the Gentiles also was poured out the gift of the Holy Ghost. 46 For they heard them speak with tongues, and magnify God. Then answered Peter, 47 Can any man forbid water, that these should not be baptized, which have received the Holy Ghost as well as we?"

In every case, speaking with other tongues was associated with the baptism of the Holy Ghost.

John said, this Holy Ghost Baptism came with fire!

(Lu 3:16)... "He shall baptize you with the Holy Ghost and with fire.
Fire Speaks of life, of energy, of intensity, of passion.
He shall baptize you with the Holy Ghost and with fire. This fire is the devouring nature of God. *Our God is a consuming fire. (Heb 12:29)*
 When I was growing up in church, it seemed every testimony had the fire in it somewhere. Every message had the fire in it somewhere.
Sadly today in many cases, I look around in our churches and I wonder, is the fire in it anywhere?
The favorite songs of the church used to be about the fire

Songs like...
• It's the Holy Ghost and fire and it's keeping me alive.
• It's just like fire shut up in my bones.
And it wasn't just words, about the third or fourth time through, the song leader would go to jerkin, her head would jerk back, it looked like it would break her neck.
Then all of a sudden one of the ladies up on the platform would start shouting, and then it was holy pandemonium, shoes came off, hairpins went flying. Then one of the brothers jumped up and started shaking like he was on fire.
Right about then my grandpa would jump up and take off running. The closest person to the outside isle joined grandpa's train, I call it a train because grandpa used to hold his hand up to his ear and holler like a train whistle.
 Today many of our full gospel, Pentecostal churches would say, that was just excessive emotions, and it was not necessary, and it's not necessary now.
Well, I will agree that there was a great deal of emotion in it, but when you got a fire in your feet it's hard to stand still.

And it may have been extremely emotional but in the middle of that dancing and shouting and running, people got saved healed delivered, and filled with the Holy Ghost and fire, and many received their call into the ministry, including me.

Today our churches have become so seeker sensitive that we have become Holy Spirit insensitive.

We're so concerned about creating an environment that is conducive to the seeker, that we've ignored the one we're suppose to be seeking.

I'll just be honest about it, I would rather risk offending a seeker than offending the Holy Spirit, because I can make it without you, but I can't make it without him.

But the truth is: a true seeker is not going to be scared off by the power of God. A true seeker is looking for truth, they are looking for something real, and when they see the genuine power of God in action they will want it.

I believe that we have a responsibility to show our generation the true manifestation of the power of God, uncensored, undiluted, full strength.

Listen to what David said: It should be the prayer of every true believer, and especially every minister of the gospel.

He said…

"Now also when I am old and gray headed, O God, forsake me not; until I have shewed thy strength unto this generation, and thy power to every one that is to come." (Ps 71:18)

Jesus First Miracle was that of turning the water into wine

First Full of Water, "Salvation"

Then Full of Wine "The Spirit"

The progression is salvation, then Being filled with the Spirit

Jesus Said: *"If any man Thirst let him come to me and drink, and out of his belly will flow rivers of Living water.* (See Jn 7:37-38)

- Coming to Jesus and drinking is symbolic of salvation. Receiving Jesus as our Savior.

- Then rivers of living waters flowing out of our bellies, represents, the Holy Spirit flowing out of us to minister to others.

I know that we are in an advanced age, and I know that technology has made tremendous strides, and we have access to information on a scale our forefathers could only dream about. We can go to the internet, or the radio, or television, or mp3 players, or I-pod's, and we can access tremendous truth in a moments time.

And I know that grandpa and grandma didn't have a lot of the advantages we have today, but grandma and grandpa could teach the church a few lessons.

They knew the power of the blood of Jesus.

They knew how to pray.

They didn't have the access to the medicines and the emergency room like we have today, they'd be out on the backside of a mountain somewhere and someone would get deathly ill, and they would pray until they prayed through and heaven invaded earth and the victory came.

They knew you need the Holy Ghost, those old timers believed that if you didn't have the Holy Ghost you weren't gonna' make it. They said without the Holy Ghost you weren't getting off the launching pad when Jesus comes back.

They knew the Holy Ghost was the power to conquer sin and live a Holy life.

Those old timers would get you to the altar and once they got you to the altar, it was get filled with the Holy Ghost or die trying.

One was pushing, the other was pulling. One said, say thank you Jesus. Another one said, say praise the Lord. Then one said, hold on, and the other said turn loose.

And it might have been a little confusing, but somewhere in the middle of all that activity, God saw the purity of the hearts and the hunger and the zeal to get everything he promised, and all of a sudden the spirit of God started stirring in their belly and a river came rushing through them and they started speaking in a tongue they never learned and it changed their lives forever, it gave them boldness to be a witness and live for God.

I'm not just talking about something my grandpa told me about. I'm not talking about second hand information of something that happened to somebody somewhere sometime.

I got it the same way. I got that same old-fashioned baptism. I layed on my face, I layed on my back, I stood, I laughed, I cried. I said thank you Jesus till I thought my tongue was going to fall off. And somewhere along the way God saw my heart and knew that I was serious, and all of a sudden at 4:00 a.m. on a Sunday morning, it was like a streak of lightning hit me in the top of my head and went through my body and shot out my finger tips and I started speaking in tongues by the unction and power of the Holy Ghost and my life has never been the same since.

Dear reader, I tell you unapologetically, you need the Holy Ghost. Every one needs the baptism of the Holy Ghost.

If you plan on going to heaven today the Blood of Jesus has qualified you to get in, but if you plan on getting up tomorrow and facing life, and dealing with a real devil, then you need the Holy Ghost.

According to Jesus way of thinking, we are not fit or I should say, properly suited or prepared and equipped for Christ's ministry until we are full of the Spirit.

Let's look at it again…

(Lu 24: 49) "Jesus said: *(And, behold, I send the promise of my Father upon you: but tarry ye in the city of Jerusalem, until ye be endued with power from on high.*

(Acts 1:8*) "But ye shall receive power, after that the Holy Ghost is come upon you: and ye shall be witnesses unto me both in Jerusalem, and in all Judea, and in Samaria, and unto the uttermost part of the earth."*

Notice that Jesus said, ye shall receive power <u>after</u> the Holy Ghost has come upon you, not before (after). There are no short cuts to the power of God, you must be born again, then you must be filled with the Spirit.

And let me go farther than that. You must not only be filled, you must keep being filled.

Paul the apostle said in … *(Eph 5:18) "And be not drunk with wine wherein is excess, but be ye filled with the Spirit."*

Literally, it means to be filled and keep being filled.

It really doesn't count for much what you had 15-20 years ago, or last year or last week for that matter…

What matters is, where is the Holy Spirit thermometer reading right now?

How fresh is your oil?

Are you full of the Spirit or are you running on fumes?

Be ye filled with the Spirit means; be full of the spirit at all times. When you are full of the Spirit, sometimes you will run over, it might run over in church, it might run over in wal-mart, it might run over while your driving down the road.

But if you're full it will run over sometime.

One of the greatest ways you can keep yourself full is by praying in the Holy Ghost.

(See *Jude verse 20*) … *"But ye beloved, building up yourselves on your most holy faith, praying in the Holy Ghost."*

The Spirit Filled Life means that you are…

- Led by the Spirit
- Taught by the Spirit
- Guided by the Spirit
- Helped by the Spirit
- Comforted by the Spirit
- Corrected by the Spirit
- Convicted by the Spirit
- Empowered by the Spirit

That is why wine in the Bible is such a fitting symbol of the Spirit. As wine exercises a controlling influence over a person's life, when we are filled with the Spirit our entire lives will be under his influence.

Before we go any farther in this book, if you have not received the Holy Ghost since you believed, you need to lift your hands and ask God to fill you. And if you have received the Holy Ghost but it's been a while since you have really felt him moving in you, and you haven't been experiencing the freedom and the liberty of the Spirit, and speaking in other tongues as the Spirit gives you utterance, then you need to lift your hands and tell him you want a fresh baptism.

Dear friend, receive ye The Holy Ghost.

Be filled now!

Receive a fresh Baptism of fire.

Receive Power from on High, in Jesus name.

14
The Jesus Life

When we make reference to the Christian life, we could just as easily call it "the Jesus life."

You may ask the question what do you mean when you say the Jesus life?

Well I would say that the Jesus life means, that the life of Christ is manifesting itself through the life of the believer.

The life of Jesus should be made manifest in our bodies.

2 Corinthians chapter 4 tells us this... that the life of Jesus should be made manifest in our bodies, manifest in our mortal flesh.

Let's read it together...

"always bearing about in the body the dying of the Lord Jesus, that the life also of Jesus might be made manifest in our body. [11] For we which live are alway delivered unto death for Jesus' sake, that the life also of Jesus might be made manifest in our mortal flesh." (2 Co 4:10-11)

I don't believe that we can truthfully, or properly, and honestly, speak of Jesus and his life and not take into account the supernatural aspect of his life.

The life of Jesus was filled with the supernatural:

- He healed the sick
- He cast out devils
- He opened blind eyes
- He made the dumb to speak and the deaf to hear
- He made the lame to walk
- He raised the dead
- He tamed the sea
- He walked through walls
- He traveled supernaturally
- He fed the multitude with a young lads sack lunch
- He turned water into wine

The fact is Jesus lived a supernatural life.

This is the life that Jesus willed to us. This is the life he purposed for his body through the power of the Holy Spirit.

The Bible says as he is so are we in this world. And it says the works that I do, shall ye do also, and greater works than these shall you do, because I go to my father.

The purpose for Jesus giving us the Holy Spirit, was to produce and reproduce in us that same supernatural life that he lived.

Dear reader, a church or an individual believer without the supernatural, is living beneath their birthright, beneath their inheritance, and their privileges.

And I must say that a church without the supernatural is a very weak representation of Jesus.

It is undisputedly the will of God that every one of his children be filled with his spirit, and live a supernatural life.

Mark chapter 16 is Jesus description of the individual that fully embraces and mani-fests the Jesus life. Here's what he says about the believers. They will…

➤ Cast out devils
➤ Speak with new tongues
➤ Be supernaturally protected
➤ Heal the sick
➤ Cleanse the lepers
➤ Raise the dead

Basically, they will do everything that Jesus did and more. As Jesus said in his Word, *"the works that I do show you do also and greater works than these shall you do because I go to my father." (See Jn 14:12)*

And then see another verse here in Luke:

Luke 10:19 says... Behold I give unto you power to tread on serpents and scorpions and over all the power of the enemy and nothing shall by any means hurt you.

But it is sad to say that the modern-day church is a mere shadow of the church Jesus intended us to be.

Jesus gave to us the church; the same supernatural capacity and power that he had operating in his life,
That power is the Holy Spirit.
(Acts 10:38) says... *How God anointed Jesus of Nazareth with the Holy Ghost and with power who went about doing good healing all that were oppressed of the devil for God was with him.*
The Holy Ghost was the power source in Jesus life.
Everything Jesus did in the realm of the supernatural, he did by one or more of the gifts of the spirit.
Now he has given those same nine supernatural gifts to the church, the body of Christ.
I believe with all of my heart God is calling his church back to their spiritual heritage, and their supernatural birthright.
We are entering a time of supernatural warfare on a scale we have never known in this nation.
We must return to our supernatural birthright, our supernatural DNA.
We must learn again how to walk in the supernatural.
- How to discern
- How to prophesy
- How to hear God's voice
- How to work the works of God
- How to cast out devils and heal the sick

Dear reader, I'm going to prophesy to you... In these coming days, if the church does not embrace their supernatural birthright, and does not operate by the power and the anointing of the Holy Ghost, they're going to be swept away by false doctrine and delusion.
You can talk about the humanity of Jesus, his love, his kindness, his goodness, his long-suffering, his compassion, and forgiveness, and you can embrace all of those qualities, and we should. But to cast out devils, to deliver the bound and oppressed, to open blind eyes and deaf ears, to drive cancer and drugs out of the body, or to raise the dead, you have to embrace his divinity. You have to receive his supernatural life.

Dear reader we are in a spiritual warfare!

There has been a dramatic increase of demonic freedom and activity in this nation.

And there's only one thing that can drive back the demons of hell, and that is a church walking in her supernatural heritage and power.

But you say what about the Angels? Yes the Angels are our helpers without a doubt, but the Angels only go into action, when we go into action. They assist us, they fight with us, and they protect us as we move forward against the enemy.

The church, or the individual that does not embrace their supernatural DNA, are going to get run over by hell.

The devil is going to trample you down. Dear reader, I feel a strong urgency in my spirit to urge you to press into the Spirit. To spend more time with God. To spend more time seeking God for his power. To spend more time asking him for discernment. To spend more time praying in the Holy Ghost. To spend more time in the Word of God.

Paul exhorted Timothy as his son in the faith to stir up the anointing that was in him. I exhort you in the faith today, to stir up the gifts that are in you.

To ask God for the gifts of the spirit to operate in you.

I exhort you to spend some time fasting.

Fast from food

Fast from the media

Fast from TV

Fast from the Internet

Fast from the social media

So you can become more aware of the spirit world. Whether you believe it or not, it's present, it's here. And if we do not engage that realm with the supernatural power of God, then the devil has the run of the camp.

It's up to you and I as believers, as the children, as the sons and daughters of God, to exercise divine authority, and manifest the supernatural power of the anointing. There is great opposition and great demonic warfare in the earth right now.

And sad to say, to a large degree, the church is not even engaged in the battle.

Sadly, the church has to a large measure forfeited her spiritual power and authority. In some cases, I believe it's because we have been trained to avoid the supernatural, and to be skeptical of anything spiritual.

We were also trained, to not seek after spiritual gifts.

We were also told to not seek after signs and wonders.

All of this has served to strip the church, of her supernatural life.

But God is waking up his slumbering   church. There is a desire for the supernatural power of God that is coming back to his church.

I desire to live the Jesus life. To have a life filled with signs and wonders and miracles, to have a life filled with visions and dreams, to manifest the gifts of the spirit, to cast out devils and heal the sick, to cooperate with angels in the ministry.

Dear reader this is the Jesus life.

This is the life the Holy Spirit wants to manifest through us.

This is the life that was purchased for us with the precious blood of Jesus.

Jesus did not shed his blood on the cross just to redeem us from sin, and just to take us to heaven when we die.

No precious friend, Jesus shed his blood on the cross to redeem us from sin, to make our bodies a dwelling place for his mighty Holy Spirit. So that he could work through us, with his supernatural life and power.

That's what Pentecost is all about.

Pentecost was the introduction, the infilling, the coming of the Holy Spirit, to live in, to dwell in, to possess, and to manifest through the human vessel, the presence, the power, and the glory of God, by the power of the Holy Spirit.

It is the will of God undeniably, and indisputably, that every child of God, and every single person that has been redeemed by the blood of Jesus, and that has been washed and cleansed by the power of the blood of Jesus also be filled with the mighty power of the Holy Spirit.

The blood of Jesus redeems us from our sins, and the blood of Jesus prepares us for heaven.

But the Holy Spirit is divine equipment, and is the power to operate and function, and to manifest the Christ life on this earth.

15
Taking Care Of Business

Dear Christian reader, I don't know if you realize this or not, but you and I are supposed to be taking care of the fathers business.

Do you remember the time when Jesus was twelve years old and he got separated from his parents, and they went three days journey before they realized that Jesus was not in their caravan? Well, when they finally located Jesus, he was in the temple with the scribes and doctors of the law, preaching and teaching. His parents were displeased that he had wandered off from them and that they had lost track of him. They scolded him, then Jesus said: Know ye not that I must be about my fathers business?

Jesus understood at a very young age that he had a destiny that was bigger than his earthly fathers carpentry business.

Now as we look at this verse here in Luke: Jesus is full-grown and he is now running his fathers business. As we study Jesus role in the fathers business, I believe we will also realize that we too are called to take care of the fathers business.

Now lets look at this very descriptive verse here in Luke,

(Luke 4:18) "the Spirit of the Lord is upon me, because he hath anointed me to preach the gospel to the poor; he hath sent me to heal the brokenhearted, to preach deliverance to the captives, and recovering of sight to the blind, to set at liberty them that are bruised, to preach the acceptable year of the Lord."

This was Jesus quoting Isaiah's words that were prophetically spoken concerning Jesus. And in a broader sense, it was a prophecy concerning the church, the church walking in the power of the Holy Spirit.

Here in Luke chapter 4 Jesus is standing up in the temple, and he speaks out boldly, and he quotes Isaiah, then he says... This day is this scripture fulfilled in your ears.

Now here's the Scripture that he was quoting,

Isaiah 61:1-4 "the spirit of the Lord God is upon me, because the Lord hath anointed me to preach good tidings unto the meek: he hath sent me to bind up the brokenhearted, to proclaim liberty to the captives and the opening of the prison to them that are bound. To proclaim the acceptable year of the Lord, and the day of vengeance of our God; to comfort all that mourn, to appoint unto them that mourn in Zion, to give unto them beauty for ashes, the oil of joy for mourning, the garment of praise for the spirit of heaviness: that they might be called trees of righteousness, the planting of the Lord, that he might be glorified."

In these two Scripture settings we are told what the ministry of Jesus is… We can expect that anywhere Jesus is, he will do these very same things.

As we read these very powerful verses our faith is stirred to believe God for everything that Jesus did.

We are to expect the gospel to be preached to the poor,

- ➢ The brokenhearted to be healed
- ➢ The captives to be set free
- ➢ The opening of the prisons to them that are bound
- ➢ The recovering of sight to the blind
- ➢ We are to expect comfort for all that mourn
- ➢ We are to expect joy, supernatural joy
- ➢ And we are to expect that praise is going to overcome the spirit of heaviness.

Everywhere Jesus went he healed the sick, he cast out devils, he cleansed the lepers, and he raise the dead. He set captives free, he opened blind eyes, unstopped deaf ears, and he healed broken hearts.

Everywhere Jesus went he undid the works of the devil.

That's what the Bible tells us here in the book of acts chapter 10,

(Acts 10:38) "How God anointed Jesus of Nazareth with the Holy Ghost and with power, who went about doing good, and healing all that were oppressed of the devil, for God was with him."

Jesus effectively and completely destroyed the works of the devil everywhere he went.

There is no question as to whether Jesus actually did these things or not, the Bible says it, and history bears it out.

The only question is how did he do them?

Some would say: he did them because he was the Son of God, and as the Son of God he had supernatural power and ability.

That is true, but that is not entirely correct.

Yes he was, and he is the Son of God, but he in fact laid aside his deity when he took upon himself humanity.

In other words, he willingly divested himself, meaning he put aside the deity he had, and walked the earth as any other earthly person, or human person.

In other words, he confined himself to operate and function on this earth, with the same capabilities, and the same limitations, as any other man or woman of God.

Well then, how did he do all of the divine, supernatural, miraculous things he did?

The Bible tells us here in Luke chapter 4,

(Luke 4:18) "the Spirit of the Lord God is upon me, because he hath anointed me."

And then again here in the book of Acts,

(Acts 10:38) "How God anointed Jesus of Nazareth, with the Holy Ghost and with power, who went about doing good and healing all that were oppressed of the devil, for God was with him."

You see the answer is, Jesus operated and functioned on this earth as any other man or woman anointed with the power of the Holy Ghost.

He was anointed by God with the Holy Spirit.

He was empowered by the anointing

Let's look at another Scripture,

1 Jn 3:8 "for this purpose the son of God was manifested, that he might destroy the works of the devil."

Do you see that dear reader? He was anointed with the power of the Holy Ghost, to fulfill a purpose.

Jesus had power with the purpose. In other words the anointing was the power to do the job.

There was a purpose set before Jesus

- There were lost sheep
- There were brokenhearted people
- There were those who were oppressed by the devil
- There were those who were blind and deaf
- There were those who were bound and 0ppressed, and even dead

The anointing was the power that was on Jesus life that equipped him… to heal them, to deliver them, and to raise them from the dead.

Everything Jesus did of a supernatural nature, he did by the anointing and the power of the Holy Spirit.

Why is that so important for us to know?

Because, Jesus has commissioned the church to carry on his work, to fulfill his ministry in the earth.

Jesus said, "*as the father hath sent me into the world even so send I you.*" *John 20:21*

Just as Jesus had a purpose before him, we have a purpose before us.

What that means to you and I dear reader is this, we can read everything that Isaiah said about Jesus, and everything that Jesus said about himself in Luke chapter 4:18 –19, and we can say, me too.

In other words, we are sent to do the same things Jesus was sent to do.

Jesus was sent by the father, and we have been sent by Jesus.

We also have a purpose, and to fulfill that purpose we must have power.

To do what Jesus did we must have what Jesus had.

The secret to the power in Jesus life was that he was anointed with the power of the Holy Ghost.

The secret to the power in our lives is the very same thing. It is the anointing of the Holy Ghost.

16
Jesus, The Pattern Son

He shows us, the life available to anyone of his sons and daughters who would operate by the power and the anointing of the Holy Ghost.

Unfortunately, I believe that to a very large measure we have failed to appreciate and appropriate this power.

Yes we definitely believe in prayer, and in asking God for the things that we need.

But the truth is, we are many times asking God to do what he told us to do.

In other words, He told us to…

- Preach the gospel to every creature.
- Cast out devils.
- Heal the sick.
- Cleanse the lepers.
- Raise the dead.

Remember Jesus said in *Luke 10:19,*

Behold I give unto you power to tread upon serpents and scorpions, and over all the power of the enemy, and nothing shall by any means hurt you.

And then again in *Luke 9:1 "then he called his 12 disciples together, and gave them power and authority over all devils, and to cure diseases, and he sent them to preach the kingdom of God, and to heal the sick."*

And again in Mark,

"And these signs shall follow them that believe, in my name shall they cast out devils: they shall speak with new tongues, they should take up serpents, and if they drink any deadly thing it shall not hurt them, they shall lay their hands on the sick, and they shall recover." Mark 16:17-18

Dear reader I hope you can see that the point I'm making is this, the disciples and the apostles were acting in the authority of Jesus name, and by his power, and they were doing the same things that Jesus was doing.

Now the responsibility is ours. Sadly religion and tradition, has robbed the church of this power.

Religion has decided we can be like Jesus in every way except in his supernatural character.

We can manifest his love, his mercy, his kindness, and his forgiveness. But if we dare to believe that we can do the same things Jesus did, then we're claiming to be God.

So the church has backed up, and we have forfeited our supernatural heritage.

Dear reader let me say something to you that may come as a shock. The greatest enemy to the supernatural character and power of God is not the devil, it has always been religion.

Religion and tradition will tell you that only Jesus had the anointing and the power of God. But the Bible says something different.

2 Corinthians 1:21 "now he which stablisheth us with you in Christ, and hath anointed us, is God."

Dear reader did you see that? He that hath anointed us is God.

We have received the same spirit, the same power, the same anointing that Jesus had.

The Bible says the same spirit that raised Jesus from the dead now dwells in us.

Let's look at another Scripture,

Acts 1:8 "but you shall receive power, after that the Holy Ghost is come upon you: you shall be witnesses unto me, both in Jerusalem, in Judea, and Samaria, and to the uttermost parts of the earth."

Did you see that? He has anointed us with the same power and the same anointing that Jesus had.

Precious friends, we did not receive some lesser version of the Holy Spirit than Jesus had. We did not get some starter pack. We did not get a baby Holy Ghost.

We have the same mighty Holy Spirit that lived in Jesus and raised Jesus from the dead dwelling in us today.

We are anointed with the same power that anointed Jesus.

And we are authorized to act on Jesus part.

That means we have authority and power to act on Jesus part.

<u>We are the ambassadors of</u>
<u>the kingdom of God</u>

As ambassadors of the kingdom of God, we have authority and power, to act on his behalf.

We must take our place as kingdom ambassadors authorized by Jesus, and anointed by the Holy Ghost, and carry on the ministry of Jesus.

17
His Purpose Is Now Our Purpose

He was manifested as the Son of God, to destroy the works of the devil.

Then the Bible tells us in Romans chapter 8,

"the earnest expectation of the creature waiteth for the manifestation of the <u>sons</u> of God." (Ro 8:19)

Dear Christian friend, the world is waiting for us to manifest our son-ship, and to take our place in Christ, and exercise the power and the authority that he has given us, and carry on his business.

The Bible says ... *"The kingdom of God is not in word but in power"* (*1 Co 4:20*)

We are authorized and anointed by God to overthrow, undo, cancel, and destroy the works of the devil.

We are authorized to set the captives free, loose the bands of wickedness, and undo the heavy burdens, break every yoke, to heal the sick, and to cast out devils.

The same spirit, and the same anointing. Yes dear reader, the very same power that operated in Jesus life is operating in you and me today.

We have been authorized, and anointed, to carry out the purpose of Jesus on the earth.

It's not our strength or our ability, or our wisdom. It's the anointing of the Holy Ghost.

"And it shall come to pass in that day that his burden shall be taken away from off thy shoulder, and his yoke from off thy neck, and the yoke shall be destroyed, <u>because of the anointing</u>." (Isa 10:27)

I believe that God is doing something; I believe that God is stirring something in you right now. I believe that you're feeling the anointing of God coming upon you.

Just like Samson's foxes, God has been setting us on fire. He's been stirring up the flame. Our hearts are burning for Jesus.

But there's a difference between us and those foxes.

Those foxes caught the fire all right, and they ran, but they ran mindlessly, they had no consciousness of what they were doing, they did nothing on purpose, it just happened because they happened to be on fire.

The difference is, we know what the fire is for. We know why God sent the fire.

God sent the fire to give us boldness and power to be a witness, and to make us soul winners.

And to give us power …

- To cast out devils
- To undo and destroy the works of the devil
- To lay our hands on the sick and see them recover
- To live a holy life in an unholy world
- To preach the gospel
- To lift up Jesus
- To be a light in the midst of this dark world

Am I talking to anybody today? Dear reader is this you? Are you receiving this fire?

Do you want this fire?

If you do, just lift your hands right now wherever you are, ask God to send the fire, tell God you want power on purpose.

Tell God you understand the purpose for the fire, and that you want his fire in your life so you can fulfill your divine purpose in Jesus name.

We need the fire of the Holy Ghost to take care of the business.

The business that we're in requires power from on high.

18

The Anointing Of Power

My precious friend, I am so excited you have decided to read this book. I love writing about the anointing. As you continue to read we will learn some very powerful things about the anointing, and how it operates in our lives.

Are you ready? Ok let's get into this. We are going to start with a couple of foundational scriptures…

(Isa 10:27)" And it shall come to pass in that day, that his burden shall be taken away from off thy shoulder, and his yoke from off thy neck, and the yoke shall be destroyed because of the anointing."

(Ezek 1:13-14) "As for the likeness of the living creatures, their appearance was like burning coals of fire, and like the appearance of lamps: it went up and down among the living creatures; and the fire was bright, and out of the fire went forth lightning. 14 And the living creatures ran and returned as the appearance of a flash of lightning."

(Lu 3:16-17) "John answered, saying unto them all, I indeed baptize you with water; but one mightier than I cometh, the latchet of whose shoes I am not worthy to unloose: he shall baptize you with the Holy Ghost and with fire 17 Whose fan is in his hand, and he will throughly purge his floor, and will gather the wheat into his garner; but the chaff he will burn with fire unquenchable."

God is referred to specifically as a consuming fire.

(Heb: 12:29) "Our God is a consuming fire."

(Heb 1:7) "And of the angels he saith, who maketh his angels spirits, and his ministers a flame of fire."

We gather from these scriptures and many others that our God is a God of fire, and that everything associated with God has fire connected to it.

19
Every Head Got A Flame

On the day of Pentecost every head got a flame.

They not only spoke with other tongues, but tongues of fire sat upon each of them.

Dear reader, I am Pentecostal, that's my persuasion, I believe in speaking in tongues with all my heart, and I believe that speaking in tongues is the initial evidence of the baptism of the Holy Ghost. And I believe that when you are baptized with the Holy Ghost you will speak with other tongues as the Spirit gives you utterance.

But if all you have is tongues, you are no threat to the devil or his Kingdom.

It's like carrying a 10 lb Bible under your arm but you don't really know what it says.

It's not the word under your arm the devil fears, it's the word in your heart that becomes the sword of the Spirit.

The Bible says, cloven tongues like as of fire sat upon each of them and they were all filled with the Holy Ghost and began to speak with other tongues as the Spirit gave them utterance.

The point I'm making is: two things happened that day…

1. They got tongues
2. They got fire

When the Holy Ghost came, He came as a rushing mighty wind and fire.

Yes I believe you need to speak in tongues, and you will speak in tongues.

(But with those tongues you need the fire)

They came together on the day of Pentecost

1. Tongues of Fire
2. Tongues on Fire

But religion has done a pretty good job of separating them.

So now days we have churches and denominations that still adhere to the belief of speaking in tongues, but they have no fire, and no power.

If the Holy Ghost Baptism is anything, it is a baptism of fire.

If Pentecost is anything it is a baptism of fire.

If the baptism of the Holy Ghost in your life means anything, it means that you receive Power.

Ye shall receive Power after that the Holy Ghost is come upon you. (Acts 1:8)

Ye shall receive Power: Strongs definition of Power = Force, ability, strength, violence, specifically miraculous power.

This is what happens when you are baptized with the Holy Ghost and Fire. (a supernatural force and ability, strength, violence, and miraculous power comes inside you).

The Fire of God is an energizing force

The fire of God is a sanctifying and purifying agent

John said: His fan is in his hand and he will thoroughly purge his floor.

His floor is where he walks, He walks in you, and he walks in me.

Your body is the temple of the Holy Ghost. (See 1Co 6:19)

When the Holy Ghost comes, and where the Holy Ghost lives, and where he rules he will clean his house.

- He will burn up everything that is of the world, the flesh and the devil.
- He will glorify Jesus in your life.
- He will give you power to say no to the flesh.
- He will give you power to crucify the flesh.
- He will give you power over the devil in your own life.
- You will be able to put the devil under your foot.
- He will give you power to be a witness.
- He will give you power to help others.
- He will make you a blessing to others.

- You will be a channel through which the miracle life power of God flows.

(Jn 7:37-38) Out of your bellies shall flow rivers of living waters.
You will become partners with Jesus in the great commission

(Mk 16:15-18) "And he said unto them, Go ye into all the world, and preach the gospel to every creature. 16 He that believeth and is baptized shall be saved; but he that believeth not shall be damned. 17 And these signs shall follow them that believe; In my name shall they cast out devils; they shall speak with new tongues; 18 They shall take up serpents; and if they drink any deadly thing, it shall not hurt them; they shall lay hands on the sick, and they shall recover."

That's why the devil doesn't want you to be baptized in the Holy Ghost and fire.

When you are on fire for God you are a threat to hell.

A lukewarm Christian is a better advertisement for the devil than for God, because our God is a consuming fire.

Samson caught 300 foxes and tied them together in pairs. These foxes were no threat to the philistines until he put a firebrand between their tails. These same foxes that previously were little more than a nuisance suddenly became the Philistines worst nightmare.

What made the difference?

"The Fire"

Dear reader I feel sorry for the devil, he isn't going to know what to do about you, because you are going to be too hot to handle.

Somebody is going to catch fire today

Maybe you've never really experienced the fire, you have a concept and a theory and a philosophy, but you've never really been touched by the fire of God. But this is your day to get your own personal flame.

Or maybe at one time you had the fire, you had the anointing and the unction of the Spirit upon your life, but you've cooled off, well, this is your day for a fresh anointing of the fire of God.

- The Holy Ghost fire is burning
- The wind of the Spirit is blowing

Just lift your hands and tell him: I want the fire.

Tell him you want the mighty baptism of the Holy Ghost and fire.

You say: I spoke with other tongues when I got baptized, or I spoke in tongues 5 years ago, or last week.

Well I'm not just talking about speaking in tongues, I'm talking about a fire in your belly.

When you have a fire in your belly you'll speak in tongues all the time. At the stoplight, Wal-mart, and the Gas station.

Paul said: I Thank God I speak with tongues more than ye all.

Why is it so important? Because it is the doorway in to the manifestation of all the gifts of the Spirit.

- It stirs up the anointing and the giftings that God has put inside of you.
- It quickens and stirs up that supernatural dimension in your life.
- It opens the spiritual atmosphere to the manifestation of the power of God.
- It builds up your inner man. *(Jude 1:20) Building up yourselves on your most holy faith praying in the Holy Ghost.*
- It stirs and quickens your faith

All of the Kingdom of God is in the Holy Ghost... *"For the Kingdom of God is not meat and drink but righteousness, peace and joy in the Holy Ghost." Ro 14:17*

Healing, deliverance, miracles, signs, and wonders, and supernatural joy and peace, these are all manifestations of the Kingdom of God. And they are all the product of the power and the anointing of the Holy Ghost.

Jesus was completely dependant upon the Holy Spirit.

The Apostles were completely dependant upon the Holy Spirit.

And we must be completely dependant upon the Holy Spirit.

"This is the word of the LORD unto Zerubbabel, saying, not by might, nor by power, but by my spirit, saith the LORD of hosts." (Zech 4:6)

All the miracles, signs and wonders and demonstrations and manifestations of the power of God from Genesis to Revelation are all the operation of the Holy Spirit.

It is impossible for us to have the demonstration and manifestation of the supernatural dimension of God without the person and presence of the Holy Spirit.

We will only have Holy Spirit operations and manifestations where we create an environment and atmosphere, where the Holy Spirit is pleased to dwell.

I'm going to speak now about something many believers may not fully comprehend.

I want to speak to you about what the bible calls unction...

(1Jn 2:20) "But ye have an "unction" from the Holy One, and ye know all things."

We have come to know the word unction and the anointing as the same thing, but there is a difference between the unction upon and the anointing within. Ok let's explore these operations of the Holy Ghost.

We need to understand and experience both dimensions of the Holy Spirit.

First, there are 4 operations of the Holy Spirit as pertains to our lives as followers of Christ.

1. With us.
2. In us.
3. Upon us.
4. Through us.

The unction or the anointing of the Holy Spirit is not only referring to his indwelling, but rather his coming <u>upon</u> us for service, for ministry, for doing the works of Jesus, for healing, for deliverance, for preaching the gospel, and for casting out devils.

It is the Spirit upon us that causes the Spirit within us to flow out of us, or through us.

We should desire not only the spirit <u>within</u> us, but also the anointing <u>upon</u> us.

Everything we do in the service of the Lord should be done under the power and the anointing of the Holy Spirit.

We know the principle of the Anointing <u>upon</u> us from the Old Testament.

1. Samson: the anointing, the unction of the Holy Spirit would come upon him, and under that unction he would perform supernatural feats and acts of strength.

2. Elijah: The hand of the Lord = The anointing, or the unction of the Holy Spirit came upon Elijah and he out ran Ahab's chariot for 20 miles.

That principle did not disappear in the New Testament.

Jesus told us in (*Lu 4:18 –19*) *"The Spirit of the Lord is (upon me) because he hath anointed me to preach the gospel to the poor; he hath sent me to heal the brokenhearted, to preach deliverance to the captives, and recovering of sight to the blind, to set at liberty them that are bruised, 19 To preach the acceptable year of the Lord."*

Jesus tells us that the key to the power in his ministry was that the Spirit of the Lord (the anointing, the unction of the Holy Spirit) was <u>upon</u> him.

One of the keys to the power in your life and mine is not just to have the spirit in us, (that's personal) but it is also for the anointing, the unction of the Holy Spirit to be upon us.

It is this anointing, this unction of the Holy Spirit on us, that causes these rivers of living water to flow through us.

It is this anointing upon us, and this unction upon us that is thrusting power. This anointing upon us engages the Spirit within us to flow through us as mighty rivers of healing, miracles, signs, wonders and gifts of the Holy Spirit.

Jesus said: *"Tarry ye in Jerusalem till you be endued (clothed upon) with power from on high."* Lu 24:49

"But ye shall receive power after that the Holy Ghost Is come upon you and ye shall be witnesses unto me, both in Jerusalem and Judea and Samaria and unto the uttermost parts of the earth." Acts 1:8

Two very specific things happened in that upper room…
1. The Spirit came upon them.
2. The Spirit came into them.

Tongues like as fire sat <u>upon</u> each of them.
They were all <u>filled</u> with the Holy Ghost and spoke with other tongues as the Spirit gave them utterance.
They are both the activity and the operation of the Holy Spirit.
We need them both: the Spirit within and the Spirit upon.
The Holy Spirits indwelling, the personal presence of the Lord in our lives comes as a gift.
But the anointing (unction, power) comes with a price. The price for the anointing is faithfulness, prayer, fellowship, death to self, study of Gods Word, yielding, obedience, and communion.
We have the Holy Spirits indwelling, but as we spend time with the Lord, he rubs us with his unction, and with his anointing, that is the anointing of power.

20
It's Worth Fighting For

Dear reader, the anointing is for action, not for recreation. The anointing is supernatural equipment for the battles that we fight. But the anointing won't work for you if you aren't willing to fight.

Judges 6: 2 -5 And the hand of Midian prevailed against Israel: and because of the Midianites Israel made them the den's which are in the mountains, and caves, and strongholds. And so it was, when Israel had sown, that the Midianites came up, and the Amalekites, and the children of the east, even they came up against them. And they encamped against them, and destroyed the increase of the Earth, till thou come unto Gaza, and left no sustenance for Israel, neither sheep, nor ox, nor ass. For they came up with their cattle and their tents, and they came as grasshoppers for multitude; for both they and their camels were without number: and they entered into the land to destroy it.

Now let's take a look at another scripture.

And after him was, the son of Agee the Harrarite. And the Philistines were gathered together into a troop, where was a piece of ground full of lentils; and the people fled from the Philistines. 2 Samuel 23:11

Notice the next verse, verse 12 *"but he "Shammah" stood in the midst of the ground, and defended it, and slew the Philistines: and the Lord wrought a great Victory."*

Dear reader it is right to understand and believe that Jesus once for all, and for all times and for everyone, defeated the devil.

He disarmed him, defeated him, and dethroned him.

Jesus defeated Satan and sin, through his crucifixion, his death, his burial and resurrection.

He spoiled principalities and Powers according to this powerful verse...

Colossians 2:15 "And having spoiled principalities and powers, he made a shew of them openly, triumphing over them in it."

Jesus regained through his obedience every thing that Adam had forfeited through his rebellion and disobedience.

Jesus left behind him an eternally defeated devil.

He crushed the Serpent's head, and took back the authority and power that the devil had usurped from Adam.

It is right to rejoice in everything that Jesus accomplished and the victory that he established. It is right to rejoice at Satan's defeat.

It is right to testify of the blood that redeemed us, that delivered us, and that set us free. That sanctifies us, and justifies us, and the blood that protects us, and the blood that destroys Satan's power over our lives.

➢ Thank God for the blood

➢ Thank God for the old rugged cross

➢ Thank God for a man called Jesus

Because if it had not been for the blood, it had not been for a man called Jesus, and if it had not been for the old rugged cross, then forever my soul would be lost.

It is right to rejoice that Jesus went to hell in our place, so we could go to heaven.

It is right to believe and rejoice that the whole kingdom of darkness and the concentrated powers of Hell combined couldn't keep Jesus in the grave.

But dear reader, it is wrong to think that there is nothing for us to do. It is wrong to think that you will not have to fight.

It is wrong to think that the devil will just roll over and play dead, and let you walk all over him.

It is wrong for you to think that you can stand by on the sidelines as a casual observer and win the fight.

It is wrong to think that what Jesus did for you, alleviates you of your responsibilities.

It is wrong for you to think that salvation, signs, wonders, and miracles will just happen because they're needed... they won't.

Yes that's what I said, they won't just happen because they're needed. Although Satan has been legally, eternally defeated. He is still here on this Earth operating illegally.

He is still killing, and destroying, everything and everyone he possibly can, until someone shows up with the knowledge of his defeat, and through faith begins to excercise the authority and power to cast him out.

This victory that Jesus has obtained for us is not automatic, it has to be enforced. Satan never gives up on anything. In other words, the devil never yields anything, the devil never simply let's go and slinks off into the shadows. No, he must be defeated. He must be overthrown. He must be evicted.

We were not saved simply to go to heaven. When you got saved, by virtue of the blood that bought you, and the spirit that filled you, and regenerated you, you became a member not only of the family of God, but you became a soldier in the army of the Lord.

As the army of God we have been given mighty weapons.

2 Co 10:4 For the weapons of our warfare are not carnal, but mighty through God, to the pulling down of strongholds, and the casting down of imaginations, and every high thing that exalts itself against the knowledge of God, and bringing into captivity every thought to the Obedience of Christ.

What are the weapons of our Warfare?

- The Word of God
- Fasting
- Prayer
- The name of Jesus
- Praise
- Binding and loosing
- The blood of Jesus

These weapons are mighty; they are lethal to the kingdom of darkness. But these weapons don't work by themselves, no gun can shoot itself, and no car can drive itself. They must be activated through use. The Bible is of no use to you lying on a shelf covered with dust.

What Jesus did for you and me is of no use to us unless we activate it through use. It's not going to cast out the devil, not going to deliver the bound and the oppressed. It's not going to heal the sick. God is not going to cleanse the lepers, and raise the Dead.

Oh yes, it is God's power that does the work without a doubt. Calvary was God stooping down as low as he could go to get this power to us.

Now it's up to us. And on the basis of Calvary, His spirit came to dwell in us. Now God says, I've done it all, I've done all I can do, if you don't do it, it won't get done.

- ◆ You cast out the devils
- ◆ You heal the sick

◆ You cleanse the lepers

◆ You raise the dead

◆ You perform the signs and the wonders

◆ You undo the works of the devil

◆ You set the captives free

I believe Jesus was saying, you take up where I left off.

In the book of Mark chapter 16, Jesus speaks these words...

"Go into all the world and preach the gospel to every creature, he that believeth and is baptized shall be saved, but he that believeth not shall be damned. And these signs shall follow them that believe, in my name shall they cast out Devils, they shall speak with new tongues, they shall take up serpents, if they drink any deadly thing it shall not hurt them, and they shall lay their hands on the sick and they shall recover." Mk 16:15-18

Jesus said ... behold, I give unto you power to tread upon serpents, and scorpions, and over all the power of the enemy, and nothing shall by any means hurt you.   Lu 10:19

And then Jesus said in *Matthew 10:7-8... As you go, preach saying, the Kingdom of Heaven is at hand, heal the sick, cleanse the lepers, raise the dead, cast out devils, freely you have received freely give.*

And then the Bible says... *And they went forth, and preached everywhere, the Lord working with them, confirming the word with signs following. Mark 16:20*

Now the Bible says in Luke 10: 17... *the seventy returned to Jesus saying, even the devils are subject to us through thy name.*

Well that shouldn't be a surprise at all, if we remember the words of Jesus, the Bible says in Acts 10:38... *"How God anointed Jesus of Nazareth with the Holy Ghost and with power who went about doing good and healing all that were oppressed of the devil for God was with him."*

Then put all this together with these words that Jesus spoke... "as the father hath sent me into the world, even so send I you." Of course Jesus was speaking to his disciples, but that includes you, and that includes me. I am one of his disciples.

Then said Jesus to those Jews which followed him, if ye continue in my word, then are ye my disciples indeed.   Jn 8:31

The point I'm trying to make is this...

God has done his part

➢ He sent Jesus

   Jesus has done his part

➢ He defeated the devil

   The Holy Spirit has done his part

➢ He raised Jesus from the dead, and came to live inside of us, and empower us

Now it's our turn. So often we say things like—we're just waiting on God. But beloved, the truth is... God is waiting on us.

   We are the link between the power and the problem.

Dear reader, there is no shortage of power, but the problem is finding those who will be that channel through which the power of God can flow.

Let's talk about the lame man at the temple gate.

Let me ask you a question; was it God's will for him to be healed?

Emphatically yes!

But if Peter and John, or some other man or woman of God, had not become the link and the channel for God's power to flow through, that poor man would have died a cripple, even though God willed him to be well.

The Kingdom of God is here now, in you, and in me.

21
The Power Supply Is In You

The authority, is yours and mine, Jesus gave it to us when he gave us the right to use his name.

Now the responsibility is ours to take the authority has given us, and act representatively in his stead and extend his kingdom...

- To destroy the devil's power

- To undo Satan's works

- To cast out the devil

- To set the captives free

- To heal the sick

The Holy Spirit Is The Power

I know you are not the healer and I am not the healer. We are not the source of the power.

- It's Christ in us!

- It's the anointing of the Holy Ghost!

- It's the same Spirit living in us that raised Jesus from the dead!

But if the Spirit of Him who raised Jesus from the dead dwells in you, He who raised Christ from the dead will also give life to your mortal bodies through His Spirit who dwells in you. (Romans 8:11)

It's resurrection power living in you and I.

Greater is he that is in you, than he that is in the world... (See 1 Jn 4:4)

You have this treasure in earthen vessels. (See 2 Co 4:7)

Your body is the temple of the Holy Ghost. (See 1 Co 6:19)

Jesus said in *Jn 14:12... He that believeth on me, the works that I do, shall he do also, and greater works than these shall he do, because I go unto my father.*

The Bible says of the disciples...

Acts 5:12 And by the hands of the apostles were many signs and wonders wrought among the people, and they were all with one accord in Solomon's porch.

Then see verses *14-16 believers were the more added to the Lord, multitudes both of men and women. Insomuch that they brought forth the sick into the streets, and laid them on beds and couches, that at the least, the shadow of Peter passing by might overshadow some of them. There came also a multitude out of the cities roundabout unto Jerusalem, bringing sick folks, and them which were vexed with unclean spirits: and they were healed everyone.*

Dear reader, precious Child of God what is it worth to you... to see your husband or your wife saved?

What is it worth to you... to see your prodigals standing in the house of God hands raised worshipping God?

What is it worth to you to see the sick healed, the cripples walk, the dumb talk, the deaf hear and the blind to see?

What is it worth to you to see the bound delivered and the captives set free?

What is it worth to you to see cancers fall off and the dead raised?

I'll tell you what it was worth to God, it was worth sending his own Son; humiliated and shamed and ultimately murdered, to get this life to you and me, and to get this life in us...

To get this authority, this anointing, this power in you and me, so that we can be ambassadors of his kingdom.

So we can exercise this authority, this anointing, and this power to set our loved ones free. How do you expect your husband, your wife, and your prodigals, to get saved, if you never pray for them, if you never fight for them?

Are they worth fighting for?

Is your home, your marriage, your sons and your daughters, your grandchildren, are they worth fighting for?

How about your health, your finances, your peace of mind, and your joy, are they worth fighting for?

How about the homosexual, the lesbian, the fornicator, the pedophile, the child molester, are they worth fighting for?

How about the drunkard, the drug addict, how about the pusher, the pimp, the prostitute, are they worth fighting for?

 In our scripture about Shammah, the Bible says, everyone left shammah standing alone in a Pea Patch.

They fled in fear from the Philistines.

The enemy came in to destroy and to plunder Shammah's pea patch,

He didn't run. He believed his peas were worth fighting for, and he was ready to fight to the death to defend his Harvest. And he fought for what belonged to him, and God fought with him, and he defeated his enemies.

The Holy Spirit is looking for some people today who believe it's worth fighting for, so he can anoint them for the battle.

22
Anointed For Battle

Ok let's go back to one of my favorite verses in the Bible; we'll find it here in the book of Isaiah chapter 10,

"And it shall come to pass in that day, his burden shall be taken away from off thy shoulder, and his yoke from off thy neck, and the Yoke shall be destroyed because of the anointing." Isaiah 10:27

This verse teaches us two things very clearly,

#1 The burden, and the yoke, are real.

One of the first things we must recognize as believers, is that the devil is real, his kingdom is real, and his power is real.

#2 The devils kingdom is invisible, but his power is real. Many people are being held in captivity and bondage and slavery and oppression by an invisible power.

The burdens are invisible, the yokes are invisible, the shackles are invisible, but they are real.

There are all kinds of yokes; the yoke is an instrument that binds two things together.

There are yokes of sickness and disease, yokes of addictions; yokes of fear and depression. There are yokes of lust and perversion. Then there are yokes of poverty and lack.

Dear readers, some of you have been under the oppression of the devil, and you've tried to get out from under it, but the truth is you're tied to it; you're yoked to it.

You're tied to alcohol, nicotine, or drugs. You're tied to sex; you're tied to fear, tied to poverty and lack. You're yoked up to depression, homosexuality, and perversity. Or you're tied to a broken spirit, tied to the disappointments of the past; yoked up with rejection.

You've tried to move forward, but that thing you're yoked to keeps pulling you back. You go so far and you think you're free, then the devil jerks the chain, then you're right back where you were.

Let me say again; the devils power is real. Yes, it's invisible, but it's real. But the yoke, the power, the bondage, the depression, and the captivity of the devil, is destroyed because of the anointing.

So here we have an invisible power, bondage, depression of the devil, being completely destroyed, by another invisible power, "the anointing."

While both powers are invisible, both powers can be felt, and their effects can be seen.

We see the effects of the devil's power in a person who is bound to drugs or alcohol. Bound to a lifestyle of lust and perversion. We see it when we see a person held in the grip of sickness and disease. We see it when we see someone living under the crushing load of debt.

But the invisible power of God, "The Anointing" can destroy every yoke and set you free.

The Holy Spirit, "the anointing" is like the wind, he is invisible, you can't see the anointing, and you can't tell it when to move, or where to move or how to move, or how hard to blow. But you can always tell when the wind is blowing, because you can feel it, and you can see its effects. You can always tell when the anointing is present and moving, because you can feel it, you can see its effects as well.

According to Isaiah 10:27 when the anointing shows up, burdens are lifted and your yokes are destroyed.

Some of us believe that the anointing is just this mild sense of the presence of the Lord. But it's much more than that. The anointing, is the might of God. The muscle of God. The anointing is the heavy equipment, the bulldozer, he is the mover.

The anointing is the supernatural power of God to smash, destroy, demolish and pulverize the works of the devil.

The anointing is the Holy Ghost dynamite; to blast the devils works to smithereens. The anointing is the supernatural ability of

God, to rebuke, cast down, and cast out, anything that is of the devil.

We see this Dynamite, devil blasting power right here in the Bible,

(Acts 10:38) "How God anointed Jesus of Nazareth with the Holy Ghost and with power, who went about doing good, and healing all that were oppressed of the devil, for God was with him."

And again here in 1 Jn 3:8,

(1 Jn 3:8) " for this purpose was the Son of God manifested, that he might destroy the works of the devil."

Just say this with me; I'm anointed for that.

Now say, I'm anointed for the battle.

Just as the devils kingdom is invisible, in like manner, the kingdom of God is invisible. But the kingdom of God is manifested every time the devil is overthrown by the anointing.

In the Bible they came to Jesus and they wanted to know how he was casting out devils, and how he was healing the sick.

Jesus answered them; it is by the spirit of God. In other words it is by the anointing, that I do these things, and it is proof that the kingdom of God is here among us now.

(Mt 12:28) "But if I cast out devils by the Spirit of God, then the kingdom of God is come unto you."

The Bible says that we now are ambassadors of the kingdom of God.

Dear friend, it is our responsibility to not only announce the kingdom of God, but to manifest it as well, through the power of the anointing.

We manifest the kingdom of God by destroying the kingdom of the devil.

By...

Getting souls saved

Getting the sick healed

Casting out devils

Delivering the bound and the oppressed

Healing the brokenhearted
And it is all the direct result of living and operating in the anointing of the Holy Spirit.

23
Razing Hell

I have met a lot of wonderful people in my life, but every once in a while, I would meet someone who really thought that they were bad, they were troublemakers, in fact they called themselves hell raisers. And sometimes it would even be tattooed on their arm "born to raise hell."

The word "raise" means, to lift up, to stir up, to encourage, to start or initiate.

Well this meant, you could expect them to stir up trouble, get in fights, and initiate trouble anywhere they went, and in most cases they lived up to it.

Sometimes they would even have a picture of a little devil underneath the words "born to raise hell."

Well I didn't know it for a long time, but I discovered, that there is another word and it sounds exactly the same, but is spelled different, and it means just the opposite…

That word is RAZE, and it means to pull down, to dismantle, to take down, tear down, as so to make level with the ground.

Then it hit me, that's exactly what the anointing does.

The anointing pulls down, tears down, and dismantles, and demolishes the devil's work, so that it is flat to the ground as though it never existed. Hallelujah, that's the power of the anointing.

You see, the anointing is not just something to make us feel good. The anointing is supernatural equipment, and it is divine empowerment to destroy the works of the devil. There are some who believe that they were born to raise hell, but as for me, I believe I was born again to RAZE hell.

This is also true for you my friend, if you are a child of God, if you have been washed in his blood and born of his Spirit, then you are also a hell RAZER.

You have been anointed to destroy hell.

Just as Jesus was manifested to demolish, dismantle, and to destroy the devil's works, we are also manifested to destroy, dismantle and demolish the devil's works.

By the anointing of the Holy Ghost, we are to wreck the devils kingdom.

Look at this verse,

(1 Jn 4:4) " ye are of God little children, and have overcome them, because greater is he that is in you, than he that is in the world."

And this verse,

Lu 10:19 behold I give unto you power, to tread upon serpents and scorpions, and over all the power of the enemy, and nothing shall by any means hurt you.

And don't forget this one,

(Mk 16:18-20) "and the signs shall follow them that believe, in my name shall they cast out devils, they shall speak with new tongues, they shall take up serpents, and if they drink any deadly thing, it shall not hurt them. And they shall lay their hands on the sick and they shall recover."

There are some people in the secular world, who specialize in demolition. When companies want to get rid of a huge old building or Coliseum or something of that nature, they call in a demolition crew. These people are specially trained in how and where to place the dynamite charges, and when to ignite them. And in a matter of seconds the building is gone as though it never existed

What I'm telling you dear friends is that God is raising up some Holy Ghost demolition specialists, and they have the power, and they know how to use it.

All around us, Satan's kingdom is being manifested. Families are being torn apart by drugs and alcohol. Homosexuality and lesbianism is running rampant. Sickness and disease steals our health and strength. Suicide is plaguing our nation. Abortion is robbing us of our future. Prophets and pastors and missionaries and teachers and evangelist in the womb, are being sacrificed upon the altar of convenience. Men and women boys and girls are being held in captivity by lust and perversion, bound by sexual addictions. Pornography is hiding behind many pulpits today.

What is the answer?

What is the cure?

Is there any hope?

Yes there is hope, and yes there is a cure, and the answer is Jesus.

The answer is, the kingdom of God.

The answer is the anointing, the power of God.

The only way to turn this thing around is to turn it over to the Holy Ghost demolition crew, to demolish the works of the devil.

There must be a Holy Ghost overthrow.

There must be a kingdom takeover.

These two kingdoms cannot exist side-by-side.

The old saying, you don't bother me and I won't bother you, won't work here.

Either the devil is king or Jesus is king.

Either you are in the kingdom of darkness or you're in the kingdom of light.

Jesus didn't come to this earth, just to be another king, and rule over his kingdom side-by-side with the devil's kingdom.

No, Jesus came to take over. He came to demolish, to throw down, to wreck the devils kingdom, and establish the kingdom of God where the devils kingdom had been.

Dear reader, the devil doesn't own anything, he is a liar and a thief.

Jesus paid for our redemption, our salvation, our healing, deliverance, prosperity, our peace and joy, with his own blood on the cross.

Jesus defeated Satan on the cross. He spoiled principalities and powers, and he made a show of them openly triumphing over them in the cross. (See Colossians 2:15)

Then the Bible says he went into hell, and took the keys of death and hell, from the devil, and rose triumphant and ascended into heaven, and set down on the right hand of God. Then he gave the keys of the kingdom to the church, and said, I give unto you the keys of the kingdom, whatever you bind on earth, is bound in heaven, and whatever you loose on earth is loosed in heaven. (See Mt 16:19)

Remember these words? … Upon this rock I will build my church and the gates of hell shall not prevail against it. Mt 16:18

Dear reader I want to tell you, the kingdom of God is nigh you.

The kingdom of God is here, to destroy the works of the devil.

The kingdom of God is here to set you free in any and every area of your life.

The power of the Holy Spirit, "the anointing" is here to wreck the works of the devil, to destroy every yoke and lift your heavy burdens.

The anointing is here to heal your broken heart and your wounded spirit. If you're ready for this anointing in your life, I want you to just lift your hands right where you are and ask God to anoint you with this anointing.

Dear friend, this is a Holy Ghost demolition anointing. It is a wrecking anointing; it is a hell shaking, wall breaking, kingdom taking, and pulverizing anointing.

Receive it right now. Yokes are being destroyed right now.

Bondages are being broken in Jesus name.

Burdens are being lifted in Jesus name.

The Holy Ghost demolition crew is on the job right now.

I feel some Holy Ghost charges going off right now.

I feel some strongholds coming down.

I feel victory right now in your life, and I decree it in Jesus name.

Receive the anointing, receive your freedom, and receive your victory. Receive power in Jesus name.

Receive the anointing to Raze Hell

Receive the anointing for battle.

24
Because You're Anointed

Scripture reference Acts 28:1-6

Dear reader, wonderful child of God, have you ever wondered why other people seem to float through life on a flowery bed of ease, and it seems like your life is one battle after another, and one trial on top of another? Well, we are going to answer that question for you.

I'm not just writing another chapter in a book, this is a prophecy: I hear the Lord saying that many of you have been going through some deep dark trials, some of you are in the fire right now, and the truth is, it's not just normal everyday trials.

Some of you have been experiencing crazy trials, things that don't even make sense. You've been hit in ways you never expected. And you've been hit harder than ever before. I'm going to tell you, it's not your imagination, that is exactly what's happening. It's because you are a threat to hell. It's because you've got something that a lot of professing Christians don't have, and a lot of churches don't have. "It's because you are anointed".

In the verses of scripture we are looking at, Paul is being transported by ship to Rome, to stand before Caesar for the testimony of his faith.

Paul warns them of calamity ahead, but they do not listen.

Dear reader, how many would be honest enough to say you could have avoided a lot of hardships in life if you would have just listened to good advice? (Even though they ignored his advice:

God was merciful.) I think somebody needs to say thank God for his mercy.

He sent an Angel to Paul with a message: God has given you all them which sail with thee.

That tells me something... "You better stay with the anointing"

I don't care how good it looks or how good it sounds, or how big it is, or how popular it is, or they are, the one question you better be asking yourself is, "Where is the anointing? Is the anointing in it? Are they anointed?

Please understand me, I am not against talent, and I am not against education, and I am not against having a big church. But the fact is: when I'm going through hell, and the devil is trying to kill me, or kill my family, or kill my ministry, it's not talent that I need, it's not education that I need, it's not a big church or a big name that I need, its something called the Anointing.

Paul was not just a man, he was a man anointed with the Holy Ghost and Power. "You need to stay with the anointing"

Your victory, your healing, your miracle, your deliverance, your destiny, is with the anointing. It's impossible to overestimate the importance of the power of the anointing on your life.

Your business may not know it but they are blessed because of you. Your family, your church, they're blessed because of you.

Why? Because you're anointed.

Because of the anointing on your life: lives are going to be preserved, souls are going to be saved, Satan is not going to succeed, and his plans are going to fail.

In our scriptures we are looking at we see the Apostle Paul has just survived a shipwreck, now a snake, a viper, bites him, and this is not just an every day common variety of snake, this viper is a deadly viper. This viper is well known on this Island. Many times these islanders have seen the horrible deaths that have resulted because of the poison of this vipers bite. As soon as they see this viper hanging on Paul's hand, they go to forecasting his death. I want to stop here and tell you dear anointed believer, there are some folk around you that know that you've been going through something and they know the devil has attacked you, and right now they're forecasting your death, I don't just mean physical death, I mean your failure.

This might shock some of you, but there are some people around you that are happy you got bit, and they are taking pleasure in your pain, they want to see you cry.

I'm reminded of Joseph's brothers who threw him in a pit and left him there to die, and sat down on the side of the pit and had lunch. They entertained themselves listening to Josephs cries for help. I know this is horrible and vicious, but the truth is… there are some people around you that are enjoying your pain, they are glad you got bit, they're saying things like…

I knew they weren't going to make it.

I knew that marriage wouldn't last.

I knew they couldn't afford that house.

I knew they would never make it in the ministry.

I knew they weren't qualified for that job.

I knew their children were going to end up on drugs or in prison.

Then they say things like: Who do they think they are anyway? They should have just settled down like the rest of us, they should have just been satisfied with what they had. And, they shouldn't have ever started that soul winning campaign, and they for sure shouldn't have started that building program. They should have just stayed in the boat with the rest of us here in the projects, what's all this nonsense about blessings and promotions, and walking on the water and healing the sick and working miracles.

Notice these words; they watched him, expecting him to die.

But he disappointed them he didn't die!

Can I just prophesy to somebody right now? You're getting ready to disappoint some people. There are some people that already had you dead, they prophesied your death, they wrote your epitaph, and they celebrated your expiration. But dear reader, you need to open your mouth and tell the devil, sorry Mr. Slew foot, I'm sorry to disappoint you "no not really sorry" but I have not expired.

Now say this with me, there's no expiration date on my anointing, this anointing abides with me forever.

Now lets make a bold confession: I'm more anointed now than ever.

I'm not saying I'll never be bit again, or I'll never fight another battle, or I'll never cry another tear, or I'll never spend another sleepless night, but (I beat "that" devil).

Come on, shout it out: I beat "that" devil.

Somebody needs to take about 30 seconds and give God some praise that you beat "that" devil.

Somebody reading these words, you're going through the fire right now, you're under attack right now.

Sickness has attached itself to you.

Debt has attached itself to you.

Family problems, marriage problems have attached themselves to you.

Fear has attached itself to you.

And right now the devil is pumping out his poison trying to take you out.

- Trying to kill you.

- Trying to kill your marriage.

- Trying to kill your ministry.

- Trying to kill your anointing.

- Kill your faith.

- Kill your peace and your joy.

- Trying to kill your dreams.

And right now it might feel like and look like the devil is winning. But I just want you to look back over your shoulder and see what God has already brought you through. You've been lied on, falsely accused, you've been rejected, you went through divorce, you went through foreclosure, you watched them tow your car to the repo-depo. You lost your job; your so-called friends stabbed you in the back. You got sick and thought you were going to die.

But guess what: You're still here. What does that mean if you're still here? It means... (I beat "that" devil) I beat "that" sickness "that" attack, "that" demon.

Yes this is bad: Yes Paul it looks bad for you. Paul this Viper is deadly, and no one has survived its bite.

Well Paul would say... his record is being broken today: because I'm not only going to survive, I'm coming out of this stronger, bolder, more anointed, and more of a threat to hell than ever before.

Somebody: needs to just look back and remember where God brought you from.

Look back at what God brought you through. He didn't bring you through all of that to be destroyed by this. The God that brought you through "that" will bring you through this. He'll do it again.

To God: "this" is no different than "that". I don't even have to mention what (that) is, you know without me even saying a word, what (that) is. That thing you thought was going to take you out.

That thing that looked so big. That thing that made you cry. That thing that broke your heart. That thing that you thought you would never recover from, but you made it. Hallelujah, somebody just needs to give God some praise that you made it through (that).

Somebody needs to tell the devil today: it ain't happening.

I'm not dying.

I'm not quitting.

I'm not giving up. I won't quit dreaming. I won't quit preaching. I won't quit prophesying. I won't quit praying. I won't quit sowing. I won't quit believing.

I've been bit before, and I'm still here.

Am I talking to anybody that's been bit before?

Am I talking to anybody who has felt the devil sink his fangs into your life before? Am I talking to anybody who knows that God did a miracle for you? God delivered you? God healed you? God brought you through?

I know I can't see you dear reader, but why don't you just lift your hand if you've been bit before but you're still here.

Every time Paul looked down at his hand and saw those scars it was a reminder: That the devil couldn't make it stick.

Now lets take the next step, just lay your hand on your heart and Prophesy to yourself: I'm going to make it, this is not the end. I've been bit before and I'm still here, and if I survived that, I'll make it through this.

Dear reader, I know it's painful but it's not fatal.

I know it hurts but God will heal it.

I know it looks bad, but God will turn it around.

I know your crying now but Joy is coming.

Weeping may endure for the night but Joy comes in the morning.

Somebody reading these words right now, maybe you're like Paul; you just survived the sea, and lived through a shipwreck, and now you've been attacked by a deadly Viper.

Or you just got out of the lions den and now you've been thrown into the fiery furnace.

Or you just got out of debt, and now sickness has hit your body.

Or you just got your car paid off and your house caught on fire.

Or you just got your job back and now your marriage is under attack.

You're wondering: Why me?

What have I done?

Why is it happening to me?

You say, I love God, I go to church, I tithe, I sow into the Lord's work, I read his Word, I try to live holy, it doesn't make sense.

You say, I thought I was anointed. I thought the hand of God was on my life.

Well I know this is going to sound crazy, but that is exactly why it's happening to you.

(It's because you are anointed)

It's because the hand of God is on your life.

It's because you are a threat to hell.

It's because you won't compromise.

It's because you are lifting a standard of holiness, in the midst of a wicked and perverse generation.

It's because every time the devil looks at you he sees Jesus.

It's because every time the devil hears you speak he hears Jesus.

Terry Sisney

It's because every time you take a step, the devil sees Jesus walking.

No my friend: It doesn't mean you have done anything wrong. It doesn't mean God is angry at you.

What it means is: You are anointed and you are a threat to hell and the devil is afraid of what God is doing in your life, and he hates you, and the anointing on your life makes you a target.

Was Joseph anointed? Absolutely

Was God with him? Absolutely

Was David Anointed? Absolutely

Then why did they go through what they went through?

Why did Joseph's brothers try to kill him?

Why did Saul try to kill David repeatedly?

(Because they were anointed)

If the devil knows about anything it's the anointing: He was the anointed cherub, the worship leader of heaven.

He knows the anointing of God and he hates it, because you have what he had and he lost it.

The anointing on your life makes you are a target.

You ought to be shouting right there: If it seems like the devil has singled you out, and all hell has broken loose against you, that means the devil has recognized your anointing.

That means, you are now on his radar screen, which means you are someone he's concerned about.

That means, you make him uncomfortable.

He wouldn't be worried about you, if you weren't anointed. He wouldn't be bothering you if you weren't a threat to him.

You make him uncomfortable.

You give him sleepless nights.

I don't know about you but I like that, I want to make the devil uncomfortable, I want him to worry about me.

I want him to be afraid that everywhere I go people are going to get saved. Somebody is going to get healed, and somebody is going to get delivered.

Miracles and signs and wonders are going to happen because I'm anointed.

Just say that again... I'm anointed.

Why has the devil launched an all out attack on your life? Your family, your finances, your ministry, your health?

Because you're anointed.

Dear Christian friend, if the devil knew what was going to happen because of his attacks, he would have left you alone.

If the devil would have known that by crucifying Jesus he was opening the way of salvation to the world, and making a way for the power of the Holy Ghost to come and live and manifest through us: He would have never done it.

The Bible says, had the princes of this world known, they would not have crucified the Lord of Glory.

And if the devil knew what God was about to do in your life because of his attacks, he would have left you alone.

But he thought he was going to kill you.

- He thought he was going to take you out.

- He thought he was going to destroy you.

- He thought he was going to break you.

- He thought you would quit.

- He thought he would crush you.

- He thought you would get full of his poison, and become bitter and critical and resentful and angry.

But he was wrong.

Terry Sisney

You see dear reader, Paul didn't die, and you didn't die.

Yes that Viper sunk his fangs into his flesh and shot that poison into his body, but when that poison hit the anointing that poison died.

- And the anointing just got stronger.
- The anointing went to another level.
- Paul's testimony went to another level.

Some of you know that the vipers of hell have been unleashed against you, and you've been bit and it hurts.

The fangs are real and they hurt.

But you're not going to die: You're shaking it off and moving up.

You're going to another level in the anointing.

You're testimony just went to another level.

You're going to walk with a greater anointing and a greater authority than ever before. You're going to cast out bigger devils than before. You're faith is going to take you places you could never go before.

The things that used to trip you up and hold you down, aren't going to bother you anymore.

More people will be healed and delivered. More be people will be blessed because of your testimony.

The anointing does not exempt you from the bite of the viper, but it gives you power over his poison.

Not only did Paul shake the viper off and survive...

He shook him off into the fire.

That means: That viper's life ended. In other words, that viper never bit another person.

That viper was destroyed because of the anointing.

I prophesy to you right now dear reader; there are Vipers that are being destroyed right now because of the anointing on your life.

Something that has plagued you for years. Something that you have wrestled with for years. Something that has dogged your heels and rode your back for years… It's being destroyed because of the anointing.

Vipers of sickness.

Vipers of financial problems.

Vipers of marital problems.

Vipers of spiritual problems.

Vipers of addictions, and habits, and bondages of the flesh.

Vipers that came to steal kill and destroy: are being shaken off into the fire right now, and their power is being broken, (because of the anointing)

That poison is dying now: Vipers are feeling the fire right now.

The anointing is rising up.

The anointing is growing.

The anointing is increasing.

The devil meant it for evil, but God meant it for good to increase my anointing.

Dear reader, if you receive this lift your hands and begin to praise him right now…

- That the anointing is increasing in your life

- That you are not going under, but you are going over

- You're not expiring, you're refiring.

Somebody needs to praise God right now, that the devil couldn't make it stick.

Somebody needs to praise God that the anointing is greater than anything the devil can devise against you.

Ye are of God little children and have overcome them, because greater is he that is in you than he that is in the world. 1 Jn 4:4

Somebody needs to praise him for a poison busting no stick anointing.

Yes I was bit, but you couldn't make it stick.

Yes it hurt and I cried, but you couldn't make it stick.

Yes I went down hard, but I hit my knees and I'm getting up stronger.

There are some vipers being burned up right now.

There are some people that are being disappointed right now, people who wanted to see you die, but they're being disappointed.

There's some stuff sliding off right now.

In that day: (This day) the burden shall depart from off thy shoulder and the yoke from off thy neck, because the yoke shall be destroyed because of the anointing. Isa 10:27

Come on dear reader, it's participation time. Shout it out: I'm anointed.

Say it with me: Thank you father for a no stick anointing.

Thank you father, the anointing delivers me now in Jesus name.

I am anointed.

Anointed For The Battle

25
We Are At War

I did a pod-cast not long ago titled "sometimes you have to push". The word push has an acronym (pray until something happens). **Pray until something happens.**
The point is we are not just sitting back in our pews waiting for something to happen but we are rising up in our faith with boldness and authority and power and we are praying for something to happen.

My friend the truth is something has already happened when the church starts praying.

What I mean is this; one of the greatest battles we fight is the battle to get into prayer.

If we can get the church into prayer and praying with power and authority, there's nothing that can't be accomplished.
Jesus said; With God all things are possible, and all things are possible to them that believe.

Beloved we are living in perilous times and dark times and there is no place for casual Christianity. There is no place for indifference; there is no place for half-heartedness, and there's no place for luke warmness.
The point I'm trying to make is that we are in a different season, and in this season there's no room for less than a full out effort. There's no room for less than a soldier in full armor.
In other words, it's going to take everything you have to make it in this season.

Paul's words are very aggressive words. They tell us that we are at war. They tell us that the only way that we are going to be able to stand is to give it everything we've got.

He said, having done all to stand.

In other words he is saying that we have to take full advantage of every weapon at our disposal, and we have to take full advantage of the armor of God. We have to take full advantage of the privilege and the power of prayer.

And we have to take full advantage of the Word of God.

We are at war. This is not boot camp, this is not just a training session, and this is not just a rehearsal run. This is for real. The bullets are real. Every attack is launched with your destruction in mind.

Every time the Devil throws something at you, his intention is to kill you, to take you out.

The church must receive a new mindset.

The church must receive a reset.

The church must return to a book of acts attitude.

The church must return to a book of acts anointing.

The church must return to book of acts praying and intercession.

The church must return to a book of acts boldness and authority and power of The Holy Spirit.

The fact is, nothing less than a book of acts Church is going to be effective and is going to be able to resist the devil and defeat the principalities and powers that are at work in the earth today.

I can talk to you about heaven.

I can talk to you about prosperity.

I can talk to you about seven steps to a better life.

I can talk to you about how to have joy in the midst of pain and trials.

I can talk to you about restoration of relationships.

I can talk to you about the promises of God.

And every one of these things are powerful, and they are wonderful, and they belong to us as part of our inheritance. And I can talk to you about everyone of these things and I will, and I have. But the truth is, if I don't talk to you about being equipped and being empowered and knowing how to use the weapons of your warfare, then my friend, I have failed you miserably.

The Bible is very clear that we have an adversary "the devil." He goes about as a roaring lion seeking whom he may devour.

I not only have a responsibility to sound the alarm, I also have the responsibility to tell you and show you how to put on your armor and how to use your sword, and how to pray effectively.

To show you how to use the power of the blood in your life, and how to use the name of Jesus in prayer, and also in warfare.

The church from its inception was never intended to be just a hospital where we splint sprained fingers, and cast broken bones, and console the tattered and battered.

Yes that is a part of our ministry. But the church was always meant to be more than an organization, she is a living organism filled with the presence and the power of God.
Living stones.
A Holy nation.
A Royal priesthood.
A Chosen generation.

Called, Chosen, Anointed and Appointed, to carry on the ministry of Jesus. To invade the darkness and to undo the works of the devil.
To heal the sick.

To cast out devils.
To deliver the bound and oppressed, and to make disciples of all nations.

In other words, the church is supposed to be a training center, an equipping center.

Now I'm going to meddle here for a minute. You know if a pastor doesn't meddle every once in awhile he's not doing his job.
When recruits don't show up at boot camp after they have been enlisted, they are categorized as a.w.o.l. Absent without leave. If they are gone very long they will be dishonorably discharged.

Why? Because, if they are not going to be there for the teaching and the training, they are not qualified to fight for their country, and they would be a liability in the heat of battle.

Well that's why we write books, to teach and to train. There's training going on all the time. Your church is a training center. Through the church you are provided with what you need to be equipped and empowered for the battle. But some folks have been a.w.o.l. You haven't been showing up for the training.
The tragedy of that is, you are disqualifying yourself. You are endangering your own soul and you are a liability to those around you who would look to you for help in the warfare.

I know it's tight but it's right.
I love you too much to let you go out on the battlefield without warning you.

The fact is if you don't go through the training, you are a problem looking for a place to happen.
God has made me responsible, to teach and train and disciple those who are positioned under me.

But God does not hold me responsible for the loss, for the wounds, or for the tragedy that happens in the lives of those who don't go through my boot camp or don't listen to what I say.

That's why I write books. My books are training manuals. I don't write them just to get rid of some nervous energy.

I write them to teach, to train, to equip, to establish.
Every one of my books carries an anointing to produce in you the spirit of a conqueror.

Paul makes a statement that if the trumpet doesn't make a clear understandable sound, then those who would hear the warning and prepare for the battle, will not prepare themselves.
That puts a heavy responsibility on those of us who God has commanded to sound the trumpet.
We must make the message clear. It must be unmistakable. That is our responsibility. But it is up to the hearer to hear the warning and prepare himself or herself.

26
Follow Your Guide

Joshua 3:2-4 And it came to pass after three days, the officers went through the host; and they commanded the people saying, when ye see the ark of the covenant of the Lord your God, and the priests the Levites bearing it, then ye shall remove from your place, and go after it. Yet there shall be a space between you and it, about two thousand cubits by measure: come not near unto it, that ye may know the way by which ye must go: for ye have not passed this way heretofore.

Over and over I have spoken the words so many times that it is getting monotonous.
I'm talking about these words, *"we have never lived in times like these."*

It seems like every time I turn on the TV or see another post on face book, or watch another you tube video, I'm reminded: We have never lived in times like these.

And the truth is it is not just a saying, and it is not just a phrase. It is reality. "We have never lived in times like these."

You've heard people say before; my dad would turn over in his grave to see something like this.
In other words they are saying that what is happening is of such horrific and dramatic departure from what is normal that it would cause the dead to turn over in their graves.

The reality is, we really have never been this way before.

We have never had to worry about our children being brainwashed by a socialistic gender confused, sex crazed school system that wants to introduce our babies to sexual exploration and child pornography.

We never had to worry about being put in jail for biblical discipline of our own children. We never had to worry about preaching the pure gospel that saves sinners, convicts saints and sets the captives free. We were never forced to choose between being biblically correct or politically correct. We never had to worry about being sued for bringing deliverance to a captive soul. We never dreamed the day would come when they would give you the legal right to kill your baby after it was born.
Today the law supports the murder of newborn babies but will put you in prison for killing a field rat.

We have never been this way before.

As I thought about all of this, I felt a question coming up in my spirit; what do you do when you're in a place you've never been before, and you don't know where you're going or how to navigate through the territory you're in.

Then I heard the Holy Spirit whisper these words to me. Follow your guide.
Hallelujah, I almost shouted. Praise God, just follow your guide.
Thank you Jesus, follow your guide.
Follow your guide. Praise God.
Wow, why didn't I think of that?

It couldn't be any easier. I don't have to know the way. I don't have to know what's coming next.
I don't have to lay awake at night tossing and turning worrying about what's coming next. All I have to do is follow my guide.

167

My guide knows the way. My guide has been this way before. Nothing surprises my guide.

My guide knows where the road narrows, He knows where all the curves are before I get to them. He knows all the cliffs and drop offs. He knows where the green pastures are. He knows where the still waters are. He knows when we need to stop and rest, and he knows when we need to run hard.

He knows where the enemies are hiding that would try to ambush us on the way.

He knows how to avoid their traps and snares.

Our guide has an aerial view; he can see everything from a higher perspective.

He may lead you down a different road than you would choose for yourself, but if he does it's because he knows something you and I don't know.

He knows that the easiest path is not always the best path. And he knows that many times the easiest path looks that way to lure those who have no guide into a trap.

There may be some guides in some countries that are new at the job and have the title but they don't really know the country. They don't really know the lay of the land. And the truth is they may be just experimenting at your expense.

But not so with the Holy Spirit, he has been guiding pilgrims through this weary land for centuries, and the truth is; he has never lost one single person who has followed him faithfully.

As I began to mediate on this I felt a sense of relief, and I felt a peace coming over me.

I felt a great fear leave me, and I felt a great burden lift off my shoulders.

I don't have to try and figure out which way to go, I already have the way. Jesus said, I am the way, the truth and the life.

All I have to do is abide in Him and let the Holy Spirit lead me.

Jesus is the way to the father, he is the way to heaven, and he is the way through this valley of confusing twists and turns.

Psalm 32:8 I will instruct thee and teach thee in the way which thou shalt go: I will guide thee with mine eye.

Psalm 48:14 For this God is our God for ever and ever: he will be our guide even unto death.

Psalm 25:9 The meek will he guide in judgment: and the meek will he teach his way.

John 16:13 Howbeit when he, the Spirit of truth, is come, he will guide you into all truth: for he shall not speak of himself; but whatsoever he shall hear, that shall he speak: and he will shew you things to come.
Over and over again David emphasizes the fact that he needed a guide through this life.

I believe It was out of this deep recognition and dependence upon the wisdom and direction of God that David pens these words, that have inspired millions and millions of people during and through the most difficult and trying times of their lives.

The Lord is my Shepherd I shall not want, He maketh me to lie down in green pastures:
He leadeth me beside still waters. He restoreth my soul:
He leadeth me in the paths of righteousness for his names sake.
Yea, though I walk through the valley of the shadow of death, I will fear no evil for thou art with me; thy rod and thy staff they comfort me.
Thou preparest a table before me in the presence of mine enemies: thou anointest my head with oil; my cup runneth over.
Surely goodness and mercy shall follow me all the days of my life:
And I will dwell in the house of the Lord forever.

Listen to this: if we follow the leader, if we stay in step with our leader and our guide, not only will we not have to worry about what is in front of us: we won't have to worry about what is behind us, because goodness and mercy will take care of that.

Goodness and mercy will follow you all the days of your life. Lets look at this again. If we follow our guide...

He will take care of our needs.
He will tell us when and where to rest.
He will lead us to the waters of refreshing.
He will restore our souls.
He will keep us in the right paths, the paths of righteousness.
He will deliver us from the fear of the dark.
He will support us in the hard and difficult places.
He will bless us in spite of and in front of our enemies.
He will anoint our lives with fresh oil, and bring overflow into every area of our lives.

But this is not a universal application provision.
This is the promise to those who are willing to be led by the Holy Spirit. To those who can admit that they need a guide. To those who are not too proud to be corrected.

"For as many as are led by the Spirit of God, they are the sons of God" Romans 8:14.
There are multitudes today who will end up ambushed, beaten and wounded, and robbed of every good thing in their lives, simply because they want to make their own way. (In other words; they aren't willing to be led).

You see it takes a certain amount of humility to be led.
It takes a willingness to leave the driving up to someone else.
Many people are too proud to trust their lives to the Lord.
The sad truth is: they are bound for destruction.

The only one who knows how to navigate through these turbulent, uncertain confusing times is the Holy Spirit.

He guided the children of Israel through the wilderness. He guided David through the valley of the shadow of death.
He guided Jesus through the garden of Gethsemane, and through the suffering of Calvary then into the eternal glories of heaven.

The Holy Spirit is your guide and he knows the way.
The question is, are you willing to be led?
Will you listen to your guide?
Will you read his Word?
Will you turn when he says turn?
Will you stop when he says stop, and go when he says go?
Will you pray when he says pray?
Will you repent when he says repent?
Will you forgive when he says forgive?
I am truly concerned about those today who are trying to make it without the trusted guidance of the Holy Spirit.

27
Tell It Like It Is

For several days now I have been hearing something going on and over in my spirit, it's these words; tell it like it is.

Tell it like it is.

To tell the truth I believe it's a response to what's been happening in the atmosphere around us. I feel like the Holy Spirit is responding to all of the lies and all of the deception and all of the confusion that is surrounding us.

As I was thinking about the way the news has been handling a lot of the things that have been happening in our world, I was struck with the term fake news.

Fake news.

Do you know what I'm talking about? We've been hearing it over and over and over. It's gotten to the point where nobody even wants to hear news anymore because we don't believe that anybody's going to tell us the truth.

The reality is that a newscaster only has one job; tell it like it is.

Tell it like it is. That's what they're supposed to do.

They're not supposed to have an agenda, they're not supposed to have an opinion, they're just supposed to tell it like it is.

I'm reminded of a scene in a movie where Tom Cruise says; just tell me the truth.

And Jack Nicholson answers him; you want the truth? You couldn't handle the truth.

And then I thought about that, there are many reasons a person may withhold the truth or tone down the truth, or color or flavor the truth.

*One reason may be Genuine concern for another's sensibilities.

*One reason may be the messengers personal distaste for the truth, so because they personally are offended by it they tone it down, or dilute it.

*Another reason may be to control the narrative, in other words; they only say the part of the truth that furthers their agenda.

But in reality, the responsibility of the news media is; just tell it like it is. Tell the truth.

When the news media begins to color and flavor the truth according to opinion, the next step is to twist the truth to fit and further their agenda.

This is fake news.

Yes it is true; there are some people that want fake news. They want to hear what they want to hear, and they will pay to hear fake news.

As I thought about this, I thought is there any scriptural back ground for this? Or is this just some personal attitude that I have.

Am I really sensing the heart of God or is this a personal tangent I'm on?

Then I heard the Holy Spirit say: Preach The Word.

I immediately turned to 2 Timothy 4:1-5 and read these words.

" I charge thee therefore before God, and the Lord Jesus Christ, who shall judge the quick and the dead at his appearing and his kingdom; Preach the word; be instant in season, out of season; reprove, rebuke, exhort with all longsuffering and doctrine. For the time will come when they will not endure sound doctrine; but after their own lusts shall they heap to themselves teachers, having itching ears; And they shall turn away their ears from the truth, and shall be turned unto fables. But watch thou in all things, endure afflictions, do the work of an evangelist, make full proof of thy ministry"(2 Timothy 4:1-5.)

Then I knew what I was sensing was correct and that it was a witness of the Spirit.

"The Scriptures are talking about fake news."

These verses tell us that within the framework of the church, there will be those who flavor and color and twist the gospel to push an agenda. And that there will be those who will go to them and support them because they say what they want to hear.

They prophesy smooth things, lies and deceit, because they love the praise of man more than the approval of God, and because they are for hire.

I begin to recognize that the fake news in the media is just a reflection of the fake news being broadcasted by so many pulpits today.

And again I felt these words impressed on my spirit, "just tell it like it is."

As the messengers of the gospel, we don't have the permission or the authority to change the message.

Our job is to carry the message and to deliver it just as it is received. If we present any other message than what is written, then we are fake news.

Paul says it like this;

Galatians 1:7-8 There be some that trouble you and would pervert the gospel of Christ. But though we or an angel from heaven preach any other gospel unto you than that which we have preached unto you, let him be accursed.

This is what Paul was saying: if we preach any other gospel than which is written in God's holy Word, then we are not faithful messengers and ambassadors of Christ, we are fake news.

Why are so many people proclaiming fake news?

Because it pays good.

Because when you tell people what they want to hear they love you.

There's an argument today that people are gospel hardened, that they are resistant to the gospel and that the gospel doesn't work today.

That's ridiculous, the gospel of Christ is the power of God unto salvation to everyone who believes...

The problem is not that the gospel doesn't work, the problem is; so many have quit preaching the gospel and have become fake news casters. And people pleasers. News for hire.

Like Baalam the false prophet who was hired to curse Israel with his fake news. Many preachers today have become prophets for hire, they're chasing the admiration and the applause of men. They're chasing the almighty dollar.

But something is happening, there is a people that are crying out, please, just tell it like it is.

Quit lying to us...

Quit sugarcoating it.

Quit smoothing it over.

Quit diluting it.

 Quit saying what you think we want to hear, and tell us the truth...

 *Tell us that all have sinned and come short of the glory of God.

*Tell us that the wages of sin is death.

*Tell us that the soul that sinneth it shall die.

*Tell us that our own righteousness is as filthy rags in the sight of God.

*Tell us that without holiness no man shall see the Lord.

*Tell us that the grace of God is not a covering or a license for sin.

*Tell us that the only cure for sin is to repent and be covered by the blood of Jesus.

*Tell us that no man can serve two masters.

*Tell us that we can't fellowship with devils and eat at the Lords table at the same time.

*Tell us that to serve God means that we come out and separate ourselves from the world.

*Tell us that friendship with the world makes us the enemy of God.

*Tell us that Jesus didn't die on the cross just so we could have a better car and nicer house and more money, but because we were lost, and were condemned to an eternal hell.

*Tell us, we need a savior.

*Tell us that the Holy Spirit is here to empower us to live a holy life.

*Tell us that the conviction of the Holy Spirit is a gift.

*Tell us that it is a very dangerous thing to grieve the Holy Spirit.

*Tell us that there is a price to pay to follow Christ.

*Tell us about the cross.

Jesus said if any man is going to follow me, he must deny himself daily, take up his cross and follow me.

Paul said it this way... preach the Word.

Preach the gospel.

Just tell it like it is.

Something is starting to happen in the natural, the fake news has been called into account. They've been caught lying for profit.

Now they're paying for their fake news-casting.

I feel in my spirit that the same thing is getting ready to happen in the church.

I believe God is going to start judging the fake news-casters, the ones that are supposed to be preaching the gospel of Jesus Christ.

Somebody might say, what's the big deal with a little fake news? Why would God penalize someone for saying something that helps people and makes them feel better about themselves?

The answer is; when you change the message that was given to you, then you become a false messenger, and the message you present misrepresents the one who sent it.

God is going to judge those who are misrepresenting him, because they are presenting a perverted and distorted view of God.

My job, my calling, as a preacher of the gospel is very clear... Tell it like it is. Preach the word. Preach the pure gospel of Jesus Christ.

*Sometimes that's easy.

*Sometimes it's hard.

*Sometimes people love you.

*Sometimes people hate you.

*Sometimes they want to celebrate you.

*Sometimes they want to crucify you.

 But as a messenger of the gospel, it doesn't matter.

It doesn't matter if they love you or hate you. It doesn't matter if they bless you or curse you. It doesn't matter, the job description never changes, just tell it like it is.

 Tell it like it is...

*Not like you'd prefer it to be.

*Not like you would make it if you were in charge.

*Not what's popular.

*Not what's comfortable.

*Not what's easy.

*Not what's profitable.

Just tell it like it is.

That's the message that has the power to save, to heal and to deliver.

That's the only message God promises to back up with his power. The gospel.

Preach the word.

 *Some will love it.

*Some will hate it.

*Some will cherish it.

*Some will despise it.

*Some will love you for loving them enough to tell them the truth. Some will hate you for telling the truth. But it doesn't matter our responsibility never changes.

"Just tell it like it is."

28

Paid In Full

Many years ago we recorded an album; one of the songs on that album was, Paid in full.

I love that song; its like a sermon in a song.

It goes like this...

1. Oh how great was the debt that I owed; bound to pay for the seeds I had sown. But in Jesus my Lord a great treasure I have found, I'm redeemed by the blood of the lamb.

2. When justice called for a payment for sin; no one worthy could be found among men, but the precious son of God with a cross and thorny crown, paid the debt by the blood of the lamb.

The chorus goes like this... Paid in full by the blood of the lamb, free from sin free to live now I am. And it reads on the page where my sins were written down, paid in full by the blood of the lamb.

Hallelujah, as I said; that's a sermon in itself, "paid in full by the blood of the lamb".
When Jesus died on the cross... when Jesus shed his blood; he didn't just die as a man hanging on a cruel cross suspended between Heaven and Earth. No my friend... when Jesus died on the cross...

➤ He died as the sacrificial lamb.
➤ He died as the sin substitute.
➤ He died as the scapegoat.

- He died as my sin bearer.
- He died in my place and your place.
- He suffered the shame.
- He suffered the humiliation.
- He suffered the ridicule and the mockery that belonged to you and me.

- He knew exactly what he was doing.
- He knew that he was dying in your place in my place.
- He knew that he was carrying the sin of the world on his back.
- He knew the stripes that he was taking upon his back were for your healing and for my healing.
- He knew he was fulfilling the scripture.
- He knew when he was hanging there on the cross suspended Between Heaven and Earth that he was the prophesied one— that he was the one Isaiah spoke about.

"it pleased the LORD to bruise him; he hath put him to grief: when thou shalt make his soul an offering for sin, he shall see his seed, he shall prolong his days, and the pleasure of the LORD shall prosper in his hand" Isaiah 53:10.

He is despised and rejected of men, a man of sorrows, and acquainted with grief, and we hid as it were our faces from him, he was despised and we esteemed him not. Surely he hath borne our griefs and carried our sorrows yet we did esteem him stricken, smitten of God and afflicted. But he was wounded for our transgressions, he was bruised for our iniquities, the chastisement of our peace was upon him and with his stripes we are healed (Isaiah 53:3-5).

You see my friends— it was not nails that held Jesus to that tree. There weren't enough nails that could have held our Savior to that tree.

The Bible says that Jesus himself said:

"Thinkest thou that I cannot now pray to my Father, and he shall presently give me (more) than twelve legions of angels? but how then shall the scriptures be fulfilled, that thus it must be?" (Mat 26:53-54).

Think about that... When Jesus cast the legion out of a man and they went into the pigs, there were two thousand pigs that drowned themselves in the water.
That means at the very least Jesus could have summoned 24,000 angels to deliver him from the murderous mob that day.
On one occasion in the Bible one angel slew 180,000 men in one night.
What are you saying pastor? I am saying that the nails weren't long enough or strong enough to hold Jesus to that rugged cross.
And there wasn't enough hate, and there weren't enough swords to put him there or keep him there.

It was nothing but love. Pure uncensored, undefinable, undefiable undeniable love.

Love that sought us.
➢ Love that bought us.
➢ Love that broke the chains of sin.
➢ Love that brought him down from the highest heaven, and took him to the lowest hell.
➢ Love that reached across the chasm of our sin and reconciled us back into the arms of our father.

Who wouldn't want a savior like that?
Who wouldn't want a father like that?

Now my precious family, I have been talking to you about the price Jesus paid.
But up until now we have only been looking at the <u>front side</u> of the cross.

In other-words we have only been looking at what Jesus saved us from. And what he delivered us from. And what he redeemed us from.

But there are two sides to that cross; there's the front side and there is the <u>backside</u>.

The front side is our Redemption from sin— from the power of sin, and from the consequences of sin.

But the back side of the cross is what he delivered us to, and what he saved us <u>to</u>, and what he redeemed us <u>to</u>.

In Isaiah 53 the prophet spoke of the front side of the cross when he said; he was wounded for our transgressions, bruised for our iniquities, the chastisement of our peace was upon him, and with his stripes we (are) healed.

But 1st Peter 2:24 looks at the backside of the cross and says; *"who his own self (bare) our sins in his own body on the tree; that we being dead to sin should live unto righteousness, by whose stripes ye were healed"*

The front side of the cross is what Jesus saved us from.
The backside of the cross is what he saved us to.
Salvation is not just deliverance from sin and from the power of Satan. Salvation is not merely the promise of heaven when we die.
Salvation is not just the mercy of God that carries us and protects us until Jesus comes.

No my precious family, my wonderful friends...
Salvation is an inclusive word:
It means..

- ➢ Redemption.
- ➢ Deliverance.
- ➢ Prosperity.
- ➢ Peace.
- ➢ Joy.
- ➢ Health and healing.
- ➢ Righteousness.
- ➢ Boldness.
- ➢ Confidence.

It means that we have not only been redeemed from the slave market of sin. But we have been reconciled back into the family of God with all the rights and privileges of son ship.

- We are the righteousness of God
- We are heirs of God and joint heirs with Jesus Christ
- We are the branches of the true vine... Jesus said: I am the vine ye are the branches — we are the fruit bearing part of the vine.
- We are the light of the world and the salt of the earth
- We are ambassadors of the Kingdom of heaven
- We have been given power and authority over all the works of the devil.

If the devil is running rampant in the earth, it's not Gods fault; because God has made the church responsible for extending his kingdom rule and dominion in the earth.

The front side of the cross was our redemption from everything that came upon us through Adams transgression.

But the backside of the cross is our restoration of everything that Adam lost.
We got it back.

Jesus bought it back and brought it back.
He didn't just die to deliver us from the consequences of sin.
(He rose again to give us back everything Adam lost).
So that through his finished work and faith in his crucifixion, his death, his burial and his resurrection, we stand today as though Adam never sinned.

Justified by faith in his blood...

We stand in Christ by faith (pre-fall) in other words; in Christ we stand in the same position that Adam stood before the fall.
With the same rights and privileges, the same benefits, the same access to the presence of God. And the same Kingdom mandate...
To be fruitful and multiply— to replenish the earth, to subdue it and to take dominion.

That's what it means when I say: Paid in full by the blood of the lamb.

Do you see what I'm saying? The blood is not just a cleansing from my sins past, present and future.

The blood is the life I live by every day.

As the blood is the life of the flesh— the human body. So also is the blood of Jesus the life of his body— the Church.

Jesus said: *"For my flesh is meat indeed and my blood is drink indeed. He that eateth my flesh and drinketh my blood, dwelleth in me, and I in him. As the living father hath sent me, and I live by the father: so he that eateth me shall live by me"* (John 6:55-57).

29
The Higher We Go

Genesis 6:5-8

[5] And God saw that the wickedness of man was great in the earth, and that every imagination of the thoughts of his heart was only evil continually. [6] And it repented the Lord that he had made man on the earth, and it grieved him at his heart. [7] And the Lord said, I will destroy man whom I have created from the face of the earth; both man, and beast, and the creeping thing, and the fowls of the air; for it repenteth me that I have made them. [8] But Noah found grace in the eyes of the LORD …

We are in dark times, there is no sense in pretending that it's not true. There is no sense in trying to whitewash it. There is no sense in trying to convince ourselves that it's just a little bump in the road, or it's Just a little turbulence and everything is going to smooth out.

We need to be honest with ourselves, we need to face the facts.

We are in the times the Bible speaks about. In Isaiah he speaks about a people that pulls sin like a cart with a rope.

And he says; there is a generation that has no shame and they can't even blush when they sin. He says: they call evil good, and good evil, they put light for darkness and darkness for light and sweet for bitter and bitter for sweet.

He says, There is no fear of God before their eyes.

2 Timothy 3:1-5

*This know also, that in the last days perilous times shall come.
For men shall be lovers of their own selves, covetous, boasters,
proud, blasphemers, disobedient to parents, unthankful, unholy,
without natural affection, truce breakers, false accusers,
incontinent, fierce, despisers of those that are good, traitors,
heady high minded, lovers of pleasures more than lovers of God:
Having a form of godliness, but denying the power there of, from
such turn away.*

Isaiah spoke with unbelievable prophetic insight and discernment about the times, the people, and the hour that we are living in.

*Ah sinful nation, a people laden with iniquity, a Seed of evil
doers, children that are corrupters; they have 'forsaken' the Lord,
they have provoked the Holy one of Israel unto anger, they are
gone away backward.*

*Why should ye be stricken any more? ye will revolt more and
more: the whole head is sick, and the whole heart faint. From the
Sole of the foot even unto the head there is no soundness in it; but
wounds, and bruises, and putrefying sores: they have not been
closed, neither mollified with ointment (Isai 1: 4-6).*

I know this is sounding really bleak, and depressing and that is intentional because it is the plain simple unvarnished truth.

The truth is; these are dark, evil, times, and I feel mandated by God to truthfully and accurately present to your minds the reality of the times we are in.

I feel like I am one of few that are really speaking accurately and truthfully concerning the conditions and the atmosphere of these times.

The majority of the voices that we are hearing today are not speaking   accurately   or truthfully.

In 6:13, 14, he spoke of these pillow prophets;

They have healed also the hurt of the daughter of my people slightly, saying, peace, peace; when there is no peace.

Jeremiah said: For from the least of them even unto the greatest of them every one is given to *covetousness;* and from the prophet even unto the priest everyone dealeth falsely.

"Then the Lord said unto me, the prophets prophesy lies in my name: I sent them not, neither have I commanded them, neither spake unto them: they prophesy unto you a (false vision) and divination, and a thing of nought, and the deceit of their heart"(Jeremiah 14:14.)

I wish I could honestly say to you that we are just going through a rough patch but we'll be through it in just a little while; but if I am going to be a true man of God, and speak truthfully and accurately to you; then I can't do that, because I would be lying to you.

The truth is; everything we have seen and experienced up until now has just been the pre-cursor, or we could say; the tremblings, the pre-birth pains of what is coming.

You may ask; Pastor Terry, why would you say such things? We need to be encouraged. We need to hear a bless me word. We want to hear how everything is turning around and how that our society is suddenly going to wake up and be good again. And we want to hear how Jesus loves everybody and he's not mad at anybody, and how he doesn't judge anybody, and how everybody is saved already they Just don't know it yet.

And we want to hear how Grace is this great big blanket that covers all of our sins, past, present and future, so it doesn't matter what we do, because it's already covered. And we want to hear that the Holy Spirit never convicts us of sin anymore, all he does now is convince us how righteous we are.

Well all I can say is this: If that's what you wanted to hear, I am the wrong person for you, and this is the wrong book for you, because I don't believe one little bit of that.

The truth is; I'm glad the Holy Spirit is still convicting the sinner of their sins. And I'm glad that I know that Grace is not Just a Giant Blanket For sin. But Grace is the divine gift of God working through my humanity to give me power over sin. Grace is not a floatie that I wear so I can float in a sea of sin and call myself saved. Grace delivers me from the Sea of sin.

The songwriter said it best with these words…

"I was sinking deep in sin, far from the peaceful shore, very deeply stained within sinking to rise no more, but the Master of the sea heard my despairing cry, from sins waters lifted me now safe am I.

Love lifted me, Love lifted me, when nothing else could help, love lifted me. Oh Love lifted Me, Love lifted me, When nothing else could help, Love lifted me".

Thank God: from sins waters, he lifted me, it doesn't say; in sins waters he joined me. He lifted me. He delivered me. He Saved Me. He gave me a new spirit.

"If any man be in Christ he is a new creature old things are passed away, behold all things are become new" (2 Corinthians 5:17.)

I might make somebody mad today. I might accidentally knock over somebody's Sacred Cow, but I'm going to say it anyway.

<u>I am not a sinner saved by grace.</u>

There's a beautiful song that says: I'm just a sinner saved by Grace.

But its not biblical, it's beautiful, it makes me emotional, but it's not biblical.

I can't be a sinner while being saved by Grace.

I can't be both. I was a sinner... by nature first, then by choice.

But now I am a new creation in Christ.

This work of salvation is not Just about saving me from the Sea of sin that I'm floating in.

This work of The Holy spirit has made me a new creature; <u>He took the sinner out of me.</u>

He didn't just pluck me out of sins Ocean. <u>He pulled the sin nature out of me</u>, He went to the roots and pulled it out by the roots, and he put a new nature in me.

If any man be in Christ he is New creature....

The Bible Says: He that committeth sin is of the devil... (See 1 John 3:8).

If you still have a nature, an appetite and a desire to sin, then you haven't been born again yet.

you may have been forgiven but you're not born again...

When you get born again, you get a new nature, and that new nature has no appetite and no desire for sin.

You see: I'm not a sinner, I was a sinner, I had the nature of sin in me. But I have a new nature, and for me to call myself a sinner now, is to repudiate the power of the blood and the transforming power of the Holy Spirit.

We are in the world, but we are not of the world. The Bible says: If any man love the world, the love of the father is not in him (See 1 John 2:15.)

"Friendship with the world is enmity with God, whosoever therefore will be a friend of the world is the enemy of God" (James 4:4).

"Come out from among them and be ye separate, touch not the unclean thing and I will receive you. And will be a father unto you, and ye shall be my sons and daughters saith the Lord" (2 Corinthians 6:17-18).

In our text God said: *I will destroy man whom I have created from the face of the earth; both man, and beast, and the creeping thing, and the fowls of the air; for it repenteth me that I have made them.*

Then listen to the words of Jesus:

" And as it was in the days of Noe, so shall it be also in the days of the Son of man. They did eat, they drank, they married wives, they were given in marriage, until the day that Noe entered into the ark, and the flood came, and destroyed them all" (Luke 17:26-27).

This is what is happening in the world today; it is no surprise, it is Jesus words being fulfilled.

And I'll be honest with you; if that was all the word said, I would be completely overwhelmed and cast down without hope. But I want us to go back to Genesis. There is a word here we need to pay attention to…

"And the waters prevailed exceedingly upon the earth; and all the high hills, that were under the whole heaven, were covered. Fifteen cubits upward did the waters prevail; and the mountains were covered. And all flesh died that moved upon the earth, both of fowl, and of cattle, and of beast, and of every creeping thing that creepeth upon the earth, and every man: All in whose nostrils was the breath of life, of all that was in the dry land, died. And every living substance was destroyed which was upon the face of the ground, both man, and cattle, and the creeping things, and the fowl of the heaven; and they were destroyed from the earth: and Noah only remained alive, and they that were with him in the ark. And the waters prevailed upon the earth an hundred and fifty days" (Genesis 7:19-24).

Somebody said: that doesn't sound very encouraging, I agree, that's not the encouraging part.

But stay with me, this is the encouraging part...

"And the flood was forty days upon the earth; and the waters increased, and <u>bare up the ark</u>, and it was lifted up above the earth. And the waters prevailed, and were increased greatly upon the earth; <u>and the ark went upon the face of the waters</u>" (Gen 7:17-18).

This is the word that we need in this hour; we don't need someone deceiving us with smooth, sweet, silky, flowery words of how great everything is. We need to know and hear the truth: it is bad, it's getting worse, Jesus said it would.

But Just like Noah and his family inside of that ark, (they were safe,) they were protected; and those who have their hope in Jesus Christ, are Just like Noah.

Just like Noah was <u>hid</u> inside of that ark, <u>we are hidden in Christ</u>.

"If ye then be risen with Christ, seek those things which are above, where Christ sitteth on the right hand of God. Set your affection on things above, not on things on the earth. For ye are dead, and <u>your life is hid with Christ in God</u>" (Colossians 3:1-3.)

As the floodwaters rose; as destruction came on every living thing upon the earth; <u>the ark rode on top of the waters</u>.

The waters increased and <u>bare up the ark,</u> and <u>the ark went upon the face of the waters</u>.

The waters increased and bare up the ark.

Which means that, that which was destruction to one was salvation to the other.

<u>And the worse it got around them, the higher the ark was lifted.</u>

The darker it gets, the brighter the light shines, and the higher the flood tide of sin and corruption rises, "The higher we go"

30

With A Whole Heart

David made a statement in the word of God. He said my heart is fixed. There are all kinds of heart conditions. There's a broken heart. There's a wounded heart. Then there are physical heart conditions that limit and restrict ones abilities and ones activities.

But David said, my heart is fixed oh God my heart is fixed.

I want to talk about heart conditions.

In particular I want to talk about one specific heart condition that I've been feeling in my spirit.

As I have been in prayer and seeking God and meditating on the word and seeking his heart I heard the Holy Spirit speak two words to me and I knew it was a word that I needed to share with you my wonderful readers.

Those two words are. "Whole heart".

Whole heart. I know there are a lot of ways a heart cannot be whole.

I know there is such a thing as a broken heart. And I know a broken heart can come from many different situations. I know that you can experience a broken heart through loss. Maybe divorce. Or maybe the loss of a loved one, or the death of a spouse.

Or it could be the absence of a father or mother in your life.

I know that it happens to young and old. There's no age limit on a broken heart. But I'm so glad that I know there is one who can heal the heart and make it whole.

Jesus is a heart fixer. The Holy Spirit is the greatest surgeon in the universe; he can perform open-heart surgery and never leave a scar.

But what I really felt the Holy Spirit was saying to me is that he is grieved over a heart condition in the church today. That condition is, "A divided heart" or we might even call it half- heartedness.

Have you ever heard this phrase; well I'll do it but my hearts not in it? Or have you heard the phrase half hearted?

*How much heart do you put into your prayer time?

*How much heart do you put into your Bible reading and study?

*How much heart do you put into your worship?

*How much heart do you put into your giving?

The sad truth is, that in many cases our lives are lived with less than a whole heart.

The truth is that God not only is not satisfied with less than our whole hearts. God demands our whole hearts.

To give God less than our whole hearts means that our hearts are divided. Which means we are holding out on God. Which means we are reserving something for ourselves that is actually not ours. That means in essence that we are robbing God.

To give God less than a whole heart means that the part you don't give him is open for business to anyone.

In other words, the part of your heart that is not yielded and surrendered to God is not filled with God and can be occupied by other things.

Which means that the part of your heart that is not filled with God and surrendered to God is not protected by God.

God can only protect what is his. He can only govern what is put in his control.

The Bible gives us several references to serving God with a whole heart.

2 Chronicles 15:15 and all of Judah rejoiced at the oath for they had sworn with all their heart, and served him with their whole desire, and he was found of them and the Lord gave them rest roundabout.

Psalms 91:1 I will praise thee, oh Lord, with my whole heart, I will show forth all thy marvelous works.

Psalms 119:10 with my whole heart have I sought thee, O let me not wander from thy Commandments.

Psalms 119:34 give me understanding, and I shall keep thy law, I shall observe it with my whole heart.

Psalms 119:69 The proud have forged a lie against me, but I will keep thy precepts with my whole heart.

Now I want you to look at the condition that we're talking about; the divided heart.

"And yet for all this her treacherous sister Judah have not turned unto me with her whole heart, but feignedly saith the Lord"(Jeremiah 3:10.)

In first Kings 11:4 it says: *"For it came to pass when Solomon was old, that his wives turned away his heart after other gods and his Heart was not perfect with the Lord his God as was the heart of David his father. For Solomon went after Ashteroth the goddess of the Zidonians, and after Milcom abomination of the Ammonites".*

And finally this is the one that really clarifies it: 2 Chronicles. It's speaking about Amaziah and it says:

"and he did that which was right in the sight of the Lord, "but not with a perfect heart" (2 Chron 25:2).

Here with Israel and with Solomon and with Amaziah, we see a condition that is very dangerous. It is the divided heart.

Now let's break this down. When we speak of the heart here we are speaking of what you love. In other words; your affections your intentions, your desires and your passion.

We are speaking of what you are invested in, and what you are committed to.

I'll do it but my hearts not in it, means: I'll perform the function, I'll carry out the duty, but I'm not invested in it.

Ok, I'm going to get raw here for a minute so give me some grace and give me some space. Many people in the Church are just like that; they are physically present, even give in the offering and sometimes pay tithes, but they are not invested from the heart.

Their affection, their passion, and their desire is absent from their actions.

Amaziah did what was right, but not with a perfect heart. (Perfect simply means, whole) ok, hold on, I told you that we're going to get raw for a minute so here we go...

That is no different than a prostitute. You ask, what do I mean by that?

Well, a prostitute performs a service.

They go through the same physical motions as a wife, but they are not invested in the activity. They are emotionally detached from the person they are interacting with. The truth is, before the day is out or the night is over they may have 4 or more repeat experiences with other men.

When we come to God with a divided heart, God looks at us just like a prostitute, because all we're doing is performing what we think is expected of us just to keep our fire insurance.

But there is no heart in it, no fire, no passion, no desire.

Friends, Jesus does not want a prostitute. He wants a bride.

He is not marrying a prostitute.

Don't get what I'm saying twisted, of course he loves the prostitute, the homosexual, the lesbian, the thief the liar etc.

But I'm talking about a prostitute church that is just going through the motions and their hearts not in it.

I'm going to be totally honest with you. I am concerned enough about your soul to tell you this.

If you cannot be passionate and emotionally and financially invested in your church. If you don't have any excitement about going there and worshiping God, if you don't have any passion and any fire and any appetite for the teaching and the preaching. Then I encourage you to get out of there before you die. You need to find the pastor that kindles the fire in your heart. You need to find a church that you are passionate about, where you don't want to miss a single service.

You need to find a place where you can give your whole heart and be emotionally and spiritually invested and go there.

I'm not trying to encourage church hopping. But I know that if you're really going to serve God you must do it with a whole heart. I'm going to tell you the truth, if I was going to a church and there was no fire, no presence of God, no power, no anointing, and no preaching and teaching the word. I would be gone so fast it would make your head spin.

Why? Because I am not looking for a place just to do my duty and just to keep me from drowning. I need a place where the fire is burning. I need a minister that stirs me, and challenges me, and so do you.

I don't want to know how to tread water and just stay afloat, I want to fly.

I'm not looking for a place that makes me comfortable. I'm looking for a place where the anointing of God is flowing. I need to be in an atmosphere that kindles the fire in my soul. I need to be around passionate people. I need to be around people that are hungry for God. People that are hungry for his Word. People that are passionately pursuing his presence. That's what we strive for in our services, and that's what I want to stir up in you.

Passion. Fire. Zeal. Intensity. Heart hunger. Desire. These are the things that mark the lives of those who are serving God with the whole heart.

John 2:17 says: "the zeal of thy house hath eaten me up".

Ecclesiastic 9:10 says: "whatsoever thy hand findeth to do, do it with thy might. In other words it is speaking about the whole heart".

My friend I want you to know that in the hour that we are living in you're not going to make it with half-hearted service.

God is not going to accept our offering without our hearts. God is not looking for people who know how to do the right thing.

The church thing.

He is not looking for people who know how to do church. He is looking for people to be the church.

A church that is in love with Jesus. A church that loves the Holy Spirit. A church that has a holy heart burn.

Their hearts are on fire for God.

I know it's tight, but it's right. I know this is what the Holy Spirit is saying today.

He is not just looking for warm bodies in the pew.

He is looking for hearts that are on fire, that are wholly devoted to him.

31

From Lost To Leader

The irrevocable invitation. The irrevocable commission. This could actually be two different chapters, but I just felt like I needed to bring these together today.

I want to talk first of all about the irrevocable invitation.

The irrevocable invitation of Jesus is to come all ye that labor and are heavy laden, and Jesus said I will give you rest.

The Bible declares, whosoever will let him come and take of the Waters of Life freely.

It also says, if any man thirst let him come to me and drink.

The invitation of Jesus is universal and irrevocable. It is for everybody everywhere.

It is for the young and the old, the rich and the poor, the up and outers and the down and outers. It's for the white the black, the red the yellow. It is universal; it is for all people, all times.

And it is irrevocable.

No one can change it.

No one can alter it.

No one can mitigate it.

No one can change the terms. It is what it is.

Whosoever means exactly that.

It means the liar, the fornicator, the adulterer, the pedophile, the homosexual, the lesbian, the abortionist, "whosoever."

So first it's come... Come unto me, learn of me. Then it's "Go."

Go ye into all the world, and make disciples of all Nations.

The Great Commission of the church has never changed, it has always been, go ye into all the world and preach the gospel to every creature. It is always been to make disciples of all Nations.

In Mark chapter 11:1-3 Jesus sent two of his disciples into the city. *"He said to them, go your way into the village over against you, and as soon as you be entered into it you shall find a colt tied whereupon never man sat; loose him and bring him. And if any man say to you why do you this? say ye that the Lord hath need of him and straightway he will send him hither."*

Now come down to verse 7 And they brought the colt to Jesus, and cast their garments on him: and he sat upon him.

Putting their clothes upon the colt symbolized, discipleship.

For Jesus to be manifested and glorified, there must be discipleship.

There were multitudes of people that followed Jesus, but there were few disciples.

Only to the disciples did Jesus say, go in my name and cast out devils, heal the sick, cleanse the lepers and raise the dead.

Elijah had many students but only one qualified for his anointing. "The one who qualified himself through discipleship."

A very wise man of God shared this revelation: The mantle wasn't draped over Elisha, it was dropped and he had to pick it up.

The church at large is filled with many attenders, but not many contenders.

Many followers, but not many disciples.

The difference between followers and leaders is the process of discipleship.

This has always been the ultimate plan and purpose of God. To process every single person that comes into the kingdom, and take them from lost to leader.

From coming to him with all your burdens, tied up, held prisoner by guilt and shame, a prisoner of sin. Receiving forgiveness and mercy, being released from the power of sin by the disciples (then the process of discipleship.)

Jesus says; come learn of me. Not just learn about me. But of me.

Why? Because Jesus wants to employ you in his Kingdom business.

My yoke is easy and my burden is light.

Leaders teach, disciples learn, then disciples become leaders and take Jesus where he needs to go.

Because, we are his hands, his feet...

We need his Spirit and he needs our flesh.

From lost to leaders.

This is the revelation of Ezekiel's bone yard. From chaos to conquerors.

From the defeated to the victorious.

From a valley of chaos... lost, confused, broken, oppressed, sick, mentally and emotionally, physically and spiritually, to victorious conquerors in Christ.

Through the gospel they are transformed, they're healed, they're restored. They discover their worth and their value. They are strengthened, they are empowered and now they are warriors.

Multitudes today are in Ezekiel's bone yard. They are lost, they're wounded, they're broken, they're confused, they're bound, and they're oppressed. They are slaves to sin.

But we must be the Ezekiel in their lives and we must have more confidence in the power of the Word of God than their condition.

I am trying to tell you today that God sees in every lost bone, every lost sheep. A leader.

We have got to get the vision and the heart beat of God for souls. Jesus came to this world to save sinners.

The invitation is still "universal" and it is still "irrevocable".

32

More Than What You See

Often the phrase we use to say the same thing is: The tip of the Iceberg.

That phrase is very often used to acknowledge that you may not be getting the full picture at first glance.

You are only seeing a small, often unrepresentative portion of something much larger or more complex that cannot yet be seen or understood.

Sometimes we even use that phrase to discourage someone from making a hasty judgment concerning a person's real character.

It is said that over 90% of an iceberg is below the surface of the water. That means that only approximately 10% of an iceberg is actually visible from the surface.

The depth of the iceberg extends down to between 600 and 700 feet below the surface of the sea.

The iceberg that broke off from Antarctica's Larsen C Ice Shelf between July 10 and July 12 is gargantuan. At about 2,200 square miles in area, and ranking as one of the largest icebergs ever observed.

Here are some size comparisons that may help you put it into context. The area of the iceberg is about equal to the state of Delaware, or four London's, and the volume of ice contained in the iceberg is about 277 cubic miles. This means that, if melted down, the iceberg contains enough water to fill <u>462 million Olympic size swimming pools.</u>

Friends, I have come to understand that the reality of it is, we rarely ever get the full picture of anything at first glance, or at face value. There is always more to it than what meets the eye.

 One of the most important lessons of your life will be; investigate before you invest.

Investigate before you invest your money into anything.

Investigate before you invest your heart into a relationship.

Take the time to research, ask questions.

Investigation provides what discernment does not.

Remember you only see about 10% of anything or anyone.

 That brings to my mind the story about little David. He was approximately 15 years old and he comes to bring some lunch to his brothers who are in Saul's army. While he is there he sees Goliath and he hears Goliath curse God and defy the children of Israel, and challenge them to a fight one on one.

 He recognizes that this has gone on for 40 days... And no one would accept his challenge.

David becomes furious that this giant of a man who is cursing God and defying the children of Israel is not being confronted. So David tells King Saul; let no man's heart fail because of him; thy servant will go and fight with this Philistine.

And Saul, who stands head and shoulders above any man in the kingdom, looks down at a 15-year-old Shepard boy and says...

You aren't able to go against this Philistine to fight with him: for thou art but a youth, and he a man of war from his youth.

Saul looks at Goliath, then he looks at David and he judges everything by what he sees and what he knows in the natural. And he starts telling David, "you don't understand what you're talking about, Goliath is not just a big guy, he has been trained to fight since he was a child."

He is a trained killer. He would as soon kill you as look at you.

He is as mean as he is big. He is the best of the best. He is the Philistines champion. He has earned his reputation.

Right there you would expect David to withdraw his request. You would expect to hear David say something like... Wow, I had no idea, I can't believe I was so stupid. Please just forget every stupid thing I just said. I'll just get back to my little sheep where I belong.

But David didn't say that. Please permit me to paraphrase David's words. I think if we were hearing David today, his words would go something like this.

Wait a minute Mr king, no disrespect to you sir, but I think you have misjudged things here. You have made a hasty judgment. You have made your judgment based on what you see. But there is more to me than what you see.

You think you see all of me, but there is more to me than what you see.

I know that what you see is all me, but what you see is not all of me.

You're just looking at the tip of the iceberg.

Yes, I am a teenager going through puberty and my voice hasn't even finished changing yet.

Yes, I am a shepherd boy and I tend sheep for my daddy.

But what you don't see is that I am also a lion killer, and a bear killer.

I know I don't look like it, but you can't always judge a book by its cover.

My friends you don't know who a person is based on what you see. You can never discern the sum total of a man or woman based on what you see.

Most of what makes me who I am is invisible. Like the iceberg, 90% of who I am is below the surface.

My struggles, my battles, my victories, my ups and downs. The times when I felt like quitting but somebody spoke a word that gave me the will to keep going. The times when there was no where to turn but to the Word, and I learned how to stand on the Word, and speak the Word until victory came.

The same is true for every one of us; you cannot judge anyone based on what you see. Every one of us has a story.

How could David face a man killer with every man in Saul's army watching him?

I will tell you how; He had already faced a sheep stealer and a sheep killer when nobody was looking.

In other words, David had already conquered his personal giants.

Let me clarify. He had learned how to control his mind. He had overcome rejection and anger. He had learned how to bring his flesh under subjection.

He had learned how to praise God regardless of how he felt.

You are not ready for Goliath until you have conquered your own Lions and Bears.

In other words, you can't lose the private war of character and integrity and dignity and go out and chop off Goliaths head. It's not going to happen.

The reality is, God gives everyone time to deal with their personal private issues, if they refuse to deal with them privately, he will either expose them publicly or he will allow your enemies to uncover you.

You see when David stepped onto the battlefield with Goliath he was fighting for Israel.

You are not qualified to fight for others until you have won your personal battles.

One of the things I love about God is, he knows how to keep a secret. He knows how to catch the devil off guard.

God hid a warrior in a shepherd boy.

Saul saw a shepherd boy, and Goliath saw a shepherd boy, and Israel saw a shepherd boy; but that was just the tip of the iceberg.

Underneath that shepherd boy was a Giant killer.

➢ I know by the spirit today that there are some secret weapons hearing my voice.

➢ The devil has underestimated you.
➢ Others have underestimated you.

Even some spiritual leaders have underestimated you, because all they could see was the tip of the iceberg.

 And some of you have felt like God has forgotten you, like God forgot that he called you and anointed you like he called and anointed David.

But God has not forgotten you; God has been working under the surface. He's been developing and processing and qualifying you, and getting you ready for the showdown, so that when he brings you onto the scene you'll be ready.

You won't run, you won't fold, and you won't cave in.

 You'll take your proven weapons and you will run to the battle and you will take Goliath down.

33
Build That Wall

Nehemiah's burden, and commission.

I believe this is one of the greatest stories in the Bible about a man with a love, and a man with a burden, and a man with an assignment from God. Please read this with me.

Nehemiah 1:1-3 "the words of Nehemiah the son of Hachalia. And it came to pass in the month Chisleu the 20th year, as I was in Shushan the palace, That Hanani one of my brethren came, he and certain men of Judah: and I asked them concerning the Jews that had escaped, of the captivity, and concerning Jerusalem. And they said unto me, the remnant that are left of the Captivity there in the province are in great affliction and reproach: the wall of Jerusalem also is broken down, and the gates are burned with fire."

Nehemiah 2:17 "then said I unto them, ye see the distress that we are in, how Jerusalem lieth waste, and the gates thereof are burned with fire: come, and let us build up the wall of Jerusalem, that we be no more a reproach."

When Nehemiah heard about Jerusalem and about the condition that the city was in, he became very concerned. As a matter of fact he began to weep and mourn certain days, and fasted before God.

Why? Because the city was broken down without walls, because the city had no defense against the
surrounding enemies. Because the city had no protection. And because the city was suffering great reproach.

It became a tremendous burden on Nehemiah's heart.

My heart has been stirred concerning what is happening in the world today, and especially as relates to us here in the United States and specifically here in our state of California.

These scriptures here in Nehemiah began to come alive in my heart, and I think I began to feel a little bit of what President Trump is feeling. I know that it's nothing in comparison to the burden that he is carrying for this nation. But I do believe I sense something of the passion and the urgency that he is laboring under.
I believe to a large degree that President Trump is at least in some measure a modern day Nehemiah, appointed and ordained of God to build the wall around Jerusalem.
Not really Jerusalem today, but the United States, and most particularly the southern border.
I don't believe it's just a Cause that president Trump picked up so he can fight with the Democrats and the Liberals and the Socialists.
I believe it is a divine burden and a mandate from the Lord.

I'm pretty sure that most of us today understand by now, that what happens in the natural is very often a reflection of something that is happening in the spirit.
Well what is happening with this wall business is no different.
This is not the first time that there was a battle concerning the wall.
We find the same battle and the same opposition here in this text.
Nehemiah has a burden and a directive from God to rebuild the wall around Jerusalem and to restore the gates.
But he is opposed by Tobias and Sanballat. They were in great opposition to the building of the wall and the restoring of Jerusalem.
They even threatened Nehemiah's life, Just like they have threatened President Trump's life. But Nehemiah was under a

divine command from God and he would not be intimidated or denied.

Let's talk about this for just a minute. Any country, any Kingdom, knows that walls are necessary to their well being —to their protection, to their safety. Only those who have no regard about the safety, or well being of a country or Kingdom, would resist the building or the rebuilding of the wall that protected it.

I've said it over and over, I am not trying to be political. What I'm saying has nothing to do with being political or racist, or hating any nation or culture.

But it has to do with loving my country and wanting to protect it, and to protect my fellow Americans and fellow citizens.

The Bible says: *"therefore he said unto Judah, let us build these cities and make about them walls, and towers, gates and bars, while the land is yet before us: because we have sought the Lord Our God, we have sought him and he has given us rest on every side, so they built and prospered." (2 Chron 14:7.)*

It always has been the first order of business to build walls to protect and to guard the inhabitants of a city.

Any city or country without walls was and is, vulnerable, defenseless.

Well when Nehemiah and the people began to rebuild the wall, that's when the Warfare started.

Nehemiah 4:1 "But it came to pass when Sanballat heard that we builded the wall, he was wroth and took great indignation on the Jews."

Why was Sanballat so angry? First of all Sanballat represents the devil and his desires.

So lets ask ourselves... why it made him so angry that the wall was being built, and restored?

➢ A wall represents strength and stability.
➢ A wall controls your environment.

➤ With a wall or walls, you keep the undesirable out, and the desirable in.
➤ A wall discourages intruders.
➤ A wall reverses incentive for illegal entry.
➤ A wall protects against harmful and destructive drugs and narcotics.
➤ A wall greatly reduces human trafficking.
➤ A wall establishes a perimeter and a territory that is governable.

I know I've spent quite a bit of time talking about walls, and I hope that you can see how important it is that we have walls. I also hope you can see the motives of those who oppose walls.

Those who oppose walls do not care for the people they represent, or they would do everything they could to protect the people they represent.

I hope that you have figured out by now that I am speaking spiritually. I've been using these natural physical elements to emphasize a spiritual truth.

This battle over the wall, it is manifesting in the natural realm, but it is spiritual in nature.

The reality is, we are a nation today without walls. Again I'm speaking spiritually.

We do not have any walls anymore.
● Walls protect.
● Walls filter.
● Walls preserve.
● Walls discourage Intruders.

We are spiritually speaking today, about a nation without walls.

I mean by that... we have no filters anymore.

Any kind of filth and immorality and perversion flows in and out of the minds of people and their lives without any kind of restriction or hindrance or conscience.

We as a nation, like Jerusalem in our text, are a city broken down, our gates are burned with fire, the walls are torn down and we are in reproach.

I want to tell you something, Sanballat was not mad at the wall, he was mad at God.

The wall represented the people being restored by God under the government of God, under the protection of God.

His anger about the rebuilding of the wall was simply his rebellion against the government of God.

Those walls represented a territory, a government and supervision.

In the natural, that rule of government is our constitution.

Well just like we have a constitution of government in the United States, there is a spiritual constitution of a spiritual government of the kingdom of God.

We are seeing today in our nation, a total disregard for the Constitution of the United States of America.

In other words a rejection of a duly appointed and administrated constitutional government.

But my friends this is just the symptoms, it is not the true problem.

➤ The root of the problem is spiritual.
➤ The root of the problem is rebellion.
➤ It is rebellion against God.
➤ The root of the problem is the rejection of God's constitutional government over our lives.

And the Constitution of the kingdom of God is the Bible.

That's why I'm going to prophesy to you now, the day is swiftly coming that they will be coming after our Bibles and any product that contains the Bible.

Because the reality is, it's not our guns that threaten their agenda, it's the Bible.

It's the government of God and the constitution of the kingdom of God —the rule of God, the order of God. That's what they're rebelling against.

Their hate is toward God and His government.

Their rebellion is against God and his government, and the Bible is the Constitution of the government of God.

I pray for president Trump and I believe that he is a modern-day Nehemiah appointed by God to rebuild the walls.

But that is a physical thing. The greatest need of our society and our nation is more than physical walls. It is spiritual walls; it is the restoration of the government of God.

You know why they hate the flag salute. It's not the flag they hate. It's not the colors, or the stripes, or the stars that they hate.

It's God, and it's that phrase; "One nation under God" because that phrase means, one nation under the government, under the rule, under the oversight, under the hand of God.

And that's where the fight is, and that's what the physical symptoms are pointing to.

Yes we need the wall. I want the wall... The wall is necessary.

The wall is important.

- The wall has a purpose.
- The wall is not immoral.
- The wall is not evil.
- The wall is not racist.
- The wall doesn't know color or race.
- The wall is not prejudice.
- The wall is not anti people.

The wall is not to hurt people, it is to protect the People it surrounds.

This is not a political word, It's not about politics.

It's about the kingdom of God, and the government of God. And it's about a people who are rebelling against the government of God.

It's about a people who are rejecting the Constitution of the kingdom of God.

Yes we need the wall, just like Jerusalem needed the wall. But that is the physical symptom.

What we really need is...

➤ The wall of integrity.
➤ The wall of honesty.
➤ The wall of humility.
➤ The wall of prayer.
➤ The wall of submission and obedience.
➤ The wall of depending on God.
➤ The wall of holiness and purity.

That's the walls that need to be built and rebuilt in this nation. And I can tell you right now... No liberal socialistic, humanistic, self-serving self-pleasing society is going to do it.

Just like in Nehemiah's case, this job has to be done by men and women of God who grieve over the condition of our nation.

Men and women of God who see the reproach that is upon us.

Men and women of God who will get a burden and won't back down to criticism and opposition and even persecution.

I will tell you how we can build that wall....

"If my people which are called by name will humble themselves and pray seek my face and turn from their wicked ways, then will I hear from heaven and forgive their sins and heal their land." (2 Chronicles 7:14).

34
Wake Up The Warrior

I know this is quite a bit of scripture but it is really necessary to fully appreciate this chapter.

"And they returned from searching of the land after forty days. And they went and came to Moses, and to Aaron, and to all the congregation of the children of Israel, unto the wilderness of Paran, to Kadesh; and brought back word unto them, and unto all the congregation, and shewed them the fruit of the land. And they told him, and said, we came unto the land whither thou sentest us, and surely it floweth with milk and honey; and this is the fruit of it. Nevertheless the people be strong that dwell in the land, and the cities are walled, and very great: and moreover we saw the children of Anak there. The amalekites dwell in the land of the south: and the Hittites, and the Jebusites, and the Amorites, dwell in the mountains: and the Canaanites dwell by the sea, and by the coast of Jordan. And Caleb stilled the people before Moses, and said, Let us go up at once, and possess it; for we are well able to over come it"(Numbers 13:25-30).

 Now let me start by saying: I believe inside of every child of God is the spirit of Caleb, or the spirit of a Warrior. The reason I say that is because you cannot even be saved without the Spirit of Christ taking up residence in you, and our Lord is a man of war according to the scriptures.
"The Lord is a man of war: the Lord is his name" (Exodus 15:3).

The purpose for this book is to stir up, to agitate and wake up the warrior in the bosom of every child of God.

219

In this portion of scripture we have chosen to look at, we are looking at the children of Israel who fail to take possession of their inheritance, not because it was not available but because they were not willing to confront their adversaries to get it. In other words; they weren't willing to fight for it.

God was angry with the rebellious self-preserving Israelites, but he took a great deal of pleasure in one Israelite named Caleb, actually two, "Joshua and Caleb." But in particular these scriptures point to Caleb as a picture of faith that possesses. He is a Warrior.

In the following scriptures we find that God is very angry with the 10 negative spies and all the children of Israel who were influenced by them.

But He identifies Caleb as one who has a different spirit and followed God fully.

"But as truly as I live, all the earth shall be filled with the glory of the LORD.
22 Because all those men which have seen my glory, and my miracles, which I did in Egypt and in the wilderness, and have tempted me now these ten times, and have not hearkened to my voice;
23 Surely they shall not see the land, which I swore unto their fathers, neither shall any of them that provoked me see it: 24 (But my servant Caleb), because he had another spirit with him, and hath followed me fully, him will I bring into the land whereunto he went; and his seed shall possess it" (Numbers 14:21-24.)

God is so pleased with the spirit that Caleb manifested, that He promised to give the land to Caleb and his seed.

Dear reader, we are living in perilous times, tempestuous times, times of uncertainty, times of struggle. We might as well just say it: (We are at war.) But that shouldn't surprise us.

We're at war in different places of the world, and we are at war right here in our own country; fighting terrorist cells that have infiltrated themselves into our society; fighting the spirit of perversion and deception that is covering our land.

The bible tells us these times would come…

"1 This know also, that in the last days perilous times shall come. 2 For men shall be lovers of their own selves, covetous, boasters, proud, blasphemers, disobedient to parents, unthankful, unholy, 3Without natural affection, trucebreakers, false accusers, incontinent, fierce, despisers of those that are good, 4 Traitors, heady, high-minded, lovers of pleasures more than lovers of God; Having a form of godliness but denying the power thereof: from such turn away" (2 Timothy 3:1-5.)

And let's read another scripture that describes the times we are in: *"And ye shall hear of wars and rumors of wars: see that ye be not troubled: for all these things must come to pass"(Matthew 24:6.)*

Yes, we are at war, but it's not just war in the physical sense, but it is war in the spiritual realm as well.

The natural is a mirror of the spiritual.

  Just as 9-11 signaled a change in the intensity and focus of our natural adversaries, it is also true in the spirit (all truth is parallel.) We are at war and now is the time for men and women of God to step to the forefront and be the men and women of valor and spiritual might that God has called us to be.

Now is the time for that spirit of Caleb, the spirit of the warrior; that God called (another spirit) to rise up.

In the following verse we see a cry going out for the warriors to wake up!

"Proclaim ye this among the Gentiles; Prepare war, <u>wake up the mighty men</u>, let all the men of war draw near; let them come up: 10 Beat your plowshares into swords, and your pruning hooks into spears: let the weak say, I am strong"(<u>Joel 3:9</u>-10.)

Dear reader, did you notice that? It says: prepare war, wake up the mighty men. In other words… Wake up the Warriors.

This scripture tells us that there are those who are of such quality of character and spiritual fiber that God refers to them as mighty men, but they are asleep.

Asleep means a state of sleep. Not attentive or alert. Speaking of a limb, in other words, a leg or an arm. Another word for it would be numb.

Sleep means a condition of body and mind in which the nervous system is inactive, the eyes closed, the postural muscles relaxed, and consciousness practically suspended.

My Friend I don't care how strong you are, how big and bad to the bone you are, if you are asleep it counts for nothing.

You may be a potential superman, or wonder woman. You may be able to pray heaven down, and blast hells gates off their hinges. You may have the Bible memorized by chapters and verse; and demons tremble when they hear your voice. But if you are asleep, you are no threat to the devil.

The tragedy of the hour that we live in is not that there are no mighty men or women of God, but that they are asleep. They have drifted into a kind of a stupor; they are in some sort of a daze. It's like they are looking at the world through rose-colored glasses furnished to them by the devil.

It's like they can hear and see what's going on around them, but it doesn't register that it's that bad.

What is it going to take for us to realize that it is that bad?
When are we going to wake up to the reality that we are in a state of war, and that Satan is after our children, and that everything that is good and decent is being perverted and twisted?

I'm not trying to promote fear and anxiety, but I am trying to provoke people to reality. We are at war and it's not with terrorists from another country, it's with terrorists from another kingdom.

Samson was awesome when he was awake and the Spirit of the Lord was upon him, but while he slept the enemy shaved his head, and stripped him of his power, and punched out his eyes and bound him, and took him into captivity.

I sense a cry of the Spirit going forth today to wake up the mighty men, to wake up the warriors in the body of Christ.

As in the verse I just read, I believe that many mighty men and women of valor have quit fighting and went to farming. Farming is good and there is a time for farming, but there is also a time for fighting.
Dear reader, this is the time to beat our plowshares into swords, and our pruning hooks into spears, and to stand strong in the strength of the Lord.

I hear the spirit saying: wake up the spirit of Caleb and wake up the spirit of Joshua, and wake up the spirit of Gideon, and wake up the spirit of Daniel. Yes wake up the Warriors!
As in Caleb's time there are Giants in the land.
As in Gideon's time there are invaders in the land.
As in Daniels time there is pressure to conform and fit in with a form of godliness that denies the power.
Friend don't be deceived. Don't think for a minute that if we just lay real still and pretend like they're not here that the enemy will

go away. He will not go away. Like our natural adversaries today, Satan needs no action from you to provoke his actions. The fact is, while we are pretending the devil is not there, he is stealing our children, wrecking our homes, and destroying countless lives.

I say again: It's time to wake up the Warriors.
Let's look at some Characteristics in Caleb's life that we desperately need in our lives today.

"And Caleb stilled the people before Moses, and said, Let us go up at once, and possess it; for we are well able to overcome it" (Numbers 13: 30.)

#1 He was a fighter: He would stand up and wage war against the prevailing spirit of unbelief and fear.

Caleb means: Forcible, attack.

The spirit of Caleb is the spirit of advancement.
Caleb was awake, alert, prepared.

Caleb was the son of Jephunneh.
Jephunneh means: He will be prepared; ever ready.

Caleb was an encourager
  (1) He encouraged himself.
  (2) He encouraged others.
* Caleb was faith motivated not fear motivated.
* Caleb was bold.

" The wicked flee when no man pursueth: but the righteous are bold as a lion" (Proverbs 28:1.)

*Caleb had the spirit of perseverance, for 40 years he held on to his promise.

*Caleb was not moved by peer pressure.

Caleb was of the tribe of Judah.
Judah of course means, Praise, Celebrate.
Caleb means, forceful. Judah means, praise. Jephunneh means, he will be prepared or always ready.
Jesus was of the tribe of Judah.

The point is: the spirit of Caleb is that of <u>an always ready, prepared, forceful praise</u>, and it is in the middle of this praise that Jesus manifests himself.

"But thou art holy, O thou that inhabitest the praises of Israel" *(Psalm 22:3.)*

"But my servant Caleb, because he had another spirit with him, and hath followed me fully, him will I bring into the land whereunto he went; and his seed shall possess it" *(Numbers 14:24.)*

"Doubtless ye shall not come into the land, concerning which I sware to make you dwell therein, save Caleb the son of Jephunneh, and Joshua the son of Nun"(Numbers 14:30.)
Then the Bible says these very powerful words:
"Now therefore give me this mountain, whereof the LORD spake in that day; for thou heardest in that day how the Anakims were there, and that the cities were great and fenced: *if so be the LORD will be with me, then I shall be able to drive them out, as the LORD said"(See Joshua 14:10-14.)*

(We need to wake up the Warrior spirit of Caleb).

Caleb was awake.

Awake means: To emerge or cause to emerge from a state of sleep.
To stop sleeping.
To become alert to, or aware of.
To cause to stir or come to life.
To be completely conscious and mentally perceptive. To be watchful, alert, conscious, and aware.

Friend, I know that life has a way of putting us to sleep. If we are not very careful we can lose our passion, and lose our vision.

Sometimes we get the breath knocked out of us, things happen and we get discouraged. Sometimes things don't happen and we get discouraged. When this happens our faith becomes weak and there is a tendency to slip into a kind of slumber or sleep, or spiritual coma.

I am convinced that we are at a critical point in time in the spiritual realm. I believe there has been a strong spirit of slumber that has fallen upon the church world. And many believers have been in a sense just sleep walking through life like spiritual zombies.

What we need is for the spirit of Caleb to rise up in the church again today; that warrior spirit. The spirit of boldness, and faith, patience and perseverance, commitment and obedience, and forceful prepared praise that goes before us into every struggle and every conflict.

"Let every thing that hath breath praise the LORD. Praise ye the LORD"(Psalm 150:6.)

"And that, knowing the time, that now it is high time to <u>awake out of sleep</u>: for now is our salvation nearer than when we believed"(Romans 13:11.)

I know that there are still some mighty men and women of God in the church, but many of them are asleep. They've been lulled into a false sense of security. They've drifted off to sleep: like Jonah in the bottom of the boat. And while they're sleeping there is a raging storm that is threatening to destroy the boat, but the prophet is asleep.

It's time for the Prophets to wake up.

Let the Men and Women of God wake up.

Let the Church wake up.

It's time to wake up the warrior!

35
Anointed For Break Through

In this chapter we will talk about the anointing for break through in every area of your life. There is possibly no greater example of a person operating under this anointing than Joshua.

Now after the death of Moses the servant of the LORD it came to pass, that the LORD spake unto Joshua the son of Nun, Moses' minister, saying,

2Moses my servant is dead; now therefore arise, go over this Jordan, thou, and all this people, unto the land which I do give to them, even *to the children of Israel. 3Every place that the sole of your foot shall tread upon, that have I given unto you, as I said unto Moses. 4From the wilderness and this Lebanon even unto the great river, the river Euphrates, all the land of the Hittites, and unto the great sea toward the going down of the sun, shall be your coast. 5There shall not any man be able to stand before thee all the days of thy life: as I was with Moses, so I will be with thee: I will not fail thee, nor forsake thee.*

6Be strong and of a good courage: for unto this people shalt thou divide for an inheritance the land, which I sware unto their fathers to give them.   (Joshua 5:1-6.)

As we enter into the spiritual realm God has promised us we must be prepared for confrontation.
There is no progress without resistance:

Jericho was a fortress city; it was the symbol of the enemy's strength and power.

It was made up of men and women wholly given up to idol worship.

This city stood directly opposed to Israel's inheritance.

This city had great walls that spoke of its great strength; and it had a reputation for being indestructible.

They had just begun to taste the goodness of their inheritance they were actually eating the fruit of their promised land.

Josh 5:12 And the manna ceased on the morrow after they had eaten of the old corn of the land; neither had the children of Israel manna any more; but they did eat of the fruit of the land of Canaan that year.

They were ready to possess their inheritance, but this Jericho stood in their way.

Josh 6:1 Now Jericho was straightly shut up because of the children of Israel: none went out, and none came in."

Some are satisfied right there, you don't bother me, I won't bother you.

Some churches are satisfied right there, we haven't gained any but hey we haven't lost any.

But God is never satisfied just with containment, containment means...

To suppress the enemy, that in itself is never victory.

To suppress lust, anger, resentment, criticism, is never victory.

To suppress means to hold it inside, certainly if you are holding it inside this is not victory. Victory is when the cross has destroyed that thing at the root.

I want us to look for a few minutes at what we'll call the anatomy of a breakthrough.

#1 He circumcised again the children of Israel. Sanctify yourself, take the word and cut yourself loose from anything of the flesh.

#2 He lifted up his eyes and looked. He looked beyond the walls. He looked to the hills from whence cometh his help.

He saw a man over against him with his sword drawn.

#3 Align yourself with God: The Angel of the Lord said: Nay as the captain of the Lords host I am come. This was actually an Old Testament theophany, an appearance of Jesus in a form before his birth in Bethlehem, because Christ was not born in Bethlehem, yes the physical body of Jesus was, but Christ has always existed in the father.

#4 <u>Joshua fell on his face and worshipped</u>; this is how we know it was the Lord, not just an angel, because angel worship is forbidden in the bible.

Worship is the keynote of destiny. After Joshua worships he is ready to hear Gods instructions.

What saith my Lord? Worship creates the atmosphere for hearing Gods voice. Worship opens the eyes and the ears of the heart to hear Gods voice.

For example look at these scriptures… *Acts 13:2 "As they ministered to the Lord, and fasted, the Holy Ghost said, Separate me Barnabas and Saul for the work whereunto I have called them."*

"And they rose up in the morning early, and (worshipped before the LORD,) and returned, and came to their house to Ramah: and Elkanah knew Hannah his wife; and the LORD remembered her.

20 Wherefore it came to pass, when the time was come about after (Hannah had conceived,) that she bare a son, and called his name Samuel, saying, Because I have asked him of the LORD" *(1Samuel 1:19-20).*

Worship is the atmosphere for the conception of the miraculous:
#5 Loose thy shoe from off thy foot: this is symbolic…
It was to the shoulders of barefooted priests that God entrusted the ark of his presence. To possess our spiritual inheritance, we must become barefooted, meaning, no personal agenda, no selfish ambitions; given up to the plans purpose and will of God.
It symbolizes an exchanged life, my plans for his plans, my will for his will, and my desires for his desires.

Now In Chapter 6 verse 2… God basically tells Joshua: Now the city is yours.
I don't know what walls of difficulties you may be facing today, but I can tell you this, God is looking for barefoot worshippers. Instead of griping and grumbling and complaining about the problems in your life, just take your shoes off and start worshipping him.
When one bad report after another had reached Jobs ears, and from a natural perspective he had lost everything. Job kept himself connected to his destiny through worship.

Then Job arose, and rent his mantle, and shaved his head, and fell down upon the ground, and worshipped, 21 And said, Naked came I out of my mother's womb, and naked shall I return thither: the LORD gave, and the LORD hath taken away; blessed be the name of the LORD."(Job 1:20-21.)

#6 Obedience is the key: God gave directions to Joshua, they were not suggestions, they were his commandments, and their victory was totally reliant upon their obedience.
You have to work with the Word.

#7 The People were forbidden to speak, which speaks of training ourselves to speak only that which edifies, and glorifies God and ministers grace to others.

"Let your speech [be] alway with grace, seasoned with salt, that ye may know how ye ought to answer every man" (Col 4:6.)
"But I say unto you, that every idle word that men shall speak, they shall give account thereof in the day of judgment"(Mt 12:36.)

"Thou art snared with the words of thy mouth, thou art taken with the words of thy mouth" (Pr 6:2.)

I think we can learn a very powerful lesson from the eagle. When the Eagles top beak starts getting out of shape, meaning; growing too long. It grows over the top of the bottom beak and can starve to death.
But the Eagle has learned that if he can get to the rock, he can beat that beak on the rock, and beat it back into shape, and have a new lease on life.

Unfortunately, many of Gods people have not learned the lesson of the Eagle and they are living far beneath their privileges, because their beaks are out of shape.
In other words, they haven't learned how to control their tongue and make it work for them. Many believers need to take their beaks back to the rock, and get them back into shape.
God commands Joshua to have the people march around the city, one time everyday for six days, then on the seventh day seven times around.

(7) Is Gods number and it stands for completion, maturity, totality, and fruition, total obedience.
(6) Is the number of man, 6 represents the efforts of man, incomplete and insufficient but necessary, meaning; you can't have a Seven without a Six.

In other words God expects us to do our part.

Seven is complete obedience, regardless of what it looks like, sounds like or feels like.

"That ye be not slothful, but followers of them who through faith and patience inherit the promises." (Heb 6:12)
"For ye have need of patience, that, after ye have done the will of God, ye might receive the promise." (Heb 10:36)

8 When you get here, it's time to shout. *"Joshua said unto the people, Shout; for the LORD hath given you the city." (Josh 6:16)*

There comes a time, when you know you have lifted your eyes above your problem, and you have taken off your shoes and stood barefooted and worshipped God, and you have aligned yourself with God, and obeyed his voice. And you have learned how to speak only that which builds up and edifies. Then all that's left is to shout.
Not because everything looks right or sounds right or feels right, but because God has said the victory is yours. " this is the victory that overcomes the world even our faith."

Praise is faith expressing itself audibly.
Faith has a voice. Faith calls those things, which be not as though they were, and those things that be as though they were not.
Faith hears God say it's done, sees God make it done and shouts because it believes it's done.

I'm talking to someone who needs a breakthrough.
What is a break through?
It is a victory over or through a wall or anything that presents a united front of opposition against you and the will of God for your life.
Everybody needs a break-through at some point in his or her life.
Every one of us will come to some place in our lives where we face something that presents itself before us as a united unbroken

wall of opposition.
The good news is that Our God is the God of the break through.

Now lets examine what we mean when we say break through.
Break through means; to break down, break forth, break out,
break up, breaker.
- To break through or down or over, burst, breach.
- To break or burst out from womb or enclosure.
- To break through or down, make a breach in, to burst open.
- To break into, to break up, to break open, break in pieces.
- To break out violently, to break over limits, and increase.
   *"So they came up to Baalperazim; and David smote them there.
Then David said, God hath broken in upon mine enemies by mine
hand like the breaking forth of waters: therefore they called the
name of that place Baalperazim" which means, the Lord of the
Breaks." (1Chronicles 14:11)*

I want to take it even a step farther: He is not only the God of the
Break through; he is the God of the breaker. Or we could say, the
God of the one who breaks through.
The Breaker is the one who goes ahead of the rest and hits the
opposition first and breaks it down so the others can go through.
The Breaker is like a Battering Ram that knocks the door down.

Just like the Marine Corps who are the first to make land fall.
                    They are the breakers.
*Micah 2: 13 the breaker is come up before them: they have
broken up, and have passed through the gate, and are gone out by
it: and their king shall pass before them, and the LORD on the
head of them.*

This Scripture tells us that God is on the head of the breaker.
In other words: there is a breaker anointing for busting through
anything that the enemy has tried to lift up against us.
Jesus said: upon this rock I will build my church and the gates of

hell shall not prevail against it. In other words, God is saying. All the united power and opposition of hell put together will not be able to stop the movement and progress of my anointed breakers. As I we come to the end of this chapter, just lift your hands and ask God for a breakers anointing.
I am not foolish enough to believe that everyone wants this, there are a lot of people that are satisfied to sit back and let someone else do the praying and fasting, and pulling down strongholds, and busting through the enemies defenses.

So I am only talking to the Elite, the Marine Corps, the Special Forces. The ones who want to be at the front, the ones who want the privilege of breaking through enemy forces and throwing down the works of the devil and opening the way for other brothers and sisters to come through.
If that's you, then the Holy Ghost wants you.

There is a breakers anointing coming on you now in Jesus Name.

36
Stepping Into Your Miracle

In the story that we are looking at, the children of Israel are standing in a familiar place. (40 years prior, their parents had stood in this same place.) Right there on the brink of a breakthrough, they had a breakdown, they had a faith failure. They forfeited their promise. They were still Gods people, and He cared for them and sustained them for 40 more years in the wilderness, until all the unbelievers and doubters died off.

We find all of this in the bible, Joshua 3:11-17
They were rich with a promise, but they died destiny poor.

One of the greatest tragedies in life is to live and never discover your destiny, but worse than that is to discover your destiny and forfeit it.

I want to talk for a minute to some people unlike this first generation. I want to talk to some people who know they have a destiny over their lives, who know there is a reason and a purpose for their existence.
I want to talk to the ones who want everything God has ordained for your life, and you refuse to let go, give in, or give up.
I want to talk to some people that have a fight in your spirit; the kind of fight like Caleb had who at 85 years old said; (give me my mountain.) That's the kind of fight that won't be denied.

Is there anybody who wants what God has promised you?
Is there anybody who refuses to settle for less than what God said you can have?
Is there anybody who has their mind made up that whatever it costs, you're going to get what God has promised you?

I wish somebody would just shout it out 3 times and make God glad and the devil mad by shouting it out...
Give me my Mountain.
Now if you're satisfied where you're at, with what you've got, seeing what you're seeing, and doing what you're doing and experiencing what you're experiencing, then this book is probably not for you.
But if you happen to be one of those rare breeds called dreamers, and if something inside of you is kicking, and if your spirit is divinely dissatisfied, and if you know God has destined you for more, then you're the one I'm talking to.

First of all, I would be doing you a disservice if I didn't tell you that every promise comes with a price.
There is no victory without a fight, and there is no testimony without a test.
There's no crown without a cross and there's no resurrection without a crucifixion.

There is something you will have to go through to get your promise. Before Joseph went to the palace he was betrayed by his brothers, falsely accused by his employers wife, and went to the pit and the prison.

Before the three Hebrew boys were promoted, they went through the fiery furnace.

And between the children of Israel and their Inheritance, their promise land, there was a river called Jordan. Jordan means, descender or the one that takes you down. That's what Jordan intends to do is take you down, kill your dreams, drown your faith.
Even in most of our songs Jordan River is used to describe death.

There is a Jordan for every one of us.

Your Jordan may be different from mine, but what is the same is the fact that it stands between my promise and me and between you and your promise.
And the only way you or I can get through it, is by faith.
You can't float over on feelings, feelings won't get you across, and you can't run over on past experiences, and you can't get through on second hand knowledge.
Religion won't get you through it.
The only thing that can conquer Jordan is a living faith in a living God.

As the children of Israel stood at the edge of a raging Jordan river at flood stage, the captain Joshua give the Priests that carried the ark of the covenant a strange order.

Joshua says, "Start walking" "Step into the water." Start moving in the direction of your promise.
You can't go by what you're seeing or what your hearing or what you're feeling, or what other people are saying.
You can't go by what your mind is saying, or the economy is saying.

You have to move because God says move.

You can't wait until you can see a break in the waves, or until it makes sense or it feels good to your emotions.
You can't wait until you see the waters open up in front of you.
Maybe the first time God did it that way for you, when you were just starting out, but you've got some history with God now and he is requiring more faith from you now.

God says, it's time to take the training wheels off.
It's time to get rid of the pacifier.
It's time to get rid of the crutches.
It's time to move from sight to faith.

It's time to move from I hope so to I know so.
It's time to move from the milk to the meat.

In other words: this time you have to get your feet wet.
You have got to have enough vision and enough faith in God to
get you off your blessed assurance and step in.

Just say it out loud: I'm stepping in!
I know it sounds crazy, I know it doesn't make sense. I know this
Jordan is at flood stage, and I know that people are saying it
won't work.
Yes I know that the circumstances are against me and the odds are
against me, but it really doesn't matter as long as God is for me,
because if God be for me, who can be against me?

You see I've got a Word.
That's all you really need is a Word from God.
When you've got a Word from God, you can sleep like a baby in
a den of lions. You can walk through a fiery furnace.
You can do the impossible.
You can bring down Goliath with a piece of leather and a rock.
You can have your meal barrel full, and your cruse of oil full in
the middle of famine.

All it takes is a Word from God.

Peter Had a Word: Launch out into the deep and let down your
nets for a draught.
(Lord we've toiled, we have worked hard all night long and
haven't caught anything.)
Nevertheless, at thy Word we will let down the net.

And when Peter obeyed the Word of the Lord, he went into
overflow.
One word from God changed Peter's circumstances.

He went from nothing to too much in one step.
He went from emptiness to overflow in one step. He went
from broke, busted and disgusted, to blessed, happy, and wealthy
in one step.

He had such an abundance of fish it almost sank his boat; he had
to call others to come and help bring in the blessings.
And it was such an overflow and abundance that it almost sank
their boat too.

Remember these words my friend, though weeping may endure
for the night, Joy cometh in the morning.
Peter went from a night season of wearied and toilsome, fruitless
endeavor, to a morning season of overflow and joy and blessings
in one step.
Let me prophesy to somebody who has the faith to reach out and
grab it: Somebody is one step away from your miracle, one step
away from your breakthrough.

One step away from a too much blessing.

You've put in your time of toiling, and trying and praying and
confessing, and waiting and watching.
And I prophesy that you are one step away from what you've
been believing for.

*Nu 23:19 God is not a man that he should lie, neither the son of
man that he should repent, if he said it he will do it, if he hath
spoken it he will make it good.*

The miracle happened for them as soon as the priest's feet
touched the waters. (The waters rolled back.)
As they walked, the water fled from before them.
 David was meditating on this miracle one day and he said:
What ailed thee O thou sea, that thou fleddest? Thou Jordan that

thou wast driven back? (Ps 114:5.)
The Message Bible says it like this:
What's wrong with you sea, that you ran away and you river Jordan that you turned and ran off.
I want to prophesy to someone right now: there are some things that have been chasing you, in fact threatening to drown you and take you under.
It may be debt. It may be sickness, or it may be fear. Or it may be a bad relationship.
I don't know what it is that's chasing you, but there's a turn around in the atmosphere and God is getting ready to flip the script, and that which has been running after you, nipping at your heels is going to be running from you.

But you have to stop where you're at, turn around and face it and step toward it in faith.
And when you do you are going to initiate a Miracle.

Sometime ago my wife broke her ankle, we had just crawled our way out of over $5,000.00 worth of debt.
We thought we were finally getting on solid ground, and, POW we we're hit with over 6,000 dollars worth of medical debt, and then our income tax came due about $1,500.00 dollars.

Then to top it all off, our income tax preparer didn't prepare our income tax and cost us a big penalty.

Wow, it felt like the Jordan River was at flood stage and was chasing us trying to drown us in a sea of debt.
But several years before that, God gave us a word that he was going to cause an abundance to fill our lives. In fact he said: more than enough, as a matter of fact the Word of the Lord even said, enough to give it away, Hallelujah!
So we stood on that word, we fought with that word. We fought fear and discouragement and worry and doubt.

We stood on that word and confessed that word through disappointment, through confusion, through fear and through tears.

I even preached that word, when everything in our natural circumstances contradicted it.

We said many times: Lord we don't know how you're going to do it, but you said it and you cannot lie. We said: Lord we believe your Word no matter what.

Then one day in the middle of our trial, God gave us a directive. He said: pay your tithes first. We heard the man of God present the revelation that by paying your tithes first, the blessing of God comes on everything that follows.

Well we had always been faithful to pay our tithes but it was not first, it was usually a check we would write on the day that we went to church and paid our tithes. Sometimes it was the last thing we paid, even though it was held back and never spent.

But this revelation struck home. I told my wife from now on as soon as we deposit our paycheck, we will write our tithe check. It seemed like such a small thing since we had always been faithful to do it anyway, even though it was fifth or sixth place, somewhere down the line.

But we obeyed the directive: It was kind of like Gods command to Joshua, it didn't make any sense, but God said step into the water.

As we obeyed the directive, we noticed almost immediately a change, a shift, something started happening.

Our money began to stretch, it was like a miracle, and we didn't have any more money it just seemed to go farther.

Then God gave us a side job, we immediately sensed God working in this and began to sow the income from that job as a seed.

Then God gave us another side job, we recognized that God was working with us now and that we had tapped into something.

So we began to use that job also as a seed.

It didn't make much sense in the natural simply to change the time we wrote the tithe check, and it didn't make a lot of sense to sow everything extra that we had coming in, because we could have used it to pay on a bill, or get cable TV or high speed internet or go shopping.

But it definitely meant something in the realm of the spirit.

So we obeyed God and now Jordan is running from us: We have debt on the run, not only have we learned how to conquer debt for ourselves, now we are helping others step into their blessings.

Our weekly seed went from 5, dollars, to 10, to 20, to 30, to 50, to 100, and sometimes more.

And it all started when like Joshua; we took the first step and started writing our tithe check first.

One step started moving us from borrowers to lenders.

From barely making it, to more than enough.

From weeping to rejoicing.

From hoping somebody would give us a Pentecostal handshake with a 10 or a 20-dollar bill in it, to being the one to give the Pentecostal handshake.

I'm trying to tell you, one step can turn your situation around and put you in charge.

I don't know what Jordan you may be facing today. Your Jordan may be completely different from what I described to you from my own life.

And I don't know what that one step is that you need to take, but if you will obey God and take that step, Jordan is going to run from you.

Poverty and lack are going to run from you.

Sickness and disease are going to run from you.

Hopelessness and discouragement are going to run from you.

Worry and anxiety are going to run from you.

Fear and confusion are going to run from you.

Deuteronomy 28:7 The Lord shall cause thine enemies that rise up against thee, to be smitten before thy face: They shall come out against thee one way, but they shall flee before thee seven ways.
One step of obedience makes all the difference: the willing and obedient shall eat the good of the land.
Whatsoever he saith unto you, do it.
The miracle is not in the knowing or even the believing, the miracle is in the doing.
In our own circumstances, there was not an overnight miracle. No one walked up to us and handed us 10,000 dollars to pay off our debts.
We didn't see immediate debt cancellation, but what we did see was that Jordan that was chasing us stopped and turned around and now it was running from us.

When Ezekiel obeyed the Lord and started prophesying over those bones, things started changing, it was a process that continued until there was a full manifestation.

Say this with me: I'm in process.
Now say this: I'm making progress.

The bible says that the priests that were bearing the ark kept moving until they were standing in the middle of the Jordan.
Precious friend, keep moving, keep praying, keep sowing, keep coming to church and prayer meetings.
Keep on confessing, keep tithing, keep believing.
Keep praising when you don't feel like it, and you don't see anything to praise him for. Praise him just because…
Just because he's God and Just because he's worthy.

The main thing is, keep moving, don't sit down, don't quit.
Then the bible says: The priest that were bearing the ark stood firm on dry ground in the midst of the Jordan. There they were

standing in a place where it was impossible to go, doing what it was impossible to do.
Somebody needs to tell the devil: take a good look at me, cause I'm getting ready to do the impossible. I'm getting ready to go where they said it was impossible to go, and I'm getting ready to do what they said it was impossible to do.
You see friend, I'm just crazy enough to believe God when he said: with God all things are possible, and all things are possible to him that believeth.

You see I believe my faith is making a way for me, and your faith is making a way for you.

Now while the priests stood in the midst of the Jordan with the ark of God raised in the air, somewhere between a half a million to three million people crossed over.

In other words, while the priests were lifting God up in the middle of their trial, and their Jordan. Somewhere between a half a million to three million people came through on their praise.

I just want to tell you beloved: Somebody's coming through on your praise. Somebody that wasn't going to make it, is going to make it because you praised God in the middle of your Jordan.

That's why it's so important that you lift him up and praise him and magnify him even in the prison. Even in the lion's den, even in the fiery furnace. Lift him up; somebody's life depends on it.

Dear reader, anybody can praise God post Jordan, post the lions den, post the fiery furnace, post the prison, after the fact, after the fight.
But there's something about a midway praise, a midnight praise, an in the middle praise, that gets Gods attention and breaks things open.

Joshua erected a pillar of stones in the midst of the Jordan where the priest's feet stood firm on dry ground.
What is this pillar Joshua? What does it mean?
Joshua would say: This is my going through it praise.

I'm going through the worst trial of my life, but I'm going to praise him anyway.
I'm going through hell in my finances, but I'm going to praise him anyway.
I'm going through the valley of the shadow of death, but I'm going to praise him anyway. I'm going through it with my family, or on my job, or they're trying to destroy my ministry, but I'm going to praise him anyway.
This is my testimony, that God has been faithful and somebody else sometime is going to come this way, and in the middle of their fiery trial they're going to see this pillar of praise, and it's going to remind them of the faithfulness of God, and it's going to tell them, that someone else has passed this way before them. And they didn't drown, they didn't burn up in the fire, the lions didn't eat them and the prison couldn't keep them.

And somebody else, who wouldn't have made it, is going to make it because of your praise.
Somebody is coming out of depression because of your praise.
Somebody is being set free from a spirit of suicide because of your praise.
Somebody is coming off of drugs, and somebody's marriage is being restored, and somebody's prodigal son or daughter is coming home because of your praise.
And at Midnight Paul and Silas prayed and sang praises unto the Lord and the prisoners heard them.
It didn't say they joined with them or even that they enjoyed their singing, just that they heard it.
And suddenly there was an earthquake that shook the foundations of the prison and every door flew open and every prisoner's bands

were loosed.

My friend as you read these words, receive this now; this praise is for you. I'm praising God for you right now. I'm praising God for your healing, your deliverance, and your miracle.
I love this part: And all the Israelites passed over on dry ground. This is perhaps the greatest part of the miracle, not just that they made it through, but that there was no evidence, no residue that they had been through what they had been through. Just like the three Hebrew children, when they came out of the furnace their clothes were not burned, their hair was not singed, and there was not even the smell of smoke on them.

And it all started when the priests obeyed the Lord and stepped into the water.

Precious friend, it's time to step into your miracle.

37
Then Came Jesus

John 20:19-28

I don't know who is going to receive this, but I prophesy to you by the Spirit of God, that somebody is going to get a breakthrough. Somebody's going to get their deliverance. Somebody's going to get some real peace, and real joy. Somebody is getting ready to come out of a prison. God is sending an earthquake your way and he's going to shake some things loose that have been bound up a long time.

In our text the disciples were gathered together in a spirit of discouragement, despair, and hopelessness. They had believed that Jesus was going to be their deliverer, which was going to liberate them from Roman rule. But now it's over. Jesus is dead. They saw the cruel crucifixion, they watched as the soldiers drove nails in his hands and his feet, and shoved a spear in his side, and they saw him die.

And they thought to themselves; it's over. Every natural, and visible evidence said it's over. They said: he tried, he was a good man, he meant well, but it's over.

But it's not over till God says it's over. The doctor may say it's over we've done all we can do. The lawyer may say it's over. The banker may say it's over. The husband or wife may say it's over. The word of man may be impossible.

But the word impossible does not exist in Gods vocabulary.

The Word of God says:

*But with God all things are possible.
*All things are possible to him that believeth.

Luke 18:27 And he said, The things which are impossible with men are possible with God.

John 9: There was a man who was blind from birth, what can man do for him? Nothing, he is destined to die as he was born, blind in darkness. Then came Jesus –Jesus spit in the dirt, made clay and put it in his eyes, sent him to wash in the pool of Siloam and he came seeing.

Mk 5: Tells the story of a woman with an issue of blood, who had been to many physicians and spent all she had and was worse than ever, she was dying, all hope was gone, what can man do for her? Nothing it's an impossible situation.
 Then came Jesus and she pressed her way through the crowd and touched the hem of his garment and she was made instantly and perfectly whole.

Luke 5: Tells the story of a leper.
Not just a leper, but a man full of leprosy. Man says lock him up, he's a menace to society. This man was destined to live his life as a dead man walking, no contact with his family and friends, no interaction with society, barred from the temple.

What can man do for him? Nothing, it's an impossible case.
(Then came Jesus) and was moved with compassion; reached out his hand and touched him, and immediately he was made clean.

What about the 3 Hebrew children thrown into the midst of a burning fiery furnace, what can man do for them? Nothing it's impossible. Then came Jesus walking in the midst of the fire and the fire couldn't burn them.

Then there was a precious mother, a widow of Nain, they were in
the funeral procession, and her child is dead in the coffin. What
can man do for her? Nothing, it's impossible, it's over.
Then came Jesus and touched the coffin and the child sits straight
up and starts talking.

Now let's go back to the disciples; gathered behind locked doors,
mourning the loss of their deliverer. Their light had turned to
darkness, their joy had turned to despair, and their faith had
turned to fear.

Fear was holding them in bondage.
I have to stop here and say that multitudes of people, including
many believers, are living their lives today behind locked doors
because of fear.
The spirit of fear is holding multitudes of people in bondage.

Fear has many facets or many tentacles. Some are living in fear of
terrorism. Some are living in fear of sickness and disease. Still
others are living in fear of gang violence.
Some are living in fear of the future, fear of failure, fear of
rejection, or fear of losing their assistance from the government.

Whatever the name you put on it, the results are the same; fear
paralyzes, fear neutralizes, fear brings bondage, fear brings
confusion, fear brings feelings of helplessness, and fear brings
torment.

But here's good news for the child of God.

*Romans 8:15 For ye have not received the spirit of bondage again
to fear; but ye have received the Spirit of adoption, whereby we
cry, Abba, Father.*

2Timothy 1:7 For God hath not given us the spirit of fear; but of power, and of love, and of a sound mind.
1John 4:18 There is no fear in love; but perfect love casteth out fear: because fear hath torment. He that feareth is not made perfect in love.

There they were in the darkness and confusion, and hopelessness and fear, and then came Jesus right through the wall.

Then came Jesus and appeared in the midst of them.
When does Jesus come? When all hope is gone.
When you've said all you can say, done all you can do, prayed all you can pray, quoted all the scriptures you can quote, cried till there's no more tears, and when every-thing and everybody agree that it's over. That's when Jesus comes.

Remember the disciples, toiling in rowing, the wind was contrary to them. In the fourth watch of the night Jesus came to them walking on the water.

Is there anybody who can testify, that Jesus can come to you when all hope is gone?
They said: don't even pray for him, he'll never get saved, man he's hopeless, but Jesus came to you.
Is there anybody who knows if Jesus hadn't come to you, you'd be strung out on dope, stuck in some ungodly relationship, locked up in some mental institution or dead?

Where does Jesus Come?

Into the midst.
He'll come right into the midst of your storm. He'll be your Lawyer in the courtroom. Your doctor in the sickroom. Your marriage counselor. He will come into the midst of your fiery furnace. He'll come to you on top of the storm. He'll go with you

251

through the lions den. He'll walk with you through the raging waters.
How does Jesus come?
"Through locked doors."

That's good news, for somebody. He'll walk into that crack house, or that bar room where that son or daughter is.
He'll come into that troubled marriage, He'll walk right through the wall. You may think you locked the door and no one knows, but Jesus knows.

He'll come right into that room where that man is sitting polluting his life with pornography, and lust.
You say the door is locked. Jesus says, I don't need a key I am the door. Jesus said I am the door, and I am the way, the truth, and I am the life.
Thank God He comes through locked doors.

What does Jesus do?

"He calms the storms."

He says peace be unto you, and He calms storms of fear, habits addictions, bondage's, emotional storms, physical storms, marital storms, family storms, financial storms. "He calms the storms."

Is there a storm in your life today that you need Jesus to calm? Maybe it's a financial storm, or a marital storm, or a storm of addiction, or lust and you need Jesus to show up and deliver you.

Maybe today I'm talking to someone, possibly even a minister that's caught up in the web of pornography. You're hiding behind locked doors, but Jesus knows where you're at, and He knows what you're doing, and… He will come to where you are, and He will set you free, all you have to do is ask Him.

Is there a problem that you are facing that you can't solve?
Is there a sickness that is threatening you?
Are you wrestling with the spirit of fear and dread?
Is there a loved one that you are holding on to God for, believing
for their salvation, their deliverance?

Sinner are you here? Sinner are you tired of sinning, carrying that
load of guilt and shame and condemnation? Are you ready to be
set free? Are you ready for Jesus to bring real peace to your life?

I don't care how many walls you have built up, or how many
doors you have shut behind you, or how many bridges you have
burned.
Jesus is the bridge, and Jesus is the door, and He is our peace that
has broken down the middle wall, and He wants to come in and
heal you, and deliver you, and transform your life.
Someone reading these words today, you are facing an impossible
situation, that's what man says about it. But God says: If you can
believe all things are possible to him that believeth.

I don't care how bad it looks, or how far it's gone, or how locked
down you feel. Jesus will come right through the wall and He will
deliver you.
Dear reader, just lift your hands right now and begin to praise
him. I feel the Spirit of God moving.
Deliverance is coming to somebody right now.
Healing is coming to somebody right now.
You've been wrestling with this bondage and this addiction for a
long time, but your deliverer has arrived.
The marriage counselor has arrived. Marriages are being healed
and restored right now.

Somebody's ministry is being restored right now. Yes you messed
up and you thought it was over, and you closed the door and
locked it behind you… but right now Jesus is restoring your

ministry.

Somebody else, you have been standing in the gap for your children, and from all natural evidence it has looked like they shut the door, locked the door, and threw away the key.
But there's a turn around in the atmosphere and God is turning their hearts.

Praise the Lord precious friend, this is your day; Jesus is passing your way and all you have to do is reach out and touch Him with your faith.

38
The People That Know Their God

And such as do wickedly against the covenant shall he corrupt by flatteries: but the people that do know their God shall be strong and do exploits (Daniel 11:32).

I believe you know by now that if you are looking for someone to tickle your ears, and pet your flesh and make excuses for living a slippy sloppy, flippy floppy, life then this is the wrong book, and I am the wrong author and preacher for you.

God did not call me from my mother's womb, separate me from sin and disgrace and fill me with his Holy Spirit just to pat people on the back and shake their hands on their way to destruction.

Sometimes the medicine is a little hard to swallow, but if you can keep it down it will deliver your soul.

I don't mean to sound cross or harsh or uncaring or unsympathetic but my spirit is stirred up and agitated by all the gobbledygook and nonsense that is being propagated today as gospel.

It is now becoming popular and accepted behavior in many churches to have what some are calling beer and hymn services.

And now we have the option if you don't like the clothes you're wearing you can go to a nude church.

"Seriously" what happened to the church?

*When did we lose our minds?

*When did it happen?

*When did our brains fall out?

Can you believe it? You don't have to hide in the dark anymore with your pornographic addictions you can just go to a nude church.

But the Bible says it's the responsibility of the priest, the preachers, the prophets, to put a difference between the clean and unclean the holy and the profane.

I know it doesn't look like it or feel like it but I can tell you, there is a whole generation of people in the church and out of the church whose hearts are crying out for someone to draw the lines and establish the boundaries of truth, and not move them back and forth to accommodate the social climate.

Grace was never meant to destroy the law or deliver us from the law. Grace came to fulfill the law, to complete what the law came up short on, which is righteousness.

The law came up short because it was not of faith: and righteousness can only come by faith. But the law, according to the Word of God, is our schoolmaster to lead us to Christ.

Why would I hate my schoolmaster that led me to Christ?

Grace came to deliver us from sin and to empower us to conquer sin and live holy by the power of the Holy Spirit.

Many preachers and teachers today leave you believing that Grace and the Law are in a fight.

It's almost as though they put Moses and Jesus in the ring and say now may the best man win. The Bible says: the law came by Moses but grace and truth came by Jesus Christ

Why is it that there is such a war against the law in the church today? I'll tell you why.

*Because the law deals with absolutes.

*The law defines right and wrong.

*The law establishes boundaries.

We need that in America today!

We need those absolutes, and we need our boundaries defined. We are quickly becoming a lawless nation.

The Bible says: the mystery of iniquity doth already work.

That word iniquity means: lawlessness, transgressing the law, contempt, and violation of the law, wickedness.

Hold onto your seats: I'm going to say something. I am convinced that the contempt we see for the law in our society today is rooted in the church that has rejected God's laws.

The world, the street, the violence, the contempt, the rebellion we have toward the law today is just a reflection of a church that said: we don't have any laws, we don't have any restrictions, there are no absolutes, and it's all about Grace, it's all about whatever we want to do.

This attitude says: there are no absolutes. Therefore there are no consequences for wrong actions because without law there is nothing to tell us what is wrong or hold us accountable.

But I thank God for his law.

David said: *The law of the Lord is perfect converting the soul;*

the testimony of the Lord is sure, making wise the simple (Psalms 19:7.)

Blessed is the man whom thou chastenest, 0 Lord, and teachest him out of thy law (Psalms 94:2.)

Remove from me the way of lying and grant me thy law graciously (Psalms 119:29.)

Rivers of waters run down mine eyes because they keep not thy law (Ps 119:36.)

In our text we are talking about an adversary not only to the children of God, but also to God himself.

This adversary hates the people of God and hates God's sanctuary. This adversary, this enemy is set to defile the sanctuary of God, to desecrate the holy place of God, to bring in the abominable, the unholy, the unclean, vile, and the profane. The Bible even calls it, "The Abomination of desolation" or the abomination that makes desolate. Of course this is talking about any sin or perversion of truth, but it clearly includes homosexuality and lesbianism which is standing today in the pulpits of many churches.

Daniel prophesied: They will bring in sin and set it up in the place where God is supposed to be honored and loved and worshiped and from the place which truth is suppose to emanate. And this adversary, this demonic spirit will carry away many weak, carnal fleshly-minded Christians.

This spirit will capture them not with great overwhelming irresistible strength and power, but with flattery.

The devil will appeal to their flesh and their fleshly appetites and desires.

And those who at one time were lovers of truth and strong preachers of holiness, and sanctification, and separation from sin, are going to do wickedly against the very law, the very truth, and the covenant that they once defended. And they shall join forces to pollute and defile and profane the house of God, bringing all kinds of wickedness and uncleanness and perversion into the sanctuary.

And they shall take away the daily sacrifice...

In other words they shall despise the crucified life, the life that Jesus lived and commands his disciples to live. Jesus said any man that will come after me: let him deny himself and take up his cross daily and follow me (Luke 9:23).

Somebody said pastor Terry, you paint a pretty bleak picture. You make it sound like we're in the dark ages or something. Precious friend, let me tell you something: we are in the dark ages, these are dark times and it's going to get worse.

Jesus said: work while it is day because the night cometh when no man can work (John 9:4).

Isaiah said: *For behold the darkness shall cover the earth and gross darkness the people (Isa 60:2.)*

That's happening right now!

Just as it did in Egypt: the darkness was so thick, so heavy you couldn't see your hand in front of your face and no one moved from their places for three days.

I know it sounds bad, but it's just that compared to all this, cotton candy, fluffy white clouds stuff, that you hear today, the truth is not near as sweet and not near as comfortable.

But the Bible tells it full strength… It will be dark, and gross darkness will come upon the people.

But I love the word of God:

"God is awesome" It's like God stands to the side and says: take your best-shot devil.

Then the announcer gives you blow-by-blow coverage of all the damage that the devil does. Then Jesus leans back and turns it loose. One-shot and knocks the devil out cold, and shows us that he is still the champ.

He is large and in charge.

He is still the boss.

The earth is the Lord's and the fullness thereof.

Now if the Holy Ghost will help me for a few minutes: I want to bring you to the heart of this chapter.

This is really what the Holy Spirit burned in my heart for us right now; everything else was just to bring us to this point.

The bible says all this bad stuff will happen, then there is this one little word "But."

That one little word changes the whole picture. That word means, now that you've heard everything else, I want you to understand that what is coming next will eclipse the rest.

It is a word that tells me what is coming next is greater, more powerful, and more significant than everything that preceded it. So here after all the bad report is that one little game changer, the word "but."

"But" means, regardless of the darkness, regardless of the evil the wickedness, the violence, the lawless-ness, and the corruption, God still has a people.

The Bible says: by the hands of the apostles, were many signs and wonders wrought among the people.

Many signs and wonders, or exploits.

The devil is trying to manipulate us and intimidate and back the church into a corner. He's trying to emasculate the church and strip us of our spiritual power and our spiritual virility. He's trying to make spiritual wimps out of us and make us spiritually impotent and powerless.

"But" There is a people…

*There is a people who do know their God.

*There is a people that aren't selling out.

*There is a people who aren't compromising.

*There is a people who aren't playing footsies with the spirit of worldliness.

*There is a people who are not sleeping with this harlot spirit, and they are not laying their head in Delilah's lap.

There is a people that do know their God and the people that do know their God shall be strong and do exploits.

I Believe I'm talking to some of those people right now: I believe I'm talking to some people who know God.

We know how to get a hold of God: we have a relationship with him. He knows our voice. He knows us by name. If you don't know him that way today, I wouldn't close this book without asking him to come into your heart. This world is a dark place and getting worse all the time, and the only safe place is in Jesus. He is our cleft in the rock. He is our hiding place.

- He is our strong tower.
- He is our defender.
- He is our deliverer.
- He is our captain.

Do you know him? I mean really know Him? Do you walk together; talk together, fellowship, and commune with each other?

My advice to you today is: Get to know him, because if you know him you won't be deceived. If you know him you won't get carried away with flatteries and fleshly desires.

And if you know him:

Instead of backing up and hiding out and quieting down, you'll be standing up and shouting out, and you'll be walking in the power and the anointing of the Holy Ghost and you will be strong and do exploits.

This is what it's going to take to make it in these last and evil days.

You've got to have the power of God in your life.

You've got to live close to God.

You've got to spend time in his presence.

If you want to be strong and you want to do exploits, let God know that there is still a people who want his presence, and want his power.

Tell God you want to know him.

39

If You Don't Know My Story You'll Never Understand My Praise

Psalm 40:1-3 I waited patiently for the Lord; and he inclined unto me, and heard my cry. He brought me up also out of an horrible pit, out of the miry clay, and set my feet upon a rock, and established my goings. And he hath put a new song in my mouth, even praise unto our God: Many shall see it, and fear, and shall trust in the Lord.

I want to talk to some people today who are going through something. I want to talk to some real people today. I want to talk to some people that know what it feels like to hurt. I want to talk to some people today that know what it feels like to cry. I want to talk to some people today who knows what it feels like to be between a rock and a hard place, to have your back against the wall, to have the Red Sea in front of you and pharaohs army closing in behind you.

Now for all the rest of you, if you are reading this book and you've got it all together, you've got no problems, your body is well, your mind is in perfect peace, you've got all the money you'll ever need, you have the marriage made in heaven, there's perfect harmony in your family and everybody loves everybody... then I'm going to ask you to bear with us for a few minutes; while with the help of the good Holy Ghost we try to encourage some people who are really hurting.

For just a little while I want to speak to the people who are down in the trenches. I want to speak to the people who have taken some hard hits. I want to speak to the people who have been wounded and broken. I'm going to direct my words now to people who are fighting a real battle; who have been going through hell. Some even on the verge of throwing up their hands in despair.

I felt the Holy Ghost say to me, there will be some people reading this book who are in the fight of their lives, and they're fighting for their lives. Some are fighting depression; some are fighting a spirit of suicide. Some are fighting with lust and perversion. Some are fighting for their health. Some are fighting the sinister spirit of fear and hopelessness. And someone reading these words today has said to yourself; I'll try it one more time, I'll read this crazy preachers book, but if something doesn't change; I quit, I give up, it's not worth it.

My friend you have picked up the right book at the right time and I am the right crazy preacher for you.

I want to tell you today, God has heard your cry. God knows and God cares about what you're going through. Precious friend, you are not alone.

There is someone who loves you and knows exactly what you are going through, and has the power to deliver you. "His name is Jesus"

The Bible declares that our Lord and Savior Jesus Christ, knows exactly what you are going through and He knows exactly what you feel.

"For we have not a high priest which cannot be touched with the feelings of our infirmities; but was in all points tempted like as we are, yet without sin" (Hebrews 4:15.)

Jesus knows your grief and he knows your pain. He didn't just leave heaven and come to this sin cursed earth and die on a cross just to get us to heaven.

He wants you well, he wants you happy, and he wants you to prosper. He wants you to have a happy marriage. He wants you to have a healthy body. He wants you to enjoy life.

John says, it's the thief who comes to steal kill and destroy, then Jesus says; but I have come that they might have life, and that they might have it more abundantly (See John 10:10.)

But you have to give it all to him. You have to give him the good the bad and the ugly.

You see over 59 years of living, I have discovered that many times we're willing to be delivered from the things that hurt us and cause us pain. But we don't want to let go of the things that please our flesh.

Let me give you a for instance. Let's say you're shacking up; you know that's wrong, but you're ok with it until he starts abusing you. Now you want God to make him quit abusing you, but you don't want to quit shacking up.

Duh'

Let me give you another example: You want the church to pray for you to get a job, or get a place to live, or healing for your body; but you don't want to serve God. You want to live your own life your own way, but you want God to jump every time you stub your toe.

Sweetheart, you can't have it both ways.

God is not an Aladdin's lamp or a little statue that you rub its belly and you get your wish granted.

God is the creator of the universe; He knows every hair on your head. You can't hide anything from God. You can't fool God. He knows your thoughts before you think them.

"Thou knowest my downsitting and mine uprising, thou understandest my thought afar off" (Psalms 139:2.)

In other words, you know my thoughts before I do.

" Shall not God search this out? For He knoweth the secrets of the heart" (Psalms 44:21.)

I know I've started meddling. I was doing real good when I was talking about God blessing and healing and delivering, and meeting all of our needs and making us happy.

Well hang on; I'm not done yet. I've got to drill a little deeper here. We want to get the poison out. We want to get the diseased part out. We don't just want to shoot you full of painkiller and laughing gas and make you believe everything is fine because you're laughing and feeling good.

The truth is you can feel good and be dying.

Let me tell you another truth. A lot of people in the church don't want a God that governs them and corrects them and tells them how to live; they just want a "sugar daddy".

They just want someone to make them feel good about their selves, heal their hurts, take care of all their financial problems, and then go to heaven when they die.

They have been in the church for 10, 15, 30 years and they haven't grown one bit. They don't have any spiritual power or authority, they can't rebuke the devil, and they don't know ten scriptures by heart.

They have no passion for the Word, they have no desire to be possessed by the Holy Spirit, and they have no spiritual roots.

By now they should be preachers and teachers, evangelists, apostles, prophets, intercessors, prayer warriors. By now they should be mentoring and discipling others. By now they should be spiritual fathers and spiritual mothers. But they don't have enough word in them to help anybody.

The church was never intended to be a spiritual nursery, for saints who had no desire to grow and mature. It was never intended to be just a place where we all come "just like we are" and get blessed and stay just like we are.

God wants to grow us up, mature us, and build spiritual character and fortitude in us. He wants to anoint us with power and authority to heal the sick, to lift heavy burdens, to cast out devils and set captives free.

So when we meet someone who is sick, bound, oppressed, confused, tormented, even possessed, we will be able to deliver them. Cast out the devil and heal their hearts and set them free.

I know by the Spirit of God that I am speaking today to some people who are hurting, who are fighting real battles, who are being tormented by the devil, and I'm telling you, you are in the right place at the right time.

Right there where you are, the anointing is flowing, to heal you everywhere you hurt.

- To heal your mind.

- To drive sickness out of your body.

- To restore your marriage.

- To deliver you from the spirit of hopelessness.

- To pull you out of the pit of depression, that pit of fear, that pit of sickness and disease, or that pit of anxiety.

Listen again to David's words: I waited patiently for the Lord; and he inclined and to me, and heard my cry. "He brought me up also out of an horrible pit" out of the miry clay, and set my feet upon a rock, and established my goings. And he hath put a new song in my mouth, even praise unto our God: many shall see it, and fear, and shall trust in the Lord.

David said: He brought me up also out of a horrible pit. Then he says, out of the miry clay.

Then something happened. He put a new song in my mouth, even praise unto our God.

This verse doesn't really tell us how emotional David was about his deliverance, but knowing David's life, and his expressions of love and thanks giving, we can only imagine that he probably shouted and laughed and cried. He probably whirled around in circles, he probably jumped up and down, and he probably fell to the ground and praised God. And I can imagine him throwing kisses to God, saying, thank you, thank you, thank you.

Let me show why I say that.

The verse we're looking at says, many shall "see it" and fear and shall trust in the Lord.

Many shall see it. In other words, it's visible, not only can they hear it, they can see it. In other words, it's expressive, it's audacious, it's outrageous, and some no doubt would say: it's extreme and it's totally unnecessary.

I think if David were here today he would say; don't worry about what people say about you or what people think about you. You need to praise God like you feel it. If that means run, then run, if that means dance then dance. If it's laughing then laugh, if it's crying then cry. If it means jumping up and down, then jump up and down.

Don't worry about your makeup running or your wig getting twisted, or your clothes getting wrinkled.

Some people around you will say: that's not necessary, it don't take all of that, you're getting carried away.

But precious friend, nobody can tell you what it takes. Here is how I respond to the critics. It's real simple, I just say; I love you, but if you don't know my story, you'll never understand my praise.

When David was bringing the ark of Gods presence back into Jerusalem, he was so excited he danced right out of his kingly garments. His wife Michal mocked him.

She said; *"How glorious was the king of Israel today, who uncovered himself today in the eyes of the handmaids of his servants, as one of the vain fellows shamelessly uncovereth himself"* (2 Sam 6:20.)

But David didn't let her criticism rob him of his joy and freedom of expression of his love and appreciation for the Lord.

David said: *"It was before the Lord, which chose me before thy father, and before all his house, to appoint me ruler over the people of the Lord, over Israel: therefore will I play before the Lord. And I will yet be more vile than thus, and will be base in mine own sight."(See 2 Samuel 6:21-22.)*

I love it; David is saying, let me remind you why I dance like I do. Let me share my story again because you have obviously forgotten what the Lord has done for me. So let me run it by you again.

And while I'm on the subject let me add one more thing; you haven't seen anything yet. If you thought I was undignified and over the top, then you don't want to be around for my next praise.

Precious friend, don't ever let anybody or anything keep you from praising God.

If they don't know your story they will never understand your praise.

40

When It Don't Make No Sense

"Although the FIG tree shall not blossom, neither shall fruit be in the vines. The labor of the olive shall fail, the fields shall yield no meat, the flock shall be cut off from the fold, and there shall be no herd in the stalls. Yet I will rejoice in the Lord, I will joy in the God of my salvation" (Habakkuk 3:17-18.)

Have you ever been there? Have you ever been in a situation like the prophet Habakkuk? If you haven't been there yet you will be. If you haven't been there yet just keep on living.

The truth is; life comes with problems built in. So you might as well understand. You're not going to get through this life without trouble, without hardships, without pain, without getting your heart broken at least once or twice. You're not going to make it without being lied on, persecuted, and despised. Then throw some betrayal and deception into the pot, because that's life.

All you have to do is look in the Bible and you will see what I'm talking about. David was a great man of God, a great King of Israel, and a worshipper.

But that did not exempt David from pain. If you study David's life, you will see a man who endured much pain.

Then look at Job: He was a righteous man, but he endured more grief and pain than would seem humanly possible.

And I could go on and on: But I believe the point is clear. Sometimes life hurts.

Sometimes you're in the pit and sometimes you're in the fire. Sometimes you're on the mountain calling fire down from heaven, and sometimes you're in the cave hoping Jezebel doesn't find you.

There are just some things that happen to us all simply because we're in the world. Then there are things that are demonic in nature, attacks straight out of hell. Your adversary the devil goeth about like a roaring lion seeking whom he may devour.

John 10:10 (a) the thief cometh not but for to steal to kill and to destroy.

I said all of this to get to this point: there will be times in your life when praise don't make no sense.

When we talk about making sense of something, we mean that it is understandable, and that it is agreeable to what is before us, and it is logical and it is reasonable.

But this man of God Habakkuk, was doing something that just doesn't make no sense. He was standing in the midst of chaos, of loss, of emptiness and confusion and disappointment and he did something that sent shock waves through hell and applause through heaven.

He said: Yet I will rejoice in the Lord, I will joy in the God of my salvation.

Basically what he said was: I have decided, I'm going to praise my God even when it don't make no sense. I may be going through a season of sickness, or I may be grieving over the loss of a loved one. Or I may be walking through the fire of divorce, or family turmoil. I may be crying myself to sleep at night over my prodigals. They may be threatening foreclosure on my house. The repo-depo just towed my car away. My company says their downsizing and might have to let me go.

Well man of God, woman of God, what are you going to do?

I tell you what I'm "not" going to do. I'm not going to let my feelings and my emotions take over. I'm not going to go into deep depression. I'm not going to run to the refrigerator and try to drown my sorrow in food. I'm not going to overdose on prescription meds. I'm not going to get angry with God and accuse him of not loving me, and not caring about me.

This is what I'm going to do. I'm going to do what David did: I'm going to encourage myself in the Lord.

Then I'm going to get my praise on. I'm going to put on the garment of praise for the spirit of heaviness. I'm going to open my mouth and praise God. I'm going to give him the praise that's due his name.

Bless the Lord O my soul and all that is within me, bless his holy name.

God never promised us a problem free life.

Isa 43:2 When thou passest through the waters I will be with thee, and through the rivers, they shall not overflow thee, and when thou walkest through the fire, thou shalt not be burned, neither shall the flame kindle upon thee.

Ps 34:19 Many are the afflictions of the righteous, but the Lord, delivereth them out of them all.

I'm going to stop right here and tell you: The church is filled with pretty praisers. These are people that will praise God when everything's pretty. When the weathers nice, when the bills are paid. When all the children are saved. When their body feels good. When they've got money in the bank, they're quick to give God that nice pretty praise.

Their face never gets scrunched up, their makeup never runs, they don't cry, they don't ever get their clothes out of sorts, their wig never gets twisted, they wouldn't jump or shout or dance if the building was on fire. But I'm going to tell you something that might surprise you: God would rather have your UGLY PRAISE than your pretty praise.

Now stay with me for a minute, let me clarify that statement...

It doesn't take any confidence, and it doesn't take any faith in God, and it doesn't take any effort to praise God when everything is going great in your life.

Oh Yes we definitely should praise during those times.

But what really gets the attention of heaven, and paralyzes Hell is that UGLY praise.

That praise that don't make no sense: that praise when you're face is all scrunched up, that praise that is hard to tell if it's a praise or a moan. That praise that runs down your face, that praise that you had to reach down deep for.

That praise that is aggressive, it's Ugly, it aint pretty.

The dictionary defines Ugly as: very unattractive, unpleasant to look at, offensive to the sense of beauty, displeasing in appearance, messy, and objectionable.

Pretty praisers get uncomfortable around Ugly praisers, cause Ugly praisers aren't worried about winning a beauty contest; they're just trying to hang on to their sanity.

Those pretty praisers have a problem with real praise: because real praise might get loud, and it might get ugly.

Dear reader, God said to tell you: it's time to quit worrying about trying to pretty it up, and just give it up.

I'm going to tell you personally: I've been in some ugly situations, and I have to tell you the truth, there wasn't a pretty praise anywhere around me. All my praise was Ugly praise.

But God Loves Your Ugly Praise!

Give him your Ugly Praise...

Let me introduce you to a couple of Ugly Praisers in the Bible.

First there was Job:

Job 1:1 Job was a perfect and upright one that feared God, and eschewed evil.

Then we see in Job 1:13-22 in ten verses, Job lost everything. The Sabeans took his oxen and Asses and killed all his servants but one, then fire fell from the sky and burned up his sheep and all the servants but one, the chaldeans took his camels and slew his servants, all except one. Then all of his sons and daughters were at the oldest brothers house, and a great wind, smote the house and all his children were killed. All of these tragedies hit Jobs life in a matter of 10 Verses.

What did Job do? He gave God some UGLY PRAISE... He arose, rent his mantle, shaved his head and fell down upon the ground and worshipped.

Lets look at another Ugly Praiser in the scriptures.

The Bible says: David and his men had returned from a military campaign, and found their city Ziklag burned with fire, and their wives, their sons and their daughters were taken captive. Then David and the people that were with him, lifted up their voices and wept, until they had no more power to weep. And then it says: David was greatly distressed for the people spake of stoning him, because the soul of all the people was grieved, every man for his sons, and his daughters. (See 1 Sa 30:1-7.)

But David encouraged himself in the Lord. This is where David gave God an Ugly Praise.

They had been weeping and crying until they had no more power to weep. No doubt David was physically exhausted, he didn't look like a great warrior or a great worshipper, his eyes were most likely swollen and bloodshot. But what he did next turned everything around.

Right there in the middle of that pain: he gave God a praise that didn't make no sense.... He Gave God an UGLY praise.

And God gave him a supernatural turnaround, and he recovered every single thing the devil had stolen.

Glory to God: I'm starting to feel an Ugly praise anointing right now!

I feel like somebody, is one Ugly praise away from a miracle. One Ugly praise away from a supernatural breakthrough, a turnaround. One Ugly praise away from your prodigals coming home. One Ugly praise away from turning that lack into abundance. One Ugly praise away from a brand new anointing.

One Ugly Praise away from a healing that has been a long time coming.
Let me introduce to two more Ugly praisers: you may know them better as Paul and Silas.

We find them in Acts Chapter 16 (they are busy working for the master.) When a certain damsel possessed with a spirit of divination, began to follow them around saying: these men are the servants of the most high God, which show unto us the way of salvation. This did she many days. But Paul being grieved, turned and said to the spirit, I command thee in the name of Jesus Christ to come out of her and he came out the same hour. When her masters saw that the hope of their gains were gone they caught Paul and Silas and began to accuse them of being troublemakers, teaching customs which are not lawful to receive or observe. Well The multitude rose up together against them and the magistrates rent off their clothes and beat them, and laid many stripes upon them. And then thrust them into the inner prison and made their feet fast in the stocks.

Then we see our two Ugly praisers there in the darkness, at midnight, humiliated, backs beaten black and blue, their clothes ripped off their bodies. And the Bible says: At midnight Paul and Silas prayed and sang PRAISES unto God, and the prisoners heard them.
They gave God an Ugly praise: A praise that don't make no sense.
Right there in the midst of the darkness, and the pain, when most people would have been crying, and moaning and groaning and complaining and deciding whether the ministry was worth it or not.
Right there they gave God an Ugly praise... through the humiliation, through the tears and fears, through the pain, beaten black and blue.

They might not have passed the qualifications for the church choir. But there was something about that UGLY PRAISE that God liked.

And suddenly there was a great earthquake, so that the foundations of the prison were shaken: and immediately all the doors were opened, and every one's bands were loose. And the Jailor and his whole family got born into the Kingdom that night. Because of two men who were not ashamed to give God an Ugly praise, and to praise God when it didn't make no sense (see Acts 16:26.)

We've already met him once in this chapter, but lets look at him one more time. His name is David. He's bringing the ark of the Covenant back to Jerusalem, and he begins to be overwhelmed with thanksgiving. He starts to dance and rejoice. He starts whirling around. And the bible says: He danced right out of his Kingly apparel.

Then lets look at what happens when Ugly Praise shows up.

Then David returned to bless his household, and Michal the daughter of Saul came out to meet David, and said, How glorious was the king of Israel today, who uncovered himself today in the eyes of the handmaids of his servants, as one of the vain fellows shamelessly uncovereth himself (2Sa 6:20.)

And David could have said: you're right honey, that was a shameful thing for me to do, and it certainly was no way for a king to act. I should have composed myself; I should have behaved myself better. I'm sorry that I embarrassed you.
I said: he could have said that; but he didn't.

(2 Sa 6:21-22) And David said unto Michal, it was before the Lord, which chose me before thy father, and before all his house, to appoint me ruler over the people of the Lord, over Israel: Therefore will I play before the Lord. And I will yet be more vile

than thus, and will be base in mine own sight. and of the maid servants that thou hast spoken of, of them shall I be had in honour.

Let Me Paraphrase for Just a minute: What David said was; I wasn't dancing for you, and I wasn't dancing for the servants or the handmaidens. But I was dancing before the Lord who chose me and made me king.

And then David said: If you thought that praise was over the top, if that was offensive and distasteful to you, if you thought that my last praise was Ugly, you haven't seen anything yet.

Dear friends, I'm going to tell you the truth: I don't really understand it all, but I know its true, there's something powerful in an Ugly praise.

God responded to Paul and Silas Ugly praise and shook the Jail off its foundation.

God responded to Jobs Ugly praise and gave him back double everything he had lost.

God responded to David's Ugly praise and he recovered everything the enemy had stolen.

After 3 days and 3 nights in whale motel Jonah gave God an Ugly praise.

Sitting in a whale's belly, covered in seaweed here's what Jonah said:

"But I will sacrifice unto thee with the voice of thanksgiving, I will pay that, I have vowed, Salvation is of the Lord. 10. And the Lord spake unto the fish and it vomited out Jonah upon the dry land" (Jonah 2:9.)

What am I saying? I'm saying that when Jonah gave God an Ugly praise that don't make no sense. God told the whale to spit him out.

When Ugly praise filled that whales belly it made him sick, and he spit Jonah out. Jonah didn't come out pretty. (He came out UGLY) but he came out.

I Just believe if you would give God an Ugly praise today, a praise that don't make no sense something would happen. I believe something would shift, and something would break. Something would spit you out.

41
The Stabilizing Factor

"And wisdom and knowledge shall be the stability of thy times, and strength of salvation: the fear of the LORD is his treasure" (Isaiah 33:6.)

Let's examine the meaning of the word <u>stability</u>: It means:

- The state or quality of being stable.
- Firmness in position, continuance without change; permanence.
- Resistance to change, especially sudden change or deterioration.
- Steadfastness; constancy, as of character or purpose.

As relates to Aeronautics, it means, the ability of an aircraft to return to its original flying position when abruptly displaced.

Dear reader, I hope that you know that I am not just an author and a preacher but I am a prophetic voice to my generation, and I have been hearing something in my spirit for many days and it has been getting louder and louder.

As we look around us today it seems as though the whole worlds gone crazy. It seems as though there are no longer any reference points.

Think about this… When the prodigal son in the scriptures came to himself in the pigpen after wasting his substance, and wasting his life on riotous, self-pleasing desires, he remembered where he came from.

He remembered his father's house. He remembered what was good and what was evil. He remembered what faithfulness and honesty and integrity and dignity looked like.

He remembered what it felt like to be loved not on the basis of what he could do or the money that he had, but just for who he was. He remembered all of that.

But this society has gone crazy, it's as though we in this society and this generation have been sucked up into a tornado and we are spinning out of control.

Elijah the prophet went up to heaven in a whirlwind of fire, but this nation and this generation seems to be going down to hell in a whirlwind of hells fire.

This is no longer just the society that sins and does wrong and does evil; no sir no mamm, this is now the society that runs with passion and zeal to find the most wicked and perverse things that they can do to pervert truth and rebel against God, to spit in his face and to make a mockery of the cross and the blood of Jesus.

We are quickly becoming a zombifide people.

A zombie is defined as: the body of a dead person given the semblance of life but mute and will-less (No will) controlled by a supernatural force for some evil purpose.

That's what is happening in this nation. People are becoming zombifide. You see in order to become a zombie you have to surrender your will. And once you surrender your will to evil then evil controls you.

That's what we see happening not only in America but around the world. Nations are being driven by evil powers as puppets on a string.

They are murderous, acting without any concern for human life. Their thirst for power and world dominance has made them mad; they're off their rockers, they've lost it. They've gone off the deep end.

There is not a shred of decency or human compassion left to stabilize their actions.

In video cameras today even in our smart phones we have something built into them called a stabilizer, so that while you're filming it keeps the pictures steady even though the phone is moving and bouncing around.

Airplanes also have these stabilizing capabilities. An aircraft is considered stable when there is no rotation motion or tendency. An aircraft is considered stable if it returns to its initial equilibrium flight conditions when it's perturbed or disturbed or experiences turbulence.

But if that initial equilibrium or point of balance and stability is lost, it is impossible to bring it back into a state of perpetual stability.

That is what is happening in America, the initial equilibrium that we had in this country that was established in our trust and faith in God and obedience to his righteous commandments, has been lost and we are a nation in free fall.

That means that there are no restraints, there are no efforts being made to pull back on the yoke or pull up, or bring us back on course. All stabilizing factors, all common sense, all goodness and decency are being rejected on every hand.

Thank God for what our president is trying to do, but a president can't fix the soul of this nation.

It's not a color thing, it's not a political party thing, and it's not even a money thing, it's a soul thing. Satan is bidding for the soul of this nation and we as a nation are in free fall and this country is spinning out of control.

As I said, to a large degree we have become a people zombifide, and we're completely oblivious to what is happening in the world. Like the zombie nothing affects us, nothing makes us happy, nothing makes us sad, nothing makes us cry, nothing makes us

angry, nothing evokes joy in us. We're just going through the motions, and the sad part about is; this society wants it that way.
Because that way there is no conscience, they can perform every evil sexually perverse thing with no sense of wrong. They can commit murder - kill babies and perform every evil sexually perverse act with no consciousness of guilt or shame.

Some days ago in Michigan in our United States of America, not some deep dark Jungle in Africa, not a deep dark corner in India, but right here in the good ole U. S. of A. (A doctor was accused of mutilating the genitals of young girls).
This doctor's defense was; it is part of our religious practices.
This doctor was one of two who were both charged with conspiring to perform female genital mutilations on minor girls. Authorities believe they have done this to several other young girls between the ages of 6-9 years old.

In 2014 an Oklahoma City man went into a woman's work place and cut off her head.

Then in February 2016 it was reported that in 16 months Oklahoma had experienced four more decapitations.
Maybe your thinking, pastor this is gruesome, why are you telling us this?
Because this is the real world: this is what America is becoming.

And because too many preachers won't tell the truth, they want to keep their people medicated and sedated and in a catatonic state, just following along in a zombifide condition, oblivious to the world around them.
They keep them drugged up on feel good messages that never deal with sin, or the consequences, and don't tell them how to have power over sin and the devil.

The bible commands those who watch over the souls of men to lift their voices like a trumpet and sound the alarm.

Isaiah said: Cry aloud and spare not, lift up thy voice like a trumpet and show my people their transgressions and the house of Jacob their sins.

America is in a free fall spiraling to destruction, and much of the church world is just sitting around singing cum-ba-yah.

Sin is in the church: Homosexuality, lesbianism, drinking, gambling, fornication, adultery, pornography, sexual perversion, lust, pride, hypocrisy, false doctrine telling everybody that it doesn't matter what they do or how they live, that its already covered, your already justified. They say, there's no judgment with God, there's no consequences to your sin, go ahead and fornicate, go ahead and lust and commit adultery, go ahead and practice homosexuality and lesbianism. They say, the blood of Jesus has it all covered, and by the way there's no such place as hell anyway, that was just something invented by some angry condemning religious zealots.

No my precious friends, hell was not the invention of law preaching condemning religious zealots.

These are Jesus words: *"Then shall he say also unto them on the left hand, Depart from me, ye cursed, into everlasting fire, prepared for the devil and his angels"* (Mt 25:41.)

And the Bible says, because of the pride and rebellion of man Hell has enlarged herself to receive them.

"Therefore hell hath enlarged herself, and opened her mouth without measure: and their glory, and their multitude, and their pomp, and he that rejoiceth, shall descend into it" (Isa 5:1.)

Beloved I am a positive preacher and I preach, teach, and write with a passion to encourage people and build them up, but you don't heal a cancer by putting a band-aid on it.
It either has to be burned out or cut out.

Our country including much of the church world today has been thrown off balance and they have lost their stability, they have lost their stabilizing factor.

For just a few minutes I want to present to you what can stabilize the church, what can stabilize America, and what can bring us back to true center and true north.
There is hope yet for America, and there is yet hope for the Laodicean modern lukewarm church.
And there is hope for you and I. No matter how out of balance and out of control things are around us,
there is a stabilizing factor: but I'm not going to lie about it, it's not going to be easy and a lot of people, even church people will not accept it.

But it is not in my power or your power to make people live right, but it is in my power and it is my responsibility to show them how.
In our text it is as though God is looking right down into the 21st century and He is seeing all the confusion, and all the perversion and all the chaos, and in His everlasting mercy and goodness He is saying...
I can help you, there is hope, I can get you back on course, I can bring stability back into your life.

Dear reader, if we've ever needed anything in this world today and in the church, it's a stabilizing factor.
This whole world is a ticking time bomb.

Many times I have been in Oklahoma before a big storm hit and even though it was a beautiful day, you could feel the "instability" in the atmosphere.

The atmosphere in this country, and the world is unstable, it's volatile, and it's explosive.
It could go off any minute, only now it's not bullets, and canon balls it's nuclear interballistic missiles that can take out a whole country.

Everybody is stretching their muscles trying to prove to each other how powerful they are.
Its not interballistic missiles that we need, and it's not missile interceptors, that we need, It's the presence the power and the glory of God that we need.

There is a path back to the glory and back to a place of protection and power, and back to the place of stability.
It's right here in this verse.

Isa 33:6 And <u>wisdom and knowledge shall be the stability of thy times, and strength of salvation</u>: the fear of the LORD is his treasure.

Wisdom and knowledge, not human intellectual wisdom or intelligence, not nuclear wisdom and knowledge, not political wisdom and knowledge.
But Godly wisdom and knowledge: Divine God given Holy Spirit imparted wisdom.
Now lets get to the heart of the matter.

What is Godly Holy Spirit imparted Wisdom?

Pr 9:10 <u>The fear of the LORD</u> is the beginning of wisdom: and the knowledge of the holy is understanding.

The Fear of the Lord is where wisdom comes from. Wisdom springs from the source of the fear of the Lord. That is why our country has gone crazy, that is why America is in a free fall, that is why we are spiraling into destruction, and that is why the church is to a large degree a laughing stock of the world today; just more material for some filthy sitcom to use to ridicule and criticize the church.

That's why the church, and I use that term loosely, because there is a true remnant church, though few by contrast, they are the pure in heart and they are true to the Word of God and true to the leading of the Holy Spirit.

But this psuedo church, this lukewarm church without a cross, without repentance, without the blood, without the presence and the power and the glory of God; they have lost the fear of God.

(See Romans 3:18) *There is no fear of God before their eyes.*

"Wherefore the Lord said, forasmuch as this people draw near me with their mouth, and with their lips do honour me, but have removed their heart far from me, and their fear toward me is taught by the precept of men"
(Isa 29:13.)

God says: Their fear toward me is taught by the precept of men; in other words God says: they have no true fear of God anymore because they have been taught by the precept of man a false fear, an unbiblical fear, a deceptive fear, a diluted fear, a comfortable fear.

And the church has largely been the guilty party because for so long we preachers have tried to make people comfortable around God, take the rough edges off, smooth him down, and make Christianity easy to take. We have tried to make it palatable and easy to swallow.

And we have stripped the true fear of God out of the church and out of the hearts of the people.

Preachers have told their people that the fear of God is just a respect, just an attitude of honor and appreciation that doesn't want to offend God.

Dear reader, please bear with me for just a couple more minutes. I want to show you from Gods Word what the fear of the Lord looks like.

Pr 8:13   The fear of the LORD is to hate evil: pride, and arrogancy, and the evil way, and the froward mouth, do I hate.

Pr 14:27   The fear of the LORD is a fountain of life, to depart from the snares of death.

2 Co 7:1 Having therefore these promises, dearly beloved, let us cleanse ourselves from all filthiness of the flesh and spirit, perfecting holiness in the fear of God.

The problem we have is we haven't been taught the true fear of God:
We've forgotten the God of the bible:
I mean the God as revealed in the Bible:
 the one who wiped out the human race except for Noah and his family in the ark.
The God of the Bible:
 the one who opened up the Red Sea and swallowed up the Egyptians,
The God of the Bible: the one who opened up the earth and swallowed up the sons of Korah, and then sent his fire down and burned up 250 that tried to take over the priests ministry.
And then sent out a plague that killed over 14,000 of them that murmured against Moses and Aaron.

I'm speaking about the God of the bible

: the one who burned up the two sons of Aaron because they offered to him strange fire.

The God of the bible:

the one who rained fire and brimstone from heaven and destroyed the cities of Sodom and Gomorrah.

The God of the bible:

the one who sent poisonous serpents among the people and many of them died, because of their sin.

The God of the Bible: the one who slew over 50,000 men because they dared to look into the Ark of the Covenant.

The God of the Bible: whose was anger was kindled against Uzzah because he took hold of the Ark, and God smote him and he died.

Maybe you're thinking, Oh but Pastor Terry, that was the Old God: He was angry in the old testament, our God is the new testament God, He's all grace and mercy, He's not angry anymore, He's calm, He's better adjusted now, He's on Prozac and valiums, and He's mellowed with age.

Somebody should have told Ananaias and Saphira about that: because they didn't get the memo.

Do you remember the story of a man and his wife who tried to deceive the Holy Ghost?

They lied about the price of the land they sold and how much they received for it.

And Ananias hearing these words fell down, and gave up the ghost: and great fear came on all them that heard these things (Acts 5:5.)

And it was about the space of three hours after, when his wife, not knowing what was done, came in.
8 And Peter answered unto her, Tell me whether ye sold the land for so much? And she said, Yea, for so much.

9   Then Peter said unto her, How is it that ye have agreed together to tempt the Spirit of the Lord? behold, the feet of them which have buried thy husband are at the door, and shall carry thee out.
10 Then fell she down straightway at his feet, and yielded up the ghost: and the young men came in, and found her dead, and, carrying her forth, buried her by her husband (Acts 5:7-10.)

What was the result of this?
"And great fear came upon all the church, and upon as many as heard these things. 12 ¶ And by the hands of the apostles were many signs and wonders wrought among the people; (and they were all with one accord in Solomon's porch" (Acts 5:11-12.)
"Then had the churches rest throughout all Judaea and Galilee and Samaria, and were edified; and walking in the fear of the Lord, and in the comfort of the Holy Ghost, were multiplied" *(Acts 9:31.)*

I am prophesying to you today: that one of the marks of this last day outpouring is going to be a drastic and sudden return to the fear of God.

That's the only thing that can put the church back on track, and back in equilibrium, we must have a new vision and desire for the fear of God to take hold on the church and on our lives
.

Pr 10:27 The fear of the LORD prolongeth days: but the years of the wicked shall be shortened.

Pr 14:26 In the fear of the LORD is strong confidence: and his children shall have a place of refuge.

Pr 14:27 The fear of the LORD is a fountain of life, to depart from the snares of death.

I don't know how this will all play out in our future and I don't know what God is going to do, or the means He is going to use, but I do know this; I am prophesying that before this last great revival on planet earth comes, there is going to be a revival of the fear of God.

We better get ready, because there is a major house cleaning coming to the church, and along with this house cleaning is coming a fresh revelation of the fear of God.

And when the fear of God comes, stability will come.
This is the stabilizing factor.

42
Armed And Dangerous

It's not unusual to hear from time to time of a person who breaks out of prison. It's also not unusual for those fugitives to immediately begin to look for a weapon. In such cases the police put out what they call an A.P.B. an all points bulletin. And very often the police will warn the public that these fugitives from the law are to be considered armed and dangerous. This is to notify and alert the public that these fugitives of the law are to be avoided at all costs and they are not to be approached under any circumstances.

Of course everything I have said up until now has been on the negative side, but this book is not written from the negative side but from the positive side. It is my desire and my goal to establish the truth of God in your heart, that you are the one who is armed and dangerous. And you are the one that hell has to fear. And you are the one that hell has to put out an all-points bulletin on because you are the one who is "armed and dangerous." While I'm on this subject I do have to tell you, this is not automatic, you don't just go to bed one night and wake up in the morning in full armor, filled with the power and the anointing of God. The Bible teaches us the pathway to power, and teaches us how to be those soldiers who are armed and dangerous.

In Ephesians chapter 6 Paul talks about the armor of God.

I am not going to go into detail concerning the different pieces of the armor. For a detailed study on the armor you can read my book, armed and dangerous.

But let's make a couple of very important points about the armor of God.

1. It is not imaginary, invisible yes but imaginary no.

2. It is not a fashion statement. In other words, spiritual armor is real and is meant for spiritual warfare.
3. You have to put it on.

Many young men and women who grew up in the land of the free and the brave enlist in the armed services; they go to boot camp, which is supposed to be extreme extensive and difficult training. Then they go into the Battle Zone. Now on the battlefield they are exposed to a new reality. What never existed before is now their everyday reality. What was at one time only stories and rhetoric from someone they considered an old war relic is now their story and it's now their life.

They do not know from one day to the next if they will live to see another sunrise. Everyday is a blessing; every heartbeat is a gift from God. Now they are bombarded with things their eyes and ears were never prepared for. The Warfare is not just physical and emotional it's also mental and it's spiritual. That's why so many soldiers come back from war with PTSD. It's because their whole internal makeup has been altered, and it's been shifted. Now when they return from war they are demanded to live by our normal. They come back with a wartime mentality and we call them dangerous and out of touch with reality and abnormal. But the truth is they are in a normal mindset for wartime.
Because their normal is war. Their normal is combat readiness. They are mentally emotionally and spiritually and physically prepared to die at any minute. Yet they are just as ready to take a life without a second thought. You may ask why am I speaking like this? Why are you sounding so negative Pastor Terry?
Well I hope you understand that what I'm saying is really positive. Yes it sounds negative to someone who has never committed themselves to this high level of commitment and sacrifice.
But I can almost guarantee you that most if not all of these soldiers would tell you, I wish I had been better prepared,

mentally and emotionally and physically for what I had to face. I wish I had been better equipped.

Okay now let's get down to where the rubber meets the road. America is changing. Our beloved America the land of the free and the brave is now a war-torn country. The truth is, there is violence taking place everywhere. Our country is divided. There's violence in the streets, there's violence in the schools, violence in the government. But it's not just the crimes of adults against adults.

It's crimes against our children and grandchildren. Crimes that are being committed against our babies, and it's by the very ones that are supposed to be their caretakers and overseers.

I'm going to tell it like it is. The government system is raping our children, sodomizing our children. In a very real sense they are saying to decent moral God-fearing God honoring parents, we are going to rape and sodomize your babies and if you say anything about it we will slap you with fines and throw you in jail. And you say Pastor Terry you're saying things that sound so dark and ugly.

Friend things are so dark and ugly. That's the world we're living in. It's a war zone.

It's time for the church to quit walking around in a daze pretending everything's fine and in a few days it'll all be back to Opie and Andy, and America will be nice safe beautiful Mayberry again. Friend I hate to burst your bubble, but it's never going to happen. It's time for the church and every child of God, to wake up.

It's time for the church to soldier up.

It's time for us to suit up.

It's time for us to stand up.

It's time to realize that we are at war and we better get dressed for the battle. So many Christians would rather pretend, than deal with reality. You hear them say things like; all this nuclear threat is just a bunch of hooey, a bunch of nonsense. They say nothing like this could ever happen. Friend we need to wake up, it has already happened. In 1945 the United States dropped two atomic bombs on the Japanese cities of Hiroshima and Nagasaki. The first bomb dropped on Hiroshima wiped out 90% of the city, over 80,000 people. Then tens of thousands died later from radiation fallout. The second bomb a couple of days later was dropped on Nagasaki. That bomb killed almost 40,000 people instantly.

Again you're saying pastor Terry why would you speak to us like this?

I'm going to tell you why. It's because I love you and I care about you. It's because I want you to know the season that were in. We are in a time of war. Yes physically, but especially spiritually, and many so-called preachers and prophets aren't telling the truth.

Having said all of that, I believe today the greatest enemy that the church faces in this hour is the enemy of indifference. This is the enemy that wants to lull the church into a false sense of security, like everything is fine. That's what the devil wants you to believe. He wants the church to go to sleep and pretend like everything is fine while the house is burning to the ground.

Prosperity, blessings, peace, they say. It's fine they say. Peace peace peace they say. Relax they say. Don't make such a big deal out of things. They say eat and drink and be merry.

But I hear the Holy Spirit saying: it's time for the church to wake up. It's time for the church and every child of God to shake off the chains of apathy and indifference and seek God like never before, and put on the whole armor of God, so we can fight effectively.

Ephesians 6 says: we need to have on the whole armor of God so we can stand in the evil day. Wonderful friends we are in the evil day (See Eph 6:10-18).

Paul said, having done all to stand, stand therefore in the armor of God.

This is no time to be walking around in your bvd's or you're under roo's. This is the time to be in full dress in the armor of God.

Yes I want a blessed Church. Yes I want a prosperous Church. Yes I want a happy Church.

But you know what I really want? Do you know what I want most of all? Precious friend I want a church that's armed and dangerous. I want to know that you as an individual are armed and dangerous. That you are equipped, that you are ready for battle.

Before David took off Goliath's head, he won the war of words. Dear reader, you are going to have to learn how to fight. We are going to have to learn how to use our mouths. We've got to open our mouths and speak the Word of God. We've got to let the devil know that we are not asleep. We've got to let the devil know that we're building our lives on the Word of God. We've got to let the devil know that we're living by the Word of God.

Please don't make this a negative word today. It may sound negative, but it is only because I have to acknowledge the spiritual environment that we're in today. And we have to call it like it is. But this word is a positive word. This word is to get a people ready, armed and dangerous, and locked and loaded.

You know the soldier may feel that boot camp is a negative experience, until that same soldier is thrust onto the battlefield and stands face to face with the enemy. Then all of a sudden what felt like a negative experience becomes the most positive thing in their life. In these last several days I've been very disturbed. The things that are coming out of Hollywood are totally demonic. What we see happening in our preschools to our babies is demonic. What is happening in our culture is demonic. I saw a girl yesterday with a shirt on it that had one word on it in huge letters and it was the foulest word that could be used in public. A few days ago the governor of New York passed the law that they could kill a baby at full term, they call it abort, but God calls it murder.

I have cried. I have been angry. I have felt helpless. I have felt the spirit of hopelessness trying to get a hold on me. And then I have felt the hand of indifference trying to wrap itself around me and tell me just let them all go to hell if they want to. The spirit of indifference says, you can't do anything about it anyway so why try.

Precious friend the devil is a liar. I know I have spoken things in this chapter that are not pretty, but that's the world we live in. And I'm trying to get you ready for the fight.

We are in the world but we are not of the world.

We are still the light of the world and the salt of the earth.

We are still the Sons and Daughters of God.

We are still here to bring the kingdom of God to the Earth.

We are still the devil's worst nightmare.

We can make a difference.

We do make a difference. Everywhere we go we change the atmosphere.

You may walk into an atmosphere filled with hell, but you bring Heaven into that atmosphere. Don't ever forget, greater is he that is in you than he that is in the world.

Don't ever forget, whatsoever is born of God overcometh the world, and this is the victory that overcometh the world even our faith.

I haven't said these things to discourage you and depress you. I have said these things to shake you yes, to keep you alert, to bring to your attention how important it is that we are fully armed and dangerous. That we put on the whole armor of God, and that we be filled with the Spirit every day. And that we are full of the Word of God, and that we are walking in the Spirit and not according to the flesh.

Yes we are at war. Yes the battle is real, but we are on the winning side. Our Captain has never lost a battle.

43
Worship – Warriors

"Thou therefore endure hardness, as a good soldier of Jesus Christ" (2Timothy 2:3.)

"No man that warreth entangleth himself with the affairs of this life; that he may please him who hath chosen him to be a soldier" (2Timothy 2:4.)

There are several different aspects of God's dealings with the church; the most familiar is that of the family of God.

We are all related by the blood of Jesus and held together by our love for God our Father and for each other, then God calls the church his building, his temple, his husbandry, which means, farmland.

Then there's the relationship of the shepherd with his sheep. Jesus is the chief shepherd and we are his sheep.

Then He called the church His workmanship created in Christ Jesus: which means we are the works of his hands like a Potter's vessel is the work of The Potter's hands and

Just like the artist takes pleasure in what he creates, we were created for his pleasure. We are his Masterpiece (See Ephesians 2:10.)

All of these are different aspects of our relationship with our heavenly father and in every different facet we will experience God's work in and through our lives in different ways.

So when I speak to you I can address you as God's flock, his sheep. Or I can address you as his building, his temple, and his dwelling place. Or as his handiwork, his masterpiece. Or I might address you as his husbandry, his farmland where he sows His good seed and produces good fruit. Or I might even call you his vineyard [as Jesus said I am the vine and you are the branches].

And all of these are wonderful aspects and facets of our relationship with the Lord, but there's one aspect of our relationship that I have to deal with today, and that is [the army of God].

The Bible calls God a man of war: *Exodus 15:3 The LORD is a man of war: the LORD is his name.*

The Bible calls Jesus the captain of our salvation. (Hebrews 2:10) …to make the captain of their salvation perfect through sufferings.

The Bible shows Gods dealings with the children of Israel who had been in slavery for 400 years: They didn't know anything about fighting and warfare because they were slaves and farmers and they farmed Pharaohs land, and they took care of his animals, and built his buildings, but they didn't even know how to hold a sword; yet they became the greatest army in the world.

Israel never was and never has been the biggest or strongest nation, but God is in her midst and God has fought with Israel and God has fought for Israel.

Let me tell you something, (whatever happens in this world let us, and let the church ever stand with Israel).

In the Bible Israel was God's army; today the church is God's army.

While we enjoy and relish all the other aspects of our relationship with God, we need to know that we are in an hour when the Church must once again become the Army of God.

As in Ezekiel 37 Where a valley of dry bones became a mighty army. The Church must rise up as a mighty army filled with the spirit and the power of God. We must understand that we may be sheep but these sheep are also soldiers. Remember the captain of this army "the Lamb of God" is also "the Lion of the tribe of Judah."

There is a time where we as sheep quietly, obediently, and faithfully follow the shepherd. But when war comes the sheep must transform into soldiers. My responsibility here in this book is not just to teach you how to be good sheep; but also how to be good soldiers. Not just a loving family, but also a bold, fully equipped, and well-trained army that is a threat to hell.

Its not just about tending sheep it's about training soldiers, raising up an army.

David is a perfect example of a sheep soldier, and a worship warrior.

He was a young shepherd, he tended sheep he smelled like sheep, he thought like sheep, he was tender and caring and loving, he was a worshipper.

But this young shepherd worshipper was also a warrior. One day he's holding a wounded little lamb in his arms, the next day he's holding a giants head in his hand that he cut off with the giant's own sword.

Why is this so important? Because we are at war in this nation, I'm not speaking on a natural level of civil unrest and hostility although it definitely exists.

I'm speaking about a spiritual war that is manifesting in the natural. The devil is stirred up, demons are stepping up their activity, they're driving people to say and do things that are total Insanity that 10-15 years ago could not and would not have happened in this country at all.

Whether you agree with America's choice for president or not, it's wrong to speak of assassinating him, to call him Hitler and to plan and plot and scheme his demise.

We are at war and the sheep must learn how to fight.

I cannot stand to the sidelines and let the sheep be slaughtered because they don't know how to fight.

People look at sheep and think them weak and timid and defenseless and powerless. But that's our relationship to the shepherd, and toward our brothers and sisters, but there's another side to the sheep also.

Wonderful friend, there's more to you than what people see.

In the show The Incredible Hulk, Bill Bixby a normal everyday man gets an overdose of gamma rays, and when he gets angry a metamorphous happens, a change, a transformation. He tells a reporter Mr. McGee, don't make me angry, you wouldn't like me when I'm angry. Because when he gets angry he transforms into this big green skinned monster with incredible power and strength, and he is fearless and unstoppable.

Somebody needs to tell the devil today: you better back off you won't like me when I get angry.

I'm talking about holy anger. I'm talking about righteous indignation.

I'm talking about the kind of anger that rises up in you when you see or hear of children being molested, abused, and raped. And the kind of anger that rises up in you when you see a disease stealing the life of a loved one, or when you see drugs and alcohol abuse destroying families. And when you see little children forced to learn things that will twist and pervert their minds and condition them to accept anything as normal.

Let me tell you something dear reader: It's not wrong to get angry; anger is a powerful force when it is channeled in the right direction.

It was an angry mother who lost her child to a drunk driver that founded (madd) mothers against drunk drivers. There is no telling how many thousands of lives have been saved because a mother got angry and focused it in the right direction.

Yes I'm a sheep, but I'm also a soldier. Yes I'm a worshipper but I am also a warrior.

David very well understood this sheep and soldier, warrior and worshipper, mentality.

In Psalms 23 He said: The Lord is my shepherd.

He also recognized he was a soldier

In Psalms 144:1 He said: blessed be the Lord my strength which teacheth my hands to war and my fingers to fight.

In the book of Jeremiah God is talking about his sheep soldiers: listen to how God refers to us.

Jeremiah 51:20-21 Thou art my battle axe and weapons of war, for with thee will I break in pieces the nation's and with thee will I destroy kingdoms and with thee will I break in pieces the horse and his rider. And with thee will I break in pieces the chariot and his rider.

God says to the church, his sheep soldiers, his worship warriors… You are my battle-axe, you are my weapons of war, you are my army.

Never have I felt a greater urgency to equip the sheep to be soldiers.

Sheep are gentle kind loving obedient, that's the nature of sheep. That speaks of our relationship to the shepherd and the family of God.

But as relates to hell and the devil's works we must be as ruthless and bold as David who went from a shepherd with a staff and a sling, to cutting off the giants head with his own sword.

And in the hour that we're living in we can't afford to be ignorant of who we are.

Your ignorance will kill you.

My people are destroyed for lack of knowledge. "Hosea 4:6 ."

I'm speaking to the soldier in you today. I'm speaking to the warrior in you. I'm speaking to the soldier in you: to be bold be courageous, put on the whole armor of God, stand strong in the power and the authority of God's Word. Be filled with his Spirit everyday, and keep yourself connected.

Stay up with the army; don't lag behind. The enemy is looking for stragglers. Keep the word of God pouring through your spirit.

Acquaint yourself with your weapons. Learn how to use the Word of God. Learn how to exercise authority in the Name of Jesus.

Never forget the importance of the blood. Learn how to war in prayer and praise. Learn how to keep your-self charged up by praying in the Holy Ghost.

We are at War!

The devil knows that in this nation we are at a turning point and he knows that the church is the only power in this world that can keep him from taking over.

Make no mistake about it, the hostility the abuse and anger and the murderous spirit that is being aimed at the White House, is not really against the White House or President Trump, it's against the church.

I don't agree with everything that President Trump is doing or the ferocity with which he is dealing with some issues, but I know this hostility and this violence, this anger is spiritual, it's demonic.

It's the change of the balance of power in this country that has caused this spirit to rise up.

It can't be fought with human weapons. Nothing President Trump can do can bind these spirits of rebellion, anger, murder and abuse.

This is a job for the sheep soldiers.

This is where the sheep have to quit eating grass, and looking for a soft spot to lay down in green pastures, and start eating our spinach, the Word of God. And get an overdose of Holy Ghost radiation gamma rays and put on the armor of God. And transform and metamorphous into the Holy Ghost filled fire baptized Sons and Daughters of God wrapped in the whole armor of God, and take the sword of the spirit and start fighting.

The Bible says: *"though we walk In the flesh we do not war after the flesh for the weapons of our warfare are not carnal but they are mighty through God to the pulling down of strongholds and the casting down of imaginations and every high thing that exalteth itself against the knowledge of God and bringing into captivity every thought to the obedience of Christ."* (1 Corinthians 10:3-5.)

We are at War, and we have to know how to fight.

Yes the Lord is our shepherd yes he leads us and guides us, yes we are his sheep, and yes we are faithfully obediently yielding and following our shepherd.

But when it comes to Hell, when it comes to the plans the plots the schemes, and the assignments of hell, we must put on the whole armor of God, and the sheep must become soldiers.

The worshipper must become a warrior, and the sheep must become soldiers fully equipped and empowered to do battle in Jesus name.

I am going to tell you as nicely as I can but in no uncertain terms: It is a cop out to lean back in your easy chair and say God is in control, everything is going to be fine.

I can tell you right now… God has left it up to the church; He's not coming down here to straighten everything out.

He came down once: and he stripped the devil of his authority, and He gave the authority to the Church, and He sent the Holy Ghost to live inside of us and give us power over the devil, and if we the church, "The good sheep of the church" do not become good soldiers of the church, the devil will rob us blind, he will kill our children, and he will ransack our homes and he will destroy our nation.

Let me say one more time... thank God for every effort President Trump is making to try to make America great again: but It's not the power in the white house that can change the spiritual climate of this nation;

It's the power in the Church House.

It's the sheep soldiers, "The worship warriors" the ones who know how to pray. The ones who know how to knock on Heavens door until Heaven answers, the ones who not only know how to be led by the Shepherd, but they know how to take orders from the Captain.

We are at war and this battle must be fought and won with spiritual weapons.

Let the worshippers arise and let the warriors awaken.

It's time to "Wake Up The Warrior"

44

Something Good Is Going To Come Out Of This

We will find much inspiration for this chapter in Dan Ch 3

My wonderful friend, I don't know what kind of fire you're walking through today, but the good news is:

" Something good is going to come out of this"

I know that right now, some of you are going through the greatest fire of your life, and it's the kind that hurts, and the kind that makes you cry, and I know that what I'm going to say to you is going to sound crazy, but what you ought to be doing is praising God, that you made it (to) the fire.

You see, dear reader, there are other people that never made it (to) the fire; there are other people that died at the door.

Do you understand what I'm saying? According to the bible, The Kings Most mighty men in his army died at the door of the furnace.

That means: It's a miracle that you made it this far, by all rights you shouldn't be here. You shouldn't have lived through that car wreck.

The officers on the scene said it's a miracle, and no one should have come out of that alive.

Somebody else reading this book, you know you shouldn't have lived through that drug overdose; you had enough drugs in your system to kill an elephant.

You shouldn't have made it. Other people didn't make it, but here you are.

Let me speak directly to someone today: I'm talking to somebody right now who knows it's a miracle that you are not in prison, if you tell the truth you know that you're just as guilty as they are and more so than some people that are serving prison terms right now. But God was merciful to you.

There's somebody listening to me right now, you know it's a miracle that you are not in a mental institution somewhere.

Other people have gone through a lot less than what you went through and they lost their minds, they went off the deep end.

What are you trying to tell me Pastor?

I'm trying to tell you that you ought to be praising God that you made it (to) the fire; there are others that died at the door.

"They died where your miracle started"

These mighty men in the king's army could represent the three greatest athletes, or the three most popular, we could say; the three voted most likely to succeed.

They had everything going for them, if anybody should have made it, it should have been them. But they died at the door.

On the other hand:

Nobody expected you to make it: Maybe like me you weren't the most popular; you weren't the captain of the football team or the head cheerleader. But here you are alive, in your right mind, serving God filled with the Holy Ghost and power.

And you want to complain because you're going through the fire, when what you really ought to be doing is praising God that you made it (to) the fire.

Come on and say it: Thank God I made it (to) the fire.

Let me make it a little clearer: you could have died at the door; you could have died in that car wreck, you could have died of a drug overdose.

You could be serving life in prison; you could have lost your mind.

But God had his hand on you.

You didn't even know him and he was watching over you, I wasn't serving him, but he was keeping his hand on me. He sent his angels to deliver me.

Can I get a witness? I mean can anybody identify with me?

Friend: I don't know about you, but I wasn't the strongest one. I wasn't the smartest one. I wasn't the most popular one. I wasn't the one expected to make it. But I made it, and there's no other explanation but God.

That's why I say: Thank God I made it to the fire.

Of course we're going to get you out of the fire, but God just wanted to remind you, that He was with you before you ever got in the fire, and He is not going to leave you now.

As a matter of fact, if you are in the middle of the fiery furnace right now, it is proof positive that you are coming out.

Because the miracle started at the door, and if God wasn't going to bring you out, you would have died at the door.

Do you see what I'm saying? You wouldn't have made it to the fire.

In other words: It was a miracle I made it this far, and you made it this far. And God wouldn't have brought me to the middle if he weren't going to bring me out, and bring you out.

I know I'm talking to some people right now that are going through the fire and I know you're feeling the heat, and I won't assume for one second that the fire isn't real, or that it doesn't hurt.

I know some of you are going through the greatest fire of your life.

For some of you, it's a financial fire.

For some body else it's a fire of sickness, and a battle for your health.

Somebody else may be going through the fire of divorce, or marriage problems.

Still, somebody else is going through the fire of dealing with rebellious children.

But I am telling you on the authority of the Word of God: Something good is going to come out of this.

I know right now that sounds like insanity, because there is no visible, tangible physical evidence of anything good in this fire.

But I prophesy to you and declare to you on the authority of God's word, something good is going to come out of this. You are going to make it, and you are <u>not</u> going to burn up in the fire. You are coming out and I don't mean you're going to come crawling out on your hands and your knees, all beat up, broke, busted and disgusted, no clothes, no money, no peace no joy, with your eyebrows burnt off, smelling like smoke.

Friend: the devil is a liar. When you come out of this fire, your coming out blessed, you're coming out healed, and delivered. You're coming out with some money, you're coming out with some joy and some peace and a greater anointing than you've ever had in your life.

Glory to God! Something good is going to come out of this.

Let me draw your attention to this phrase in the story:
" THE KING CHOSE HIS MOST MIGHTY MEN"

In other words: He chose the best, his strongest, his meanest, his best-trained soldiers in his army, to bind the three Hebrew boys.

Some of you may have wondered why it feels like you're fighting on a different level, it feels like the enemy is stronger than before, and even smarter than before.

Well, friend: That ought to tell you something: The devil wouldn't be bringing out his best, his meanest, his strongest, his best trained, if you weren't a threat to him.

The fact that he is bringing out the big dawgs, tells me that you must be a threat to him, and that you are getting close to your destiny, and close to walking in your purpose.

You're getting ready to step into a greater anointing than you've ever had in your life, and the devil is trying to intimidate you, and back you down.

"THEY BOUND THEM"

This is the first thing the devil wants to do is to bind you, meaning to restrict you, limit you, confine and contain you. To take away your liberty and your freedom in God.

One of the devils greatest grief's is to see the children of God walking and living in their liberty, expressing themselves in joy and peace, and worshiping and praising God without constraint, without fear or reservation.

So he sends things our way to push us down, to back us up, to quiet us down, to put a lid on us, to dampen our praise, to get us all tangled up in fear, and anxiety and worry.

Why? Because he knows the power of our praise.
The devil knows that there is no prison pit or furnace that can hold a praiser.

I will bless the Lord at all times his praise shall continually be in my mouth, my soul shall make her boast in the Lord, the humble shall hear thereof, and be glad, O magnify the Lord with me and let us exalt His name together. Ps 34:3

Then the Bible says:
HE CAST THEM INTO THE FIERY FURNACE. 7 Times hotter!
Not just a fiery furnace: (which speaks of adversity, trials, hardship, pain, sorrow,) but 7 times greater, or hotter, or more intense, more painful.

Does that describe you right now? Do you feel like you are fighting something you've never fought before, the attack is more severe the enemy is more aggressive, the pain is deeper the night is darker, the weight is heavier and the hurt lasts longer.

I wish I could tell you I had an easy button that you could push and it would make all the bad stuff go away, but I don't.

But there is something I know for sure, and I know from personal experience and I know it on the authority of the Word of God, And so I remind you again: Something good is going to come out of this.

And then we read these words:
THEY FELL DOWN BOUND in the midst of the fiery furnace.
I know we're faith people, at least I know I am, and we don't want to be negative, but how many would just be honest enough to tell the truth and say that you have been down a time or two?
I mean, since you started this Christian walk, you have fallen down once or twice.
The fact is, sometimes the devil will hit you with something you never expected and it knocks the wind out of you and you find yourself lying on the ground saying what happened.
Well, here in this story the Hebrew boys found themselves lying on the ground bound in the midst of the fire.
But I'm so glad the story doesn't end there, because it says that wicked king looked into the furnace, and he was astonished which means: he was amazed. He expected to see 3 Hebrew boys lying on the ground turning into crispy critters, but instead he saw 4 Men UP LOOSE WALKING AROUND and the fourth looked like the Son of God
And he was AMAZED!!!
Come on and just declare it for yourself. (I'm amazing).
I'm amazing the devil that thought he had me.
I'm amazing the devil that thought because he hurt me and made me cry it was over.
I'm amazing my enemies, the ones who saw me go into the fire, and took pleasure in it.
The ones who said I'd never make it.
The ones who said I'd burn up in the fire.

The ones who said drugs would kill me.

The ones who said I'd probably die an alcoholic like my dad or my brother.

The ones who said he'll lose his mind, she'll lose her mind.

But I'm still here, but you're still here, and you know something? I'm amazing myself.

Does anybody know what I'm talking about?

Yeah, I went through hell, but I'm still here. Yeah the devil hit me hard, and I went down and it hurt and I cried for a while, but I'm still here.

Yes, I went through a divorce, and my heart was broken. But I'm still here.

Yes, it's true, I fell down: I got in trouble, I made some bad decisions, and I served some time for it.

But I have a news flash for the devil.

I'm up again, and I'm on my feet again, and I'm Loose, hallelujah, I said: I'm loose.

The devil tried to bind me, and he had me all tangled up for awhile, but I'm loose now.

I got my joy back, I got my peace back, I got my dance back, and I got my praise back.

And if the devil thought I was a problem before, he ain't seen trouble yet.

Cause while I've been in this fire, I've been working on my praise. I've been working on my shout. I've been working on my dance.

As a matter of fact, I need to say something. I need to say, thank you mister devil cause in the fire is where I really learned how to dance. That's where I really learned how to shout. That's where I really learned how to put my praise on.

And I'm getting ready to praise like I've never praised before, and shout and dance like I've never danced before.

Because now I know, not only can the God I serve keep me from evil, keep me from the snares and from the traps that the devil sets for me.

But the God I serve can walk right into the middle of my fiery trial, right into the middle of the hell I'm going through, and he can lift me up and he can liberate me in the middle of my pain, in the middle of my grief in the middle of the darkest hour of my life.

Can I get a witness? No God can deliver after this sort. I'm talking about the God that can shut the Lions mouth and they can't even take a bite. I'm talking about the God that can breathe through his nose and create a super highway through the red sea and 3 million people can walk across on dry ground.
No other God can deliver after this sort.
And friend let me give you some good news. This same God who walked with the three Hebrew boys through their fiery furnace, is getting ready to show up in the middle of your fire.
And this God is getting ready to show the devil whose boss.
Let me give you some more good news.
The same fire that was intended to burn up the 3 Hebrew boys actually burned up the ones who threw them in.

Did you get that? God said to tell you, don't worry about those enemies anymore, don't worry about those nay Sayers, haters and agitators.
God said he's going to take care of them for you, you aren't going to have to say a word, and you're not going to have to lift a hand.
Stand still and see the salvation of the Lord.
Vengeance is mine, saith the Lord, and I will repay.
That may not mean anything to some of you, but for those who know you have some enemies, it means a lot.
Praise God it's getting good now:

THE FIRE LIBERATED THEM

Yes, brother and sister, that's right: The fire burned off the things that had them bound.

315

I can't speak for everyone, but I found out when I got in the fire, there were some things in my life that I didn't need. There were some things that were holding me back and it took the fire to set me free.
The truth is: There was some stuff I didn't want to let go of, and it took the fire to get it out of me.
The bottom line is: I got free in the fire.

The fire burned a lot of stuff off me, but it also burned some stuff out of me. The fire set me free from pride, and self-righteousness and the fire set me free from religion and the fear of man.
I won't presume to suggest that you had the same issues that I had, but there was some stuff, that didn't belong in my life and it took the fire to deliver me.

Is there anybody glad you're free?

Now I want to say something to those who are going through the fire right now, and you know the devil has turned the thermostat up and he has intensified his attacks against your life, (You're the one who ought to be shouting and dancing and praising God right now.)
I know you're thinking: there he goes with that goofy thinking again, but if you'll hang with me, I think you'll see what I mean.
You see: what the devil has done by increasing and intensifying the fire against your life… is accelerate your process, and your preparation.
Hallelujah: right there is a good place to shout. Somebody knows that the devil has turned the heat up in his attacks against your marriage, your health, your finances, and your ministry. Your faith has been stressed to the limit.
But I came to tell you: what the devil meant for evil God is going to make it work for your good.

See (Gen 50:20) How God turned Josephs darkness to light, his sorrow into joy.

And God is going to turn it around, and God is going to take the very thing that the devil sent to destroy you and (incinerate you and burn you up, and he is going to use it to accelerate you and to speed you up.

Go ahead devil and turn the heat up, heat it up seven times, and I'll come out with a 7th degree blessing.
Do you see it? Heat that furnace seven times hotter, and I'll come through seven times faster. 7 times more joy. 7 times more peace. 7 times more money. 7 times more anointing.
Glory to God: Dear reader just open your mouth and prophesy… I'm being accelerated!

Praise God: I'm getting ready to go into warp drive.
Somebody's being accelerated right now: while you're reading this book, something is happening, the Holy Spirit is moving, the Anointing is falling on you.
Let me tell somebody today who has been going through the fire: It's not punishment it's preparation.
I'm talking to somebody, who feels like you've been in low gear, like you've been in granny gear, like you've been walking in quicksand, like nothing seems to work out, you go one step forward and two steps back.
But I prophesy to you, God is getting ready to accelerate you.
Come on and lift your hands and tell God: Accelerate me.
You're going into high gear.
Something good is going to come out of this.

Precious friend: God never said we wouldn't ever have to go through anything. In fact, it's just the opposite.
Isa 43:2 When thou passest through the waters I will be with thee, and the rivers, they shall not overflow thee, when thou walkest

317

through the fire, thou shalt not be burned, neither shall the flame kindle upon thee.

Kindling is what you use to get a fire, started, to catch, to take hold.

God never said you wouldn't have to go through the fire, but he said it couldn't catch you; it can't take hold on you.

I felt the flames reaching for me, but they couldn't take hold on me

Poverty couldn't take hold on me, sickness, couldn't take hold on me; depression couldn't take hold on me.

Fear and anxiety couldn't take hold on me, it reached for me, suicide reached for me, alcoholism, and drug addiction reached for me but God wouldn't let it kindle on me.

See, the truth is; we are all going to walk through some fire, and we are all going to cross some deep waters, but you're going to make it.

Ok, let's look at the most amazing part of this story: I'm sure you're thinking "Yeah, now we get to see the three Hebrew boys come out of the fire."

Surprise: Nope, that's not the most amazing part of this story.

I can't wait so I'm just going to jump ahead and say it: The most amazing part of this story is that the three Hebrew boys actually didn't want to come out of the fire.

I know I know you're thinking: Now I know he's crazy.

Well, I can't blame you for thinking that, to tell the truth, I wouldn't believe it myself if I hadn't read it for myself.

So let's get it straight from the book, The Holy Bible.

Dan 3:26 Then Nebuchadnezzar came near to the mouth of the burning fiery furnace, and spake, and said, Shadrach, Meshach, and Abednego, ye servants of the most high God, come forth, and come hither. (Then) notice, then. Not before, not until he called them out.

He said: come forth, and come hither and the bible says: *Then Shadrach, Meschach, and Abed-nego came forth of the midst of the fire.*

So this wicked, heathen king looked into the fiery furnace and called the 3 Hebrew boys out and publicly declared them to be the winners.

The king had to call them out of the fire.

When did they come out? After they were up loose, walking around.

So maybe you're asking God, when am I coming out of this fire?

I know this almost sounds impossible: But here's the revelation: (when it doesn't matter anymore) when it doesn't matter whether you come out or not. In other words: when you've learned how to dance in the fire, praise him when you don't feel like praising him, lift him up when you don't feel like lifting him up. Give when you don't feel like giving.

And when they came out of the fire immediately they were ELEVATED in the kingdom.

They were elevated by the Fire.

I'm trying to tell somebody: Something good is going to come out of this.

You're being: LIBERATED, ACCELERATED, and ELEVATED, by the fire, by the very thing the devil sent to burn you up, it's speeding you up, and lifting you up.

Finally: somebody is thinking, I've never experienced this kind of fire before.

(There's a reason for that)

It's because God is getting you ready to go where you've never gone before, and do what you've never done before.

And I close this chapter with this revelation:

[THE SHORT CUT IS THROUGH THE FIRE].

I know it's not something you would have asked for, but my friend: The Gold is not afraid of the fire.

319

The fire is not your enemy.
The hotter the fire, the purer the gold.

    I can't tell you that God is going to put the fire out, but I can tell you this:

Something good is going to come out of this.

45
When God Says Seven
Six Won't Do

Seven is a principle that releases God to work supernaturally in our favor. Learn how to put it to work in your life.

Naaman was:
- A great man.
- God had wrought deliverance by him.
- Naaman had a problem.

It would be appropriate to say right here, that great men are not perfect men. Regardless of how strong someone may appear to be they are only human, and as humans they have problems too.

This is good news because it tells us that God uses imperfect people.

In other words: You and I do not have to be perfect, without fault or weakness or shortcomings for God to use us.

In fact, it was the apostle Paul that said: His strength is made perfect in our weaknesses.

That ought to encourage somebody right now who has been sitting on the sidelines because you're still wrestling with an issue in your flesh, or you are still fighting certain fleshy desires, or you are struggling with a habit.

You did not have to answer a questionnaire or pass a physical or spiritual exam to be saved. You just had to call upon the name of the Lord.

Naaman was a great man not only because he was a great warrior, but also because he was willing to admit he had a problem.

It takes a certain amount of greatness in a man or a woman, to admit they have a problem (most people are quick to point out everybody else's problem) while conveniently overlooking their own.

There was something else that was great about Naaman, he had learned the art of listening, and he heard from a little slave girl that there was a prophet in Israel who could help her master.

We have to stop here and talk about this little maid: What a wonderful Christian spirit she showed.

While most slave girls would have been happy to hear of their captor's illness, she desired his well-being.

She exemplifies Jesus teachings.

Matt 5:44 But I say unto you, Love your enemies, bless them that curse you, do good to them that hate you, and pray for them which despitefully use you, and persecute you.

If she would have been like most people she would have enjoyed watching her enemy suffer, and called it pay back.

She directed Naaman to the Prophet: She knew where the power was.

One of the most important things in your life is to know where the power is.

Padded pews and stained glass windows do not add up to power.

A five-pound cross around your neck and a family bible under your arm does not add up to power.

There can be great talent, great skill, great recognition among men, but that still does not add up to power.

Too many people are looking for prestige, when they should be looking for power.

Paul the Apostle Said: *But I will come to you shortly, if the Lord will, and will know, not the speech of them, which are puffed up, but the power. For the kingdom of God is not in word, but in power… (1 Cor 4:19-20.)*

Naaman appeals to the King.

Naaman assumes that position is power; if there is any power he assumes it must be with the King.

The king interprets Naaman's request as an effort to start a fight.
Why? Because he is powerless to help him, so rather than to admit his own impotency, he accuses Naaman of being a troublemaker.
Just because a person has a position before men, does not mean they have a relationship with God.
Religion can never substitute for the reality of relationship.
When religion can't produce, it always shifts the blame.
Religious people will never say: It's my fault, I'm not where I need to be with God, I'm sorry I haven't been praying and fasting like I should, I'm sorry it's not God, and it's not you, it's me.
No, when religion can't produce it will always shift the blame.
-It's your lack of faith.
-It's your environment.
-It's just one of those things, Only God knows.
-It's probably just not his will.
The prophet of God sends a message to redirect Naaman (Send him to me) Sometimes God has to redirect our faith. Yes Naaman had faith, enough to get him moving, but it was misguided, he assumed that power was with the position, he assumed that he who had power with men, also had power with God.
Naaman arrives at the prophet's home.
The prophet does not meet him personally, but sends out a messenger.
This is the first blow to Naamans pride.
The messenger tells Naaman to go and dip 7 times in the Jordan River and he will be healed.
Naamans pride takes another hit (he becomes very angry).
Why is he so angry?
1. Because he had preconceived ideas of how he would receive his blessing.
Oh, I think we could preach there for awhile, (how many of us have our preconceived ideas of how we want God to bless us, (we want to tell God when, how, where, how much, and who to use) to get our blessings to us.

*He thought the prophet would come out wave his hand over the place, and the job would be done and he would go home with his blessing.

We're just like Naaman a lot of times, we are willing to throw out to God what we want him to do, we are willing to show him the places we want him to see, (we are quick to let God see those surface issues) the stuff that really doesn't matter anyway.

Or I could say the stuff that is just flesh.

What I'm saying is, God wants to do more than just fix your flesh issue, (your money problem, your habit problem, your relationship problem).

God wants to heal your heart.

It is the diseases of the heart that is the source of most sickness.

They are heart diseases…

-Unforgiveness

-Anger

-Bitterness

-Jealousy

-Envy, Strife

-Rebellion

-Pride

Pride was killing Naaman.

Yes, he had leprosy in his body, but pride was killing his soul.

Before Naaman could be healed of the disease in his flesh, he had to be delivered from the disease in his soul.

What good is a lot of money, or a new car, or a new house, or a healthy body if your heart is full of disease?

The bible says: Guard your heart with all diligence, for out of it are the issues of life.

Then there is another blow to Naamans pride.

Why do I have to go dip in this dirty mud puddle, when we have got big beautiful clean rivers where I come from?

Then there is one final blow to Naamans pride.

Seven times (Seven = completion, total obedience).

Anything less would <u>not</u> be partial obedience it would be disobedience.

Anything less than seven would be disobedience and would disqualify him for the blessing.

Some of you are wondering right now why you haven't got the blessing you desired, you have done something right, but you haven't done it all right.

It won't work (when God says seven, six won't do).

Many times we're like Naaman; we're willing to obey God as far as it makes sense to us.

We're willing to obey God as long as it doesn't make us look weird, or goofy.

We're willing to obey God as long as it's convenient, as long as it's comfortable.

If you're going to receive the blessing God has for you it will cost you something, it's more than money that God requires from you, (its obedience).

It will cost you your pride.

It will cost you your plans, and preconceived ideas.

It will cost you your feelings and emotions.

Every dip in muddy Jordan was stripping pride from Naaman's heart.

One thing I admire about Naaman was: He was a finisher, he understood commitment, and he understood perseverance. Once he made up his mind to do it, he was totally committed.

That's what we need in the church, men and women who are not just here to get blessed, but they are committed to the work, they're here to see it through, they're faithful, you can count on them to finish what they start.

No matter what the cost, no matter how long it takes, no matter what people might say about them, (they're in it to win it).

Perseverance wins the prize:

- God never said everything would always be easy.
- God never said there wouldn't be any rain.
- God never said you wouldn't have to fight hell sometimes.

- God never said you would understand it all.
- God never said you wouldn't be criticized and persecuted.
- God never said there wouldn't be delays.

But perseverance always wins.

When God says seven, six won't do.

Seven is the number of completion; it's the number of maturity, of harvest.

 (Seven is where mans obedience and Gods Power Intersect).

If Naaman were to have stopped at 3, 4, 5, or even 6 (Nothing would have happened, there would have been no manifestation of the power of God, no healing, no miracle).

Whatsoever he saith unto you, do it.

Not think about it, pray about it, talk about it, or sing about it.

Do it, and when you do, your natural human finite ability will intersect with the supernatural infinite power of a miracle working God, and you will see the glory of God.

Take away the stone: This is the human ability of obedience.

   "Lazarus, Come forth = The Supernatural ability of God"

There is a word from God for every situation in your life. Through your obedience your faith will intersect with the power of God and you will see the manifestation of Gods power in your life.

Examples:

1. The widow woman "I'm gathering sticks to make a small cake for my son and myself and we're going to eat it and die".

The prophet says, make me one first, and your meal barrel will not be empty and your cruise of oil will not run dry.

She obeyed the word of the Lord, from the prophet and was sustained, through the famine.

2. The widow woman of 1 Kings 4, (Her husband died and left her in debt.) The prophet said borrow empty vessels not a few, take your little pot of oil and pour into them, setting aside that which is full.

She obeyed the word of the Lord through the prophet and went into supernatural multiplication and provision.

3. The wedding of Canaan of Galilee (they ran out of wine). The prophet = Jesus, says: Fill the water pots with water.

It didn't make any sense to them, it was a difficult job, but they obeyed and their obedience intersected with the power of God and water became wine.

I don't know the miracle you stand in need of today, but I know all you need is a word from God. One word from God can turn that situation completely around.

The Prophet Ezekiel looked at a valley of dry bones, a hopeless situation, (but God gave him a word.) Prophesy,

That was the word of the Lord to Ezekiel. (Prophesy upon these bones).

He could have cried, he could have prayed, he could fasted, he could have sung songs and danced all over the place and nothing would have changed).

But when he obeyed that word and began to prophesy; even though it looked impossible, even though it felt ridiculous, even though his natural senses were arguing with him. When he began to prophesy, there was a manifestation of the power of God and bones began to come together, bone to his bone, sinew, and muscles and skin began to come upon those bones and finally the breath of God filled them and they stood upon their feet a great army.

Because one man dared to obey God.

My precious friend: I dare you to obey God.

I dare you to jump out of the boat, and go to Jesus on nothing but a word.

I dare you to fill the water pots with water, when they're wanting wine.

I dare you to prophesy to a hopeless situation.

I dare you take your little pot of oil and start pouring and expect it to multiply until you're out of debt and in the oil business.

I dare you to march around the walls of Jericho for Seven days.

Once each day for 6 days, then on the Seventh day seven times.

You say: Pastor Terry, (That doesn't even make any sense, I can't walk around Jericho that city doesn't even exist any more).

It's not the physical Jericho we're talking about (it's the principle of total obedience that never changes). 1 time around every day for 6 days, then on the Seventh day 7 times around (Then shout).

You see, it would not have mattered if they had faithfully and obediently got up every morning and made that journey and took that trip around the walls, once, twice, or five times; nothing would have happened.

And it wouldn't even have mattered if they had faithfully obediently made that trip for six days, and even on the seventh day made six trips.

God said seven and six won't do.

It was when they made that final lap in total obedience to God, that Joshua said shout (for the Lord hath given us the city).

When they shouted, the walls fell down flat.

I'm talking to somebody today your on your final lap around. I don't know who I'm talking to but you're one act of obedience away from a release of Gods supernatural miracle working Power. Even after their seventh lap, it wasn't until they shouted that the walls fell.

For somebody today, it's one more shout!

One more Hallelujah!

One more Praise the Lord! One more thank you Jesus. One more crazy praise.

I don't know who I'm talking to, (but somebody needs to know, your miracle is in your dance.) Your deliverance, your release is in your dance.

The devil has tried to steal your dance because he knows there's deliverance in your dance, there's liberty in your dance, there's power in your dance.

You can sit there if you want to and let the devil rob you of your blessing or you can get on your feet and obey God.

Somebody needs to shout, somebody needs to run, somebody needs to break out into a dance, and somebody needs to start speaking in tongues and glorifying God.

My friend (Why would you come all this way, then stop short of your miracle?) Naaman why would you come all this way, then turn around and go home because it didn't happen the way you expected it?

Why would you walk around these walls once a day for six days, and seven times on the seventh day, and not shout.

That shout was a shout of faith.

That shout said: I believe God.

That shout said I've done all I can do, I've prayed, I've fasted, I've confessed, I've sown.

And now it's time to shout.

What is it today that you would allow to cheat you out of the blessings of God?

Is it your pride?

Is it your fear?

Is it what people might think or say about you?

Is it your feelings or your emotions?

Is it just plain old laziness?

Is it Luke warmness and indifference?

Dear reader, I have to tell you, there are no short cuts to the power of God.

When God says seven (six won't do).

46
The Anointing Has Found You

The Anointing found Elisha and changed his life, that same anointing is on the move again, it's in your neighborhood and coming down your street.

I King 19:19 so he departed thence, and (found Elisha) the son of Shaphat, who was plowing with twelve yoke of oxen before him, and he with the twelfth: and Elijah passed by him, and cast his mantle upon him.
Notice these two words, (found Elisha).

I'm going to pause right here, and I'm going to prophesy that somebody's life is going to change today. Somebody is going to another level in God.
Somebody is going to finish this book with the fire of God burning hot in your life.

Elijah (found) Elisha, which means he was looking for him.

You need to know that God is always watching and God is always evaluating and God is always on the lookout for someone he can elevate.

Elisha had God's attention: Here he was <u>not</u> working in a corporate office, <u>not</u> living in a palace, <u>not</u> driving a Rolls Royce or a Mercedes.
No, he was out in a field plowing, covered with dirt, but he had God's attention.
Dear Friend; God notices everything.
Sometimes you may feel as though you are so far down the line that no one even notices what you do.

But God notices. He notices your sacrifice. He notices your faithfulness and your commitment. He notices your willingness to do the jobs no one else wants to do.

Elisha had God's attention.

Growing up I remember from time to time my Dad would say (I think you need some attention.) He was usually referring to the board of education being applied to the seat of understanding.

I did not like that kind of attention.

But I want God's attention, I want Gods good attention.

How did Elisha get Gods good attention?

#1 He was busy, (he wasn't sitting around with his hands folded, waiting for a perfect ministry opportunity).

He was busy where he was at, working with what he had.

#2 He was dependable, responsible. (That means his father knew the job would get done).

Elisha's father knew that he could trust Elisha alone in a field with twelve yoke of oxen. He didn't have to stand over him watching him all the time. He knew whatever was placed in Elisha's hand would be completed.

#3 He was self-disciplined.

The number twelve represents discipleship, (meaning a disciplined life.) A life that is in order. (Order is the proper arrangement of things).

It is a tragedy that so many in the body of Christ view discipleship and the disciplined life as some kind of punishment and deprivation of all the fun things in life.

#4 He was willing to work with no immediate reward.

As a farmer, he understood, there is a lot of work to do before you enjoy the fruit or the reward of your labor.

#5 Elisha was a hard worker: (he gave himself 100 % to his work.) Some people work harder trying to get out of working than if they would just buckle down and do the job.

Elisha didn't have to be sweet talked to work. He didn't have to be patted on the back to work.

Everybody needs to be appreciated, and everyone wants to be recognized and praised, but a mature believer understands that we are working for the Lord and the Lord will reward us for our labor.

These were the qualities in Elisha's life that attracted God's attention.

There are people in the church who are always talking about a double portion, but they have never yet qualified for the first portion.

I think I need to say something very important here:

The anointing is great, it is the yoke-destroying burden removing power of God and we will never accomplish the work of God without it.

But (the anointing is no substitute for hard work).

- The anointing is no substitute for training and education.
- The anointing is no substitute for Character.
- The anointing does not produce Character.

Jesus did not say: Ye shall know them by their gifts, or by their anointing. (He said ye shall know them by their fruits).

The fruit of the spirit are the qualities and attitudes of Jesus manifested through our humanity for the benefit of humanity.

Many of God's people mistakenly assume that the anointing is everything.

- The anointing does not replace practice.
- The anointing does not replace study.

And while we often say the anointing is more important than talent, we should also realize that talent is a gift from God, and when your talent is anointed by God, It glorifies God at the highest level.

In other words Excellence is talent and training yielded to the anointing.

- The anointing is the power of God for service.
- Character is the nature and attributes of Christ.

When you put the Power of God and the Nature of God together, you have a full manifestation of Jesus Christ.

He was a full representation and manifestation of the father in every way.

The Anointing without Godly Character or without the fruit of the Spirit is a confusing contradiction.

Example is the life of Samson; (There was no question he had a supernatural ability, strength by the anointing of God. But his life was out of balance, there was no character, no fruit of the spirit.

While Elisha was waiting for his anointing he was working on his character. Elisha was becoming the kind of man that God could trust with his anointing. He was becoming the kind of man God could use.

Say that for yourself right now: I'm working on my character.

Elisha was waiting for something; he was working while he was waiting.

- He didn't know what it was, or where it would come from, He didn't know what it would look like or feel like.
- He just knew he needed something he didn't have.
- He just knew he needed something more.
- He was plowing and he was waiting, He was praying and he was waiting.
- He was plowing and watching, He was praising and watching
- He was plowing and expecting.

His spirit was reaching out; something on the inside of him was stirring.

Something on the inside of him was telling him; (You're bigger than this.) Something was telling him, (There's more to life than this).

Something down on the inside of Elisha was telling him:

*Something's getting ready to change, it's in the atmosphere (I can't explain how I know it, I just know something's getting ready to change).

I believe I'm talking to somebody that knows something's getting ready to change, nothing in your circumstance is saying anything different (but your spirit is stirring, your spirit knows something your head don't know, something your eyes can't see, something your ears can't hear.

But God has revealed it unto you by his spirit.

Elisha said: Momma, Daddy, I love you, but I'm gonna have to leave you pretty soon.

Where you are going son? (I don't really know).

What are you going to do son? (I don't really know for sure).

I just feel something on the inside pushing me, telling me there's greatness in you, and I know there's something I'm supposed to do.

There's something I was born for, I'm here for a reason.

My life is supposed to count for something.

Somehow I just know (I'm supposed to make a difference in this world).

Come on and confess it for yourself, I'm a world changer   (My life counts).

So here's Elisha "Walking in the light he had" faithful to what had been put in his hand to do.

Then Elijah comes by: "Elijah represents the anointing."

Elijah walks out into the field where Elisha is plowing behind twelve yoke of Oxen.

"Covered with dirt"

And Elijah throws his mantle on him.

Let me ask you my friend: Is there anybody, just glad that God saw something in you that he could use?

Other people couldn't see it because you were all covered up with dirt.

You didn't look too spiritual with dirt all over your face and oxen dung all over your feet because you've been walking in a mess.

But God said: I can use him, I can use her, I can do something with him, or her, I'll put my anointing on them and they'll plow for me.

I'll make them a vessel of honor.

I'll make them a diadem in my hand and a crown of glory.

I'll use them to tear down Satan's kingdom and establish the Kingdom of God.

When Elijah's mantle touched Elisha; Destiny jumped in Elisha's spirit and said: This is it, this is what I've been waiting for, this is what I've been praying and asking God for.

This is what my heart has been crying out for "It's The Anointing".

The first Anointing immediately launched Elisha into serving, ministering to and being discipled and mentored by the man of God Elijah. (He positioned himself for the double portion anointing).

He left all, and Elijah became his spiritual father.

He placed himself as a son under Elijah's jurisdiction, because he discerned the anointing of God in Elijah's life.

He put himself in school. He became a disciple, a follower, a student.

A lot of people want the kind of anointing that is on Benny Hinns life to get people saved healed and delivered.

But few people want to do what he did to get it.

They want the anointing and the power of God in their lives, but very few want to position themselves in humility and submission to the man of God over their lives and say teach me, lead me, correct me when I'm wrong, rebuke me when I need it.

The first anointing that touched Elisha's life was the anointing of the student, the disciple, the servant (the son).

Everybody wants the double portion anointing, but the double portion doesn't come until you've walked and lived and served under the first anointing.

When Elijah's mantle touched Elisha the Bible says: Immediately he went after Elijah.

He left all to follow and minister to and be schooled and mentored by the man of God.

Elisha knew he was not going to get where Elijah was overnight, but he committed himself to the process.

Elijah Says: Go back again, what have I done unto you?

This is Elisha's first test:

Right here is where a lot of people fail, they've been touched by the anointing, but the price of following on, the price of discipleship and sacrifice and commitment is too high and they settle back down into their comfortable predictable routine way of life.

I'm going to pause here and tell you, that if God ever brings an Elijah, across your path and he or she is pleased to throw their mantle over you, you better run, not walk to catch up with him or her.

Because they may very well be the door to your next level of destiny, your next anointing, and there is no guarantee that, that door will ever open again.

The first step to a new level in God is Exposure "you have to see it".

When it's time for promotion God will bring someone across your path, into your life that can demonstrate, and manifest where you want to go.

(But you have to discern the Elijah Spirit in the man or woman of God, and connect with them).

While Elisha is plowing, praying, watching, waiting, just being faithful with what he had been given; (just a little ways away God is telling Elijah, I want you to anoint Elisha the son of Shaphat for he will be prophet in your room).

So while Elisha is plowing:

Just taking care of business, faithful in the little things, willing and obedient.

(The anointing is coming).

He can't see it, but it's coming.

He can't hear it, but it's coming.

He can't tell it by looking at his present circumstances, but its coming.

I came to tell somebody today:

It's coming…

- Just keep on plowing because it's coming.

- Keep on praying because it's coming.
- Keep on pressing because it's coming.

Don't grow weary in well doing, for in due season you shall reap if you faint not.

It's coming:

- Your anointing is coming.
- Your dream is coming.
- Your destiny is coming.
- Your victory is coming.

What you've been praying for, it's coming.

Keep on plowing, keep pressing, keep praying, don't quit, you may not see it Elisha but the anointing is coming your way.

You might not see it yet Elisha, but the anointing has just turned the corner.

You might not feel it yet Elisha, but the anointing is coming down your row.

I just thought I'd give you an advanced warning (if I get a little crazy here, if I start to run, or jump, if I break out in a dance or start speaking in tongues) it's just the anointing.

Don't even think about telling me it's not necessary to be so emotional. (I've been out plowing in this field too long, dreaming about this anointing. I've been waiting on this anointing too long. I've got up and pulled this plow when I was sick. I pulled this plow when I was cold. I pulled this plow when everybody else had left the field.

This is what I've been waiting for.

The anointing destroys the yoke.

Where the spirit of the Lord is, there is liberty.

Its here (the anointing is here).

The anointing has found you.

My friend this is your time, this is your kairos moment, this is your visitation, (The anointing has found you).

I don't know who it is, but somebody just now felt the anointing touch you. This is another level for you. If you'll reach out and

take hold of this anointing your life is never going to be the same.
(Because the Anointing has found you).
Everything you do for God should have the anointing on it.
Sing with the anointing. Play your instruments with the anointing.
Make phone calls with the anointing. Cook with the anointing.
Usher with the anointing. Clean the church with the anointing.
Everything that belongs to God should have the anointing on it.
The anointing makes the difference between_
-Pretty and powerful.
-Talent and Ministry.
-Activity and Productivity.
-Gold and Glory.
I just stopped by to tell somebody, the anointing has found you.
Your whole life is getting ready to change because the anointing
shifts you.
The anointing doesn't come just to sit. It comes to shift.
When Elijah passed by (Elisha's life was shifted forever).
Praise God my friend; I feel a shift coming on.
We're getting ready to shift into the anointing, but I have to warn
you, when you go into this shift, (this next level of anointing)
some people aren't going to make the shift.

Some people will even get mad at you, and call you extreme,
radical, fanatic.
Some people will try to stifle you, and settle you down.
Somebody needs to declare this over your life: I can't help it if
I'm high performance.
The anointing has found you.
Is there anybody ready to go to another level in the anointing?
Then why don't you make a prophetic declaration and just shift
like you're shifting into high gear, and tell the devil goodbye. And
say goodbye to low living, and low performance, and low power.
The anointing has found you.

47
If You're Willing To Stretch

There is nothing really out of reach for the child of God, but there are some things that you have to stretch for to get.

You can have it (if) you're willing to stretch.

God has put a word in my spirit for the body of Christ, and I must prophesy to any one with ears to hear: God is setting his people free. You say But Pastor; I'm a child of God.

Yes, you may be a child of God and yet be bound, bound by religion, bound by traditions and the philosophies of man, bound by the limitations of past experiences, bound by the fear of failure, bound by the fear of man, bound by insecurities, and personal doubts.

But I prophesy that by the end of this message, somebody is going free, you are coming out and you are coming up, and you are going to get what the devil said you couldn't have, and you are going to do what people said you could never do.

I wish somebody that believed that prophetic word would give God a shout of praise for what he is going to do.

You can have it (if) you're willing to stretch.

Read Mark 3:1

Our story begins by telling us that: Jesus entered again into the synagogue (we could talk about that one phrase all day). Jesus entered again into the synagogue.

The number one need of the church is the manifest presence of Jesus.

We've got talent, we've got central heat and air, we've got carpet on the floors and padded pews and we've got over head projectors and power point presentations, we've got theology.

But what we need is some old fashioned kneeology.

What we need is the firepower of the old saints who knew how to get a hold of the horns of the altar and persevere in prayer until

339

the very atmosphere was pregnant with the tangible presence of Jesus.

Somebody say it out loud: Come on in Lord Jesus.

I like the modern conveniences of our day as much as you do, but if it's a choice between modern conveniences and the manifest presence of Jesus there is no competition.

I would rather be in a barn with sawdust on the floor and hay bales for our pews, and have the presence of Jesus than the finest cathedral with every comfort and convenience money could buy.

When Jesus shows up miracles happen, when Jesus shows up the drug addicts, the alcoholics, the homosexuals, the demon possessed are instantly set free.

No wonder the old timers used to sing: Take this whole world but give me Jesus.

Now I want you to notice something: Not all religious people really want Jesus to show up at church.

They like to sing about him, talk about him, preach about him, but when Jesus really shows up, he messes up their routine because Jesus always comes with his own agenda.

*and there was a man there, which had a withered hand.

*And they watched him, whether he would heal him on the Sabbath day; (that they might accuse him.)

Many times it's religion itself that is the greatest hindrance to the manifest presence of Jesus.

I can't get past this part, cause it's such a blessing to know:

Everybody doesn't have to agree with you for you to get blessed, they don't even have to like you.

I know it comes as a shock to many of you, but everybody in the church don't want you blessed, there are some people that are happy to see you struggle and happy to see you have to pinch pennies, and worry about how you're going to pay your light bill.

There are some people that take pleasure in your pain; they take pleasure in your loneliness, and your hardships.

It makes them feel superior to be able to look down their self-righteous noses at you.

But I came to tell you: when God gets ready to bless you, he's not going to consult with the self-righteous long nosed hypocrites;
He's not going to ask their opinion,
He's just going to do it.
You see religious opposition couldn't stop Jesus from ministering the power of God to needy people. Everywhere Jesus went religious Pharisee's and hypocrites opposed him.
But he just chewed em` up and spit em` out, healed the sick, cleansed the lepers, raised the dead, and cast out devils.
The person on either side of you may be as dead as four o clock in the morning and as dry as last years corn shucks, but if you are hungry and thirsty for God, he will climb over the top of a thousand satisfied, petrified, fossilized, relics of religion, and he will come to you and he will meet you at the point of your need and he will touch you and your life will never be the same.
Is there anybody hungry for Jesus to touch you?
The fact that this mans hand was withered, tells me he either contracted some kind of disease or had some kind of accident
In other words: He wasn't born that way.
Let me just tell somebody right here: You weren't born that way...
You weren't born addicted to porn.
You weren't born prejudice.
You weren't born a liar or a thief.
You weren't born a pedophile.
You weren't born a homosexual or a lesbian; I don't care what they're saying today.
But the disease called sin, deformed your life and made it into something ugly and painful.
But the good news is: There is a cure for you today.
It's the power of the blood of Jesus.
What can wash away my sin, nothing but the blood of Jesus, what can make me whole again, nothing but the blood of Jesus?
I wish somebody would take about 60 seconds, and praise God for the power of the blood, the power that set you free, some of

you were drug addicts, some of you were addicted to pornography, some of you had one immoral relationship after another, and went from one partner to the next, but the blood of Jesus washed you, the blood of Jesus set you free.

I know you're all looking good today and smelling good, but there was a time, way back when, that you didn't look so good and you didn't smell so good.

Thank God for the power of the blood of Jesus.

I'm talking about the power of the blood of Jesus, to heal your heart, to heal your mind, to purge your conscience.

Somebody needs to know: You weren't born that way.

You weren't born depressed, angry, discouraged, fearful and lonely, full of doubts and dreads about the future.

You weren't born with a broken heart, aborted dreams and lost visions. You weren't born with a history of disappointments and failures.

But life happened, and life is not always kind and life is not always fair. And it withered up your hand of faith, it withered up your expectation of better days.

And now you have quit dreaming, you have quit reaching, you have quit expecting and you've just settled down into an existence.

One of the worst things that can ever happen to a person is to quit dreaming and settle down into just existing.

Jesus said: The thief cometh not, but for to steal, and to kill, and to destroy, but I am come that they might have life and have it (more abundantly.)

Jesus looked at this man, and he saw more than just a withered hand, he saw a withered life.

He saw all his anger and frustration, he saw all his disappointments and broken dreams, he saw every time he had tried and failed.

Then Jesus said to him: Stretch forth thy hand.

I know it's going to be hard, I know it's going to take some effort, I know you're going to have to push past bad experiences of the past; I know there is going to be some pain.

I know you're going to have to overcome some religious opposition, I know it's going to make some people mad.

But go ahead and stretch forth thy hand.

Child of God, if we are going to go anywhere in God, we are going to have to stretch, it may cause some discomfort, it may upset some people, some people may turn their backs on you, some people may lie to you, (but to walk with Jesus you have to be willing to get out of the boat.)

Part of the stretching is separation from the crowd: Every body can't go where God is taking you, everybody don't want to go where God is taking you.

(The bible teaches us to follow the cloud, not the crowd).

The glory of God is in the cloud not the crowd.

That withered hand represents all the can't do's of religion and all the opposition to your dreams and visions and desires, and all the negative elements in your life that contradict the promises of God.

You don't have enough money, you don't have a good enough education, you're too young, you're too old, you don't have enough faith.

What they're saying is: You can't have that, (you can see it,) somebody else can reach it, but it's always going to be just out of your reach, too far back on the shelf.

You feel like gravity is just pulling you down, and you are destined to live the withered life.

But I came to tell you that even gravity itself can't hold you down if you've got enough power and it doesn't matter if all the forces of the universe are waged against you (greater is he that is in you than he that is in the world).

And if God be for us, who can be against us?

When Jesus spoke those words to that man: It ignited an explosion in his spirit, and faith came alive and instantly the impossible became possible.

Instantly he was able to do what everybody said he could never do.

Instantly every can't do and can't have of religion and past failures broke off his life.

And instantly that which was withered, became whole and complete.

Somebody I'm talking to right now is getting ready to breakthrough, you're getting ready to break loose it's taking some stretching but your gonna' make it.

- Somebody's mind is being stretched.
- Somebody's faith is being stretched.
- Somebody is breaking out of status quo.

Somebody is seeing themselves right now, doing what they said you could never do.

I come to you today with a word for somebody: I came to loose you from human limitations, from religious limitations, and from demonic limitations, placed on you by the world.

It is my pleasure to tell you, it's yours. You can have it. (It is your father's good pleasure to give unto you the keys of the kingdom).

That house, that car, that ministry, that new level of anointing.

That household salvation, those open doors you've been praying for.

That Joy that you've needed.

That fire you used to have, it's coming back.

That peace you've desired it's yours.

I came to tell you today that the devil is a liar: and I came to tell you (you can have it).

You can reach it (if) you're willing to stretch.

You're gonna have to stretch: You're going to have to stretch out beyond religion, beyond tradition, you're gonna have to stretch beyond the comfort zone. You're going to have to stretch beyond peoples opinions of you.

If I had let what people said about me, or thought about me enter my heart I wouldn't be preaching the gospel today, but I made up my mind I'm not going to let small minded, people limit the power of a big God in my life.

You're gonna have to stretch.

To go to this next level you're going to have to pray like you've never prayed before.

And Praise like you've never praised before.

And sow like you've never sown before.

You can have it; you can reach it (if) you're willing to stretch.

Isa 54:2-3 Enlarge the place of thy tent, and let them (stretch) forth the curtains of thine habitations: spare not, (lengthen) thy cords, and strengthen thy stakes;

For thou shalt break forth on the right hand and on the left; and thy seed shall inherit the Gentiles, and make the desolate cities to be inhabited.

Notice all the words that speak of stretching (going beyond) Enlarge, Stretch forth. Spare not, lengthen.

And after the enlarging, the stretching, the lengthening, the strengthening, then he says: for thou shalt break forth on the right hand and on the left and thy seed shall inherit the Gentiles and make the desolate cities to be inhabited.

In other words: God is saying there is so much power released in your stretching that it will even reach your seed, and bring them into blessings they would never have had if you hadn't stretched.

There are generational blessings that are released when you stretch into the faith realm.

I wish somebody had enough faith right now to just stretch out your hand into the faith realm and take a hold of that Ministry you've been believing God for.

Take hold of that husband's salvation.

Take hold of those rebellious children, and pull them into the kingdom.

Take hold of that degree.

Take hold of that miracle healing God promised you.

Take hold of divine prosperity, God never called you to the withered life; He called you to abundant life.

I dare somebody to get up right now and stretch (and start reaching into the faith realm.)

Everything doesn't just drop in your lap; sometimes you have to stretch for it.

Say this with me: excuse my reach but I see something God promised me, and I have to stretch to get it.

I feel a stretching anointing touching you right now.

(Somebody's breaking out, somebody's been held back by religion, by tradition, by people's opinions of you, by fear of failure, by the disappointments of past defeat, but today you're breaking the barrier).

Your breaking the limitations: When a jet breaks the sound barrier it creates a sonic boom.

Right now, we're creating some sonic booms in hell. Right now we're rattling the walls of hell.

This is the day Satan has feared: The day you got the revelation, that you can have it (if) you're willing to stretch.

God said: Abraham lift up your eyes look to the east, west, north and south. Abraham, I want to bless you I want you to have all that land. Everything your eyes can see… but you have to stretch, you have to leave where you're at, you have to take down your tent and start walking.

I'm talking to somebody: You've been camped out in the same place too long, everything in your life is stagnate, you haven't made any progress in God for years, your prayer life is at the same level, your praise life is at the same level, your sowing is at the same level and your faith is at the same level it was 10, 15, 20, years ago.

It's time to stretch again: It's time to take the tent down and start walking, there are blessings waiting on the activity of your faith.

Why sit we here till we die? When 4 lepers made the decision to walk over to the enemy's camp, God amplified their footsteps and their enemies ran for their lives, and left their gold and silver, their food and even their donkeys.

When the lepers moved (God moved.)

Some of you are sitting around saying: when God gets ready I know it's going to be great, when God gets ready I'm going to walk in a greater anointing, I'm going to see miracles signs and wonders, When God gets ready I'm going to walk in divine prosperity.

I'm just waiting on God to move.

The truth is beloved: (Gods just waiting on you to move). Your activity of faith is what activates the power of God in your behalf.

Jesus said: Stretch it out (and when he stretched it out, it was made completely whole).

I made up my mind a long time ago, I want what God has for me, and I'm willing to stretch to get it.

So if you see me getting more emotional than usual I'm just stretching.

When I sow a bigger seed than usual I'm just stretching.

If I get a little more crazy in my dance than usual I'm just stretching.

If I bump into you while I'm shouting, I apologize but I'm just stretching; (because there's something I see in the faith realm,) and God said I can have it (if) I'm willing to stretch.

I don't know what it is that God has promised you that you haven't seen manifested in your life yet, but I came to tell you, God is not with holding it from you he is just requiring you to stretch to get it.

48
What's In Your Hand?

God wants to do something awesome and powerful in your life, but it starts by giving him what you have in your hand.

What do you have?
What is available to you, at your disposal, in your possession?
This rod was nothing special of itself; it was just a rod (a stick).
What was significant about this stick was: It was what Moses had.
Note: God did not ask Moses what he <u>didn't</u> have.
We could all make a long list if what we don't have.
• We don't have enough money
• We don't have a good education
• We don't have a high social standing.
The list can go on and on.
But God never directs our attention to what we don't have, but to what we do have even though it seems small.
Remember the Little widow woman whose husband had died and left her in debt, and they were coming to take her two sons as bond slaves to work off her debt?
She called the prophet of God: And he did not run down the list of negatives in her life, he did not bring attention to everything she was lacking.
(No he said: What do you have in your house?)
What do you have that you can put in your hand? (She said: I have nothing but a little pot of oil).
Then the prophet said: Use what you have in your hand.
Borrow empty vessels then take that little pot of oil and pour into them until their full, then set them aside: She obeyed the prophet and went from nothing to more than enough, from debt to profit, from helpless to helpful, from stressing to blessing.
(Because she used what was in her hand).

Note: God gave us everything we need to get the job done; we just have to use it.

Scientist say that there are very few human beings who ever use over 10% of their brain. That means that 90% of brain power is wasted.

Why? Because most people never put a demand on that other 90%.

We have to use what we have to the best of our ability before we'll get more.

Even though what we have seems small, weak, and insignificant; this is on purpose, because God has designed it so that what we have must be connected to him to work.

The difference is the power of God.

It is not your ability, your knowledge, your brain size, your talent, or the size of your gift or the beauty of your gift that matters...

All that matters is: How much of God is in your stick?

Your stick represents that which you have that you surrender to God.

When God gets in it, it's enough.

When God gets in it, it will surprise you (Moses fled from before his rod when it turned into a serpent).

The anointing is the supernatural power of God operating through the natural to produce results that are humanly impossible.

We need to ask God to get in our stick.

That is to say; the great need of the hour is God in our song. God in our preaching. God in our marriage. And God in our business.

God in our gift. And God in our talent.

When God gets in a thing; it is not the same.

When God gets in a thing; it can scare some people.

Just like Moses who had never seen his rod do anything like that before, it had never turned into a snake before God got in it..

*God got in a rock and caused a river to flow out of it that quenched the thirst of 1to 3 million Israelites.

*God got in a donkey and caused it to speak and rebuke a rebellious prophet.

*God got in an axe head of Iron and caused it to swim up to the top of the water so the young prophet could reach out his hand and take hold of it.

*God got in a little pot of oil and caused it to multiply till it met every need and provided an abundant overflow.

*God got in a rock, and a piece of leather and brought down the philistine champion, the giant Goliath.

*God got in Aarons rod and it budded, and blossomed and produced almonds (over night).

*God got in a box, and they called it the Ark of the Covenant.

They placed this box inside the most Holy Place of the tabernacle. (The Ark was made out of wood, but it was covered with Gold.) This is symbolic of the natural and the supernatural, the human and the divine nature of Jesus.

The Most Holy Place from the inside was covered in gold, but from the outside the tabernacle was covered with badger skin.

No one would know by looking at the outside, that there was such a valuable treasure inside.

In similar fashion Today God has chosen to place his presence and glory in human tents.

Our bodies are the temples of God.

2 Corinthians 4:7 But we have this (treasure in earthen vessels,) that the Excellency of the power may be of God, and not of us.

Moses rod symbolizes something that is weak, it has no life or energy of its own, it can only do what the natural human power of Moses enables it to do.

Until the power of God got in it.

In like fashion: We are weak, we have no life or strength or power of our own.

It was only as Moses released his rod to God, that Gods power came into it.

It is only as we surrender ourselves to God that his power will be manifested through us.

Too many times we are unwilling to give up what we have.

We want to hold on to what we know, what we understand, what we are comfortable with, what we have leaned upon and had control of for so long.

God is wanting to give us something new, something greater, but you have to be willing to let go of what you have.

Trust God with your stick, with your slingshot.

Before God could fulfill his promise to Abraham that all the nations of the earth would be blessed in his seed, God asked for his seed back. He asked Abraham to sacrifice his son.

Abraham trusted God with his seed Isaac, and Isaac became the seed that gave to us Jesus and because of that seed we are saved today.

We are today the seed of Abraham because Abraham was willing to give what he had to God.

The rod of Moses became the rod of God.

That rod became the symbol of Gods authority and Power; the instrument by which God's Word and will were enforced.

So it is today: It is through you and I who carry the Spirit and the Word in us that Gods will is enforced in the earth.

God told Moses what he was going to do, and how he would deliver Israel But he still had to stretch out the rod.

In like fashion God's word reveals his will to us, but we still have to speak it, (Stretch out the rod).

Jesus said we had mountain moving power, but he said in order for the mountain to move we have to speak to it.

Every time Moses stretched out the rod it was a type of speaking the Word out of a believing heart.

Just as Moses and the rod were Gods instruments for bringing his Power against Egypt and setting the Israelites free, we today are God's instruments to afflict satans kingdom, to bind the enemy of the souls of men and women and set them free.

One of the greatest problems we have as Believers is we have a tendency to underestimate what we have.

I have just enough meal and oil for one little cake said the widow of Zarephath.

I have just a little pot of oil, said the widow woman who was in debt and in danger of losing her sons to a life of slavery.

There is a lad here with two fish and five loaves of bread, but what is that among so many asked Philip a disciple of Jesus.

I just have a rock and a slingshot: said David the shepherd boy.

But in each case their little bit was enough.

When they put it in Gods hands it became more than enough.

When Samson was assaulted by the philistines there were no superior weapons of quality design to be found.

He started looking around him for something, (anything that he could use).

He found the jawbone of an ass and with it slew a thousand men.

What made this jawbone Samson's weapon of choice? Its material? No. it's superior design? No. Because everybody else was using one? No.

The answer is simple…

- It was there.
- It was available.
- It was within reach.

When The Angel of the Lord appeared to Moses as a fire in a bush. What made that bush Gods choice to manifest himself through?

It wasn't any special kind of wood, it wasn't a beautiful bush that people would go miles out of their way just to look at.

The answer is: It was available.

Now my wonderful friend; (I've got some really good news for you. (Any old stick, any old bush will do).

Hallelujah: God is not looking for greatness. He's not looking for beauty. He's not looking for perfection. (All God needs is for you to make what you have, and make yourself available to him). Put it in his hands.

When Samson looked at that jawbone of an ass, he saw something no one else saw, (he saw an instrument of mass destruction,) and that's what it became in his hand.

Had he despised that jawbone and thought that it was too weak, or too insignificant or too foolish, he may have died at the hands of the enemy.

I believe many of Gods people have been defeated in life because we have allowed the enemy to cause us to despise our gift, or our talent, like the servant who went out and buried his one talent, many have buried their talents because it seemed so weak, so small, and so insignificant.

But the Holy Spirit is saying to us: It's time to take the harp off the willow tree, dig up that hidden talent and put it in the master's hands.

- Look what God did with a stick.
- Look what God did with the jawbone of a donkey.
- Look what God did with a slingshot and a rock.
- Look what God did with two fish and five loaves of bread.

What's In Your hand?

I'm praying for you right now for God to anoint your hands for service, for His use. (So that whatever it is that God has put or is going to put in your hands, will be used in the power and the anointing of the Holy Ghost to build the Kingdom).

If it's a song you're going to sing it.

If it's a testimony, you're going to give it.

If it's a gift of hospitality you're going to use it to bless others.

If it's a desire to call others and encourage them and lift them up, you're going to do it.

There are many gifts and ministries in the body, such as, teaching, administration, compassion, and self-sacrificing, service.

There are (9) Specific gifts of the Spirit that are the work, the operation and the manifestation that are supernatural in origin and operate by and through the unction of the Holy Spirit.

But anything that you can do, want to do, enjoy doing, have a natural inclination to do can be a gift that comes from God.

And God will anoint you to use your gifts for him, if you will put them in his hands.

49
Created For Power

We were created in Christ Jesus as new creatures to carry the power and anointing of God in our lives, that this power may flow out of us as rivers of living waters, to the lost the hungry the thirsty, and the dying.

Acts 1:8 But y shall receive power after that the Holy Ghost is come upon you ....

We serve a God who makes his presence known (He manifests himself in supernatural ways).
In Exe. He appears to Moses as a flame of fire in a bush.
He manifests himself as a pillar of fire and a pillar of cloud.
He is the rock that followed the children of Israel and he is the water from the rock.
He manifested himself in the cloud of glory that filled the tabernacle upon completion.
In (1 Kings 18) He was the fire falling from heaven and consuming the sacrifice, altar and all.
(Acts 2:17-19) Tells us that God is a sign and a wonder God.
And I will show wonders in heaven above, and signs in the earth beneath, blood, and fire, and vapors of smoke.

Acts 5:12 And by the hands of the apostles were many signs and wonders wrought among the people;
It is Gods choice to use us to manifest his power to the world.

You were created for the power of God.
We are born of the Spirit. Filled with the Spirit, led by the Spirit, taught by the Spirit. Kept by the Spirit and empowered by the Spirit.

Isa 43:7 for I have created him for my glory, I have formed him; yea, I have made him.

There are only two essential powers in the earth.
#1 The Power of God #2The Power of the devil
Good - Evil
Light - Darkness
Love - Hate
Both are supernatural both have Kingdoms.
You are either in Gods Kingdom or you are in Satans Kingdom, There is no middle ground.
You can't live in Gods kingdom and derive your pleasure and your enjoyment from Satans kingdom.
1Co 10:21 Ye cannot drink the cup of the Lord, and the cup of devils: ye cannot be partakers of the Lord's table, and of the table of devils.

1Jn 1:6 If we say that we have fellowship with him, and walk in darkness, we lie, and do not the truth:

Eph 5:11 And have no fellowship with the unfruitful works of darkness, but rather reprove them.

You have a High and a Holy Calling on your life.

Mt 5:14 Ye are the salt of the earth.
Salt has healing influence, It preserves, it seasons, It makes thirsty.
Christ in you causes your life to be a channel of healing and comfort, a seasoning and preserving influence, Making your life exciting and joyous.
Mt 5:14 Ye are the Light of the world
Christ in you causes your life to be a beacon in the night. Sin is darkness. Righteousness is light.

Your life, your words, your attitude, your actions can be and should be a light to those who are in darkness.

This is no time for an attitude of indifference of who cares or what difference does it make, or I can't make a difference anyway so why even try.

 One day a young man was walking on the beach, and he saw an old man throwing the drying starfish back into the ocean; the tide had washed them ashore, and they were dying.

The young man said to the old man… you're wasting your time you'll never make a difference there are millions of starfish here.

As the old fellow lifted one starfish and threw him back into the ocean he said with a smile; it made a difference to that one.

Satan's best friend is a lukewarm Christian. They're a false representation of Jesus, and they drive people away from Christ rather than draw them to him.

Satan's attitude toward a lukewarm Christian is; Keep up the good work.

What is Gods attitude toward a lukewarm Christian?

Re 3:16 So then because thou art lukewarm, and neither cold nor hot, I will spue thee out of my mouth.

There is nothing Satan fears more than to see people who are on fire for God.

A fitting description of people on fire for God is that of the 300 foxes Sampson set on fire.

All he had to do was turn them loose, There was no planning committee, no strategic outlays of the city, No survey of God consciousness in the community.

They just ran and took the fire, and destroyed all the enemy's crops.

Their fire was all consuming, Contagious, Outrageous, and Unquenchable.

There is nothing Satan desires more than to see our energies perverted in the pursuit of natural earthly, carnal and selfish desires, or wasted, wrapped up in a don't care, so what, it's my life so what it's to you attitude.

Your life, your strength is a gift from God: You can return it to God or you can give it to the devil.

God wants to set your life on fire. Fill you with his power, Turn you loose in the fields of the philistines, give you power to be a witness, to cast out devils, to lay your hands on the sick and see them recover.

It's a wholly Life: God wants everything.

It's a Holy Life: God wants you to live a separated life.

2 Ti 2:21 If a man therefore purge himself from these, he shall be a vessel unto honor, sanctified and meet for the masters use, and prepared unto every good work.

<u>You were created for power.</u>

Multitudes of young people today are following after things like, Harry potter, and Ouiji boards, and tarot cards, and the physics'.

These are only the devils counterfeit for the power of God.

Acts 1:8 Ye shall receive Power.

Ps 63:1-2 O God, thou art my God; early will I seek thee: my soul thirtieth for thee, my flesh longeth for thee in a dry and thirsty land, where no water is;

2 To see thy power and thy glory, so as I have seen thee in the sanctuary.

Ps 71: 18 O God, forsake me not; until I have showed thy strength unto this generation, and thy power to every one that is to come.

There is only one answer for the ills of this world, and it's not physcology, or AA. or 12 Step, or sexual reorientation. (It's the Power of God).

You were created for the Power of God.

2Co 4:7 But we have this treasure in earthen vessels, that the excellency of the power may be of God, and not of us.
As a fish was created to live in the water, We were created to live in the atmosphere of the supernatural Power of God.
As a fish living on land would be unnatural and abnormal, So is it unnatural and abnormal to be called a Christian and have no fire of God in our lives, and no taste or desire for the supernatural presence of God.
Yes you were created for power.
Someone may say: That's too strong, we can't handle this.
The fact is while we are content or satisfied to be powerless, and not pursue The supernatural power of God. The door to the supernatural power of Satan is wide open.
And multitudes of spiritually hungry young people as well as adults, are streaming in.
You were created to receive the power of God and to be a channel for his power to flow through to meet the needs of humanity.

50
No More Crumbs

God never intended for his children to live a crumby life, just getting by on left overs, ours is life abundant in Christ.

Judges 1:1-7 Now after the death of Joshua it came to pass, that the children of Israel asked the LORD, saying, Who shall go up for us against the Canaanites first, to fight against them?
2And the LORD said, Judah shall go up: behold, I have delivered the land into his hand.
3And Judah said unto Simeon his brother, Come up with me into my lot, that we may fight against the Canaanites; and I likewise will go with thee into thy lot. So Simeon went with him.
4And Judah went up; and the LORD delivered the Canaanites and the Perizzites into their hand: and they slew of them in Bezek ten thousand men.
5And they found Adonibezek in Bezek: and they fought against him, and they slew the Canaanites and the Perizzites.
6But Adonibezek fled; and they pursued after him, and caught him, and cut off his thumbs and his great toes.
7And Adonibezek said, Threescore and ten kings, having their thumbs and their great toes cut off, gathered their meat under my table: as I have done, so God hath requited me. And they brought him to Jerusalem, and there he died.
This was to demonstrate his superiority over these kings.
With no thumbs they could not hold a sword, so they were no threat to him.
With no Great toes they were unstable, could not stand to fight. If you can't stand you can't fight.
Kings eating under his table means… oppression, slavery. They lived off the scraps they could gather under his table, which was very difficult with no thumbs.

Judges 1:7 (RSV) …

He said 70 kings Used to pick up scraps under my table.

This king is just like the devil, he wants to oppress you and rob you of the benefits of your salvation. Many of God's people live a beggar's life style while they are the rightful heirs to the kingdom of God.

Here were 70 KINGS who had kingdoms somewhere, but they were living a beggar's life.

1 Sam 20:14-15

14And thou shalt not only while yet I live show me the kindness of the LORD, that I die not:

15But also thou shalt not cut off thy kindness from my house forever: no, not when the LORD hath cut off the enemies of David every one from the face of the earth.

2 Sam 9:1And David said, Is there yet any that is left of the house of Saul, that I may show him kindness for Jonathan's sake?

2 Sam 9:3-4 And the king said, Is there not yet any of the house of Saul, that I may show the kindness of God unto him? And Ziba said unto the king, Jonathan hath yet a son, which is lame on his feet. 4And the king said unto him, Where is he? And Ziba said unto the king, Behold, he is in the house of Machir, the son of Ammiel, in Lo'debar.

Mephibosheth means: Dispeller of shame.

Ammiel means: People of God.

Lodebar means: Pastureless, dry, empty, barren.

Machir means: Slavery.

Here was Mephipbosheth, the grandson of King Saul, living like a beggar. Why? (He didn't know anything about the covenant, between his father Jonathon and David).

Satan is holding many of God's people in bondage to guilt and shame, (slavery) living like beggars because they don't know what the covenant says.

The syrophenician woman said to Jesus: Just let me have the crumbs that fall from the childrens table, even the dogs under the table eat the children's crumbs, (She was an alien, she didn't know or have any part in the covenant).

But the sad part is when we are covenant Sons and Daughters of God and because of ignorance, Satan oppresses us and brings us into bondage, and has us living like beggars.

Luke 16:19-21

19There was a certain rich man, which was clothed in purple and fine linen, and fared sumptuously every day:

20And there was a certain beggar named Lazarus, which was laid at his gate, full of sores,

21And desiring to be fed with the crumbs which fell from the rich man's table: moreover the dogs came and licked his sores.

Lazarus was a son of Abraham (Yet he was living like a beggar).

Here is the bottom Line: You are not a beggar, Satan has no authority to hold you in bondage of guilt or shame to your past. You are a covenant Son and Daughter of God.

The King is calling you to his banqueting table and at his table no one see's what you were; only what you are.

When you take your rightful place at the table, you rule and reign as kings, and it is then that Satan (adonibezek is defeated in your life).

Its time for you to tell the Devil: I know who I am. I know I am the Son of a King, and I know the covenant and I know my rights, and I refuse to settle for crumbs when the Kingdom is mine.

51
The Fight Is Fixed

Good news Child of God, I don't care what you are going through right now, you are destined to win.

Child of God, God wants you to know; (The fight is fixed).
Don't worry neighbor the fix is in.

Wow, what kind of boldness and confidence would it give you to know that you are guaranteed to win, that you cannot lose? That no matter how powerful or how strong your opponent is, no matter what tricks they pull, no matter what their advantages over you may seem to be, you are the declared winner, and you haven't even thrown the first punch?

Well as unbelievable as it may sound it is the truth.
I know it may not make sense; but from a God perspective, victory is (not) determined by the outcome, it is established by the income (In other words it is established by faith, and faith comes by hearing and hearing by the word of God.   (Ro 10:17).

In other words you can know you have won the fight, before you ever step into the ring.
Let me say it again: The fight is fixed.
I don't know what battle you are facing right now, I don't know what enemy might be raised up against you right now, and I don't know what the devil is trying to do in your life tonight, and I don't know what mountain is standing in your way, but I came to tell you, no matter who you are or what your facing, the answer is the same; (FAITH) #1firm belief in the integrity, ability, effectiveness, or genuineness of, belief and trust in and loyalty to God,

363

#2 something that is believed especially with strong conviction. "Faith is the victory".

Victory is not external, victory is internal.

Men in the world determine victory by what's going on around them or not going on around them. They determine victory by the absence of external conflict,

But God determines victory by what's going on inside of us. (This is the victory that over cometh the world, even our faith).

Victory is first of all an attitude: (The attitude of faith).

Attitude from the dictionary means #1 A position assumed for a specific purpose, #2 A mental position with regard to a fact or a state.

When we get Gods word in our hearts it produces an attitude (A position assumed for a specific purpose and a mental position with regard to a fact or a state.

Dear reader you need to get an ATTITUDE!

See if this doesn't help you assume a position for a specific purpose; see if this doesn't help develop a mental position with regard to a fact or state or conditions.

- We are more than conquerors through him that loved us and gave him-self for us.
- Greater is he that is in us than he that is in the world.
- I can do all things through Christ which strengtheneth me.
- No weapon formed against me shall prosper, and every tongue that riseth against me in judgment I shall condemn.
- And they overcame him by the blood of the lamb and the word of their testimony.

I just believe somebody's getting an attitude adjustment right now.

Victory begins with a decision: (The decision to believe that God told the truth).

Who hath believed our report and to whom hath the arm of the Lord been revealed (Isa 53:1).

Who is he that overcometh the world, but he that believeth that Jesus Christ is the son of God? (1Jn 5:5).

<u>Victory is a discipline</u>: It takes a disciplined person to manifest victory, since our victory is faith and faith is born of the Word, We must discipline ourselves to believe the word regardless of what circumstances say.

Like the widow woman with her little pot of oil. She went in and shut the door. You have to shut the door to every thing that contradicts the word. You have to shut yourself in to faith, and shut out everything else, (doubt, fear, confusion, feelings, pain, sometimes friends and family).

<u>Victory demands determination:</u> Victory is not a one-time experience, victory is a way of life, it is a Spirit life that is born in us. (This is the victory that overcometh the world even our faith.)

<u>Victory is the spirit of perseverance.</u> Victory is the spirit that stands at the door and continues to knock even though the answer is no.

Victory is the spirit that hears the criticism but keeps on pressing.

Victory is not a life without problems; <u>Victory is a life that faces problems with a promise.</u>

For every problem there is a promise: <u>Victory is the faith that (clings to the promise) until the problem is defeated.</u>

2 Samuel 23:9 And after him was Eleazar the son of Dodo the Ahohite, one of the three mighty men with David, when they defied the Philistines that were there gathered together to battle, and the men of Israel were gone away:

2 Samuel 23:10 He arose, and smote the Philistines until his hand was weary, and (his hand clave unto the sword): and the LORD wrought a great victory that day; and the people returned after him only to spoil.

Here is a man who became one with his sword, his hand clave unto his sword, that means his hand became welded to his sword, he held on to the promise until the problem was defeated, and your victory and mine is in becoming one with the word.

Victory is not based upon people; sometimes people actually stand in the way of victory.

As in the case of Jairus Daughter (Jesus put everyone out except Peter James and John).

The old saying is, there's strength in numbers, well that is only true to a certain extent.

That is… if the numbers are in faith, and the numbers are anointed, and if the numbers believe the Promise.

(God does not recognize numbers, he recognizes faith).

Jonathon said: 1Sam 14:6 it may be that the LORD will work for us: for there is no restraint to the LORD to save by many or by few.

Victory is (not) never going through a trial, Victory is (going through) a trial.

1 Peter 1:7 That the trial of your faith, being much more precious than of gold that perisheth, though it be tried with fire, might be found unto praise and honor and glory at the appearing of Jesus Christ.

Victory is not in never going through a trial, Victory is in How you go through the trial.

This is how victory goes through a trial: Victory goes through a trial knowing that it is working for you.

2 Cor 4:17-18 This light affliction which is but for a moment (worketh for us) a far more exceeding and eternal weight of glory, while we look not at the things which are seen but at the things which are not seen for the things which are seen are temporal, but the things which are not seen are eternal.

Ro 8:28 And we know that all things (work together for good) to them that Love the Lord, and are called according to his purpose.

Job said it this way…

The Lord knoweth the way that I take; when he hath tried me I shall come forth as gold. (Job 23:10).

In other words, I will be better for this.

I want to tell someone, I don't care what you're facing right now. (Faith has fixed the fight). Faith has never lost a battle. From Genesis to Revelation to 2018 True Bible believing faith has never lost a battle.

But you say (Pastor) you don't know what I'm going through. I'm going through hell. I've never been through a storm like this before; I've never been through a fire like this before.

(Well you ought to be shouting right now, because you just prophesied your own victory). You said I'm going through, (Say it again so you get used to hearing yourself say it, I'm going through, I'm going through, I'm going through.

I don't care what the devil does, I don't care what he throws at me, I'm going through.

David Said: Yea though I walk through the valley of the shadow of death I will fear no evil for thou art with me, thy rod and thy staff they comfort me.

David made it through his valley of the shadow of death, and you are going to make it too.

It may look bad right now but the fight is fixed and at a certain point the devil is going down because he has to.

It may be the first round, the second round or the third round. (But my faith tells me the devil is going down).

Jesus said: *Lu 10:19 Behold I give unto you power to tread upon serpents and scorpions and over all the power of the enemy and nothing shall by any means hurt you.*

Jesus said: *Mr 16:17-18 And these signs shall follow them that believe; In my name shall they cast out devils; they shall speak with new tongues; 18 They shall take up serpents; and if they drink any deadly thing, it shall not hurt them; they shall lay hands on the sick, and they shall recover.*

1Jo 4:4 Ye are of God, little children, and have overcome them: because greater is he that is in you, than he that is in the world.

1 Jn 5:4 whatsoever is born of God overcometh the world, and this is the victory that overcometh the world even our faith.

The fact is; (as long as the child of God stays in the arena of faith, victory is guaranteed).

Ro 16:20 And the God of peace shall bruise Satan under your feet shortly.

In other words; it's just a matter of time.

It may be tonight, it may be tomorrow, it may be a month from now, but that battle is going to end, that fiery trial is going to end, that storm is going to end and when it does you are going to still be standing.

Dottie Rambo wrote a song: I've weathered storms before.

This is not your first fight, this is not your first storm, this is not your first trial, I know it looks bad but you're going to make it. I prophesy to you, you are going to make it because the fight is fixed, and the only way you can lose is to not fight in the arena of faith.

So take unto you the whole armor of God, strap on your shield of faith and jump into the ring, the victory is yours in Jesus name. The fight is fixed.

52
Moving Time

Are you ready to move to the next level? I believe that in your spirit you know it's moving time.

Re 4:1 After this I looked, and, behold, a door was opened in heaven: and the first voice which I heard was as it were of a trumpet talking with me; which said, (Come up hither), and I will show thee things which must be hereafter.

I believe that many today are hearing the call of the Spirit to a higher place in God, God is always calling us to a higher place.

Ex 40:37 But if the cloud were not taken up, then they journeyed not till the day that it was taken up.

Nu 9:19 And when the cloud tarried long upon the tabernacle many days, then the children of Israel kept the charge of the LORD, and journeyed not.

Nu 9:22 Or whether it were two days, or a month, or a year, that the cloud tarried upon the tabernacle, remaining thereon, the children of Israel abode in their tents, and journeyed not: but when it was taken up, they journeyed.

All this was to teach the children of Israel how to get from the prophecy to the promise, or from the dream to the reality, or from faith to sight.
It was to teach them that on the journey their provision and their guidance and their protection was all dependant on staying with the cloud.

One of the most important lessons it taught them was never get too comfortable.

Intentionally God would vary the time that they would stay in a place, to teach them that no matter how comfortable or convenient a place it was, it was not the promise.

God did not tell them when he was going to move, he did not send advance notice…

Because he wanted them to stay in a condition of readiness for change.

One of the greatest battles we fight is that of the familiar. Even though something or some place may be dry, desolate, and difficult once we become familiar with it we become comfortable with it.

Once it becomes comfortable to us, we resist anything that threatens our normality or our familiar.

Moving is one of the most interesting things:

There is in the moving process something called …

(Ordered chaos)

That means: chaos with a purpose.

#1. Everything is chaotic, everything is moved out of it's place, the familiar routine is replaced by what seems to be confusion and disorder.

#2. Nothing is convenient, everything you want seems to be the hardest thing to get to.

#3. Another thing is: When you start to move, you begin to realize all the things you have accumulated over the years, (a lot of it just plain junk,) or at least stuff that is outdated, and unnecessary.

#4. It's a time of shifting and sifting, it's when you lighten your load, it's when you separate the useful from the useless and the valuable from the worthless.

A lot of what you accumulate at one place you don't need at the next place.

This is a spiritual truth we learn from moving in the natural. As we move from one level to another there are things that we will leave behind.

I don't know about you but there are some things I am ready to leave behind.

I'm ready to leave behind some doubts, and fears, and discouragements, and disappointments.

I'm ready to leave behind some enemies that I've been fighting.

I'm ready to leave behind some traditions that have no power.

I'm ready to leave behind some excess baggage that's been slowing me down.

Many times moving is difficult because you are leaving the familiar, the comfortable, and the normal.

You're leaving behind Jobs, families, friends' acquaintances, routines, lifestyles, and experiences.

And you are entering the unknown = (The unknown zone).

(Unknown people, unknown Jobs, Unknown surroundings, new experiences).

Heb 11:8 By faith Abraham, when he was called to go out into a place which he should after receive for an inheritance, obeyed; and he went out, not knowing whither he went.

God is looking for some people that will follow him into the unknown zone.

Isa 42:16-19 And I will bring (the blind) by a way that they knew not; I will lead them in paths that they have (not known): I will make darkness light before them, and crooked things straight. These things will I do unto them, and not forsake them.

17 They shall be turned back, they shall be greatly ashamed, that trust in graven images, that say to the molten images, Ye are our gods.

18 Hear, ye deaf; and look, ye blind, that ye may see.

19 Who is blind, but my servant? or deaf, as my messenger that I sent? who is blind as he that is perfect, and blind as the LORD'S servant?

Is anybody ready to move on?

Is anybody ready to let go and let God?

Is anybody ready to go to the unknown zone?

Is anybody ready to obey even when it doesn't make sense? To obey when it looks foolish, to obey and go when every natural instinct says stop?

It is said that the African impala can jump 10 feet into the air and cover the distance of 30 feet in a single stride, but this great animal can be imprisoned for the span of it's life behind a 3 foot wall, because it will not jump (if it can't see where it's feet are going to land).

It refuses to go into the unknown zone.

This is what it means to be blind= to trust God.

To be able to jump when I can't see where my feet are going to land.

To move into the unknown Zone.

Re 4:1 After this I looked, and, behold, a door was opened in heaven: and the first voice which I heard was as it were of a trumpet talking with me; which said, Come up hither, and (I will show thee things which must be hereafter).

There are some things that are not going to happen until we make the transition into the unknown zone or we could just call it the faith dimension.

One of the greatest motivations for moving to the next level is I am more afraid of staying where I am than of moving into the unknown.

This next level that God is calling you to is going to take a faith step into the unknown.

53
Don't Miss Your Move

When you move with God you cannot fail, when you move without God you cannot win. There is a time to be still, but there is a time for making a move.

Multitudes of feeble folk surrounded that pool waiting for the moving of the water.

This was a multitude of people that testified by their very presence in that place, that they were in need of something there that they couldn't get anywhere else.

The same thing is true for you and I today, we all need something that the world can't provide for us.

It's not in a bottle, it's not in a pill, and it's not in drugs or sex, or money.

The doctor can't do it for you; you won't find it in motorcycles, boats, or sports.

What we need is nothing less than the supernatural presence and power of the living God.

I know sometimes it's hard to come to the place where we're ready to admit our desperation and our impotency.

But here I am today admitting that I'm no different than the multitude gathered at that pool.

I'm impotent, I'm powerless, and I'm helpless, and without his touch I'm nothing.

Without his anointing I can do nothing.

And I found out that one of the greatest keys to that touch and that anointing is learning how to wait on God.

God doesn't operate on my timetable, so I have to wait on him.

Ps 62:5 My soul, wait thou only upon God; for my expectation is from him.

Ps 27:14 Wait on the LORD: be of good courage, and he shall strengthen thine heart: wait, I say, on the LORD.

La 3:25 The LORD is good unto them that wait for him, to the soul that seeketh him.

Lu 21:19 In your patience possess ye your souls.

Isa 40:31 But they that wait upon the LORD shall renew their strength; they shall mount up with wings as eagles; they shall run, and not be weary; and they shall walk, and not faint.

When I come before God in prayer and I get quiet before him and I just wait. I'm admitting to God I'm powerless without you.
I'm impotent without you.
I can't even walk without you holding my hand.
But you have to realize there is a time for waiting and there is a time for stepping.
A lot of people sit around on their hands excusing their fear, their doubt and their laziness by saying (I'm just waiting on God).
There's a time for waiting and there is a time for moving.
In 2 Sa 5:18... David was anointed to be king and when the philistines heard about it, they all came to fight with David.
David enquired of the Lord, shall I go up and will you deliver them into my hand? God said go up, and David did, and won a great victory.
A short time later the philistines came back, and David again enquires of the Lord. And the Lord says go up, I will give you the victory; again David wins a great victory.
Then a Third time the Philistines come up against David.
Most people would have assumed that God was with them based upon past victories and rush into battle.
But David understood the need to get Gods Help and Gods direction.
When David enquires, God tells him…

2 Sam 5:23-25 Thou shalt not go up; but fetch a compass behind them, and come upon them over against the mulberry trees.
24 And let it be, when thou hearest the sound of a going in the tops of the mulberry trees, that then thou shalt bestir thyself: for then shall the LORD go out before thee, to smite the host of the Philistines.
25 And David did so, as the LORD had commanded him; and smote the Philistines from Geba until thou come to Gazer.

In other words, God said to David, (wait.) If you want me to be with you, and you want my power on your behalf then wait.
The revelation here is that there is a time for waiting and there is a time for moving. Now let's look back our text again…
When the water moved, there was an angel present. Whatever their need was, it was met immediately when they stepped into the water.
When the water moved there was a miracle in the water, but only when the water moved.

In my imagination I see this crowd of people spread out around this pool waiting for the moving of the water.
They did not know when it was going to happen, so they had to watch the water.
I can imagine all of these people anticipating their miracle concentrating on the water, getting as close as they could to the place of Blessing.
I can imagine the struggle to be in the front and how over a period of time those who started out in the back made it to the front.
I can also see in my imagination people becoming discouraged because it didn't happen soon enough for them.
I see them begin to lose interest and lose faith and their focus shifted to other things, they began to grumble and complain that it was too cold, or too hot, their seat was too hard, the music was too loud the songs weren't their style.

They even started talking about looking for another pool where there was more action and more activities for the kids.

Then all of a sudden someone comes climbing over the top of a hundred people.

I can see people getting angry at this person, this person has completely forgotten his manners he has not said please or thank you or excuse me, or what time is it, or isn't this nice weather we're having.

He's stepping on fingers and toes; he's bumping heads on his way.

See this person I'm talking about is the one who saw the water moving. He recognized the presence of the supernatural power of God.

He is the one who made up his mind… I'm not going to miss my move.

He didn't come for the company, he didn't come just to get out of the house, and he didn't come for the weather.

He was there for only one reason; he was there for his miracle, the touch of God.

I just have to believe that there is somebody like that I'm speaking to right now.

You're reading this for a reason; you need the supernatural power of God to touch you.

This man saw the water move and he went crazy.

I'm going to stop here for a minute and say: Many of Gods people have become too familiar with the presence of God.

We're too casual with his presence, and many times we miss his glory because we have forgotten how to entertain his presence.

What began as a ripple in the water became a tidal wave of blessing, and of healing and deliverance to the one who recognized the presence of the angel of the Lord.

I am convinced that many times we miss the miracles and the glory of God simply because we are insensitive to the gentle stirrings, and the ripples in the water.

We're wanting Earthquakes Wind and Fire, but many times he's in the still small voice. Many times he is in the gentle ripples and stirring.

But we miss it because we're in such a hurry to get to the buffet bar first.

There's an old saying, anything worth having is worth waiting for.

That means that the best things require some time, and if you want the best you have to have some patience.

Good things come to them who wait.

But some one added (But not to those who wait too late).

The bottom line is, there is a time for waiting and there is a time for stepping.

David had the revelation of waiting on God.

He realized that if I wait on God, and I move when God moves, then I'm going to have a miracle, I'm going to get the victory.

The Bible says:

Whosoever first, after the troubling of the water stepped in, was made whole of whatsoever disease he had.

When the water moved the miracle power of God was present.

The healing, the deliverance, the breakthrough was present in their midst, (but the only person who got their miracle was the one who moved when the water moved).

It was the stepper.

I'm just going to warn you, I don't plan on missing my move.

When the water starts moving I'll be stepping.

So you might want to pull your feet in a little bit.

I don't mean to be pushy or rude, but I need a miracle. I need a breakthrough, and I don't have time to be worried about being cute or comfortable.

This is my move and I don't know when or if he will ever move like this again.

I can't sit here worrying about what you think about me.

I can't let your attitude hold me back. I may be a little undignified but this is my move, and I've been waiting for it for a while. I've been praying for it. I've been believing for it. I've been preparing for it, and I've been expecting it.

This may sound a little aggressive, but it's the kind of attitude you need if you're going to get your miracle and your breakthrough.

I'm starting to feel a stepping anointing right now. I believe you're getting ready to step into a breakthrough in your finances, somebody's getting ready to step into a divine connection, somebody's getting ready to step into some joy, some peace.

Have I got any steppers with me?

If I were in a crowd of bystanders and spectators, I would politely say, excuse me, I don't want to offend you, but if I can't get around you, I'll go over you.

Because I'm not going to miss my move.

Somebody needs to put your faith into action and start stepping. Step into your miracle, step into your breakthrough, Step for that husband or wife you've been praying for, step for those children who are running from God, hooked on drugs.

Step for your ministry, step for your destiny.

Somebody is one step away from your miracle. One step away from a fresh anointing.

The move is on, the waters are troubled. (The waters are moving, don't miss your move).

Jesus asked this man at the pool: wilt thou be made whole? He said I have no man to put me into the water but while I am coming another steppeth down before me.

You see when it comes to your miracle and your breakthrough… you have to be a little pushy, its first come first serve.

Yes I want you blessed and I want you healed too, but this is my move, and I'm not missing it.

Others were healed before this man (why?) because they stepped in.

I know for some of you it's going to be a little out of character, but you have to get aggressive when it comes to getting a miracle. You need to get an attitude.

You can either step in or you can watch me, it's up to you. But I'm not missing my move.

54
When Jesus Says Come

When Jesus Says Come: He has just opened a door for you to a greater life than you could imagine, but it will cost you something to get it.

I prophesy right now that before you're through reading this book, somebody is going to hear Jesus say come.

It's going to be just as real for you as it was for Peter on that stormy night. Jesus has not changed and he is still calling people to walk on the water, and somebody listening to this message is going to hear that unmistakable voice and your life is never going to be the same.

Come: It's really just another way of saying...

You can do it; it's your turn. Start, Jump, Go. Quit making excuses, break free of your fears and live your faith.

So many of Gods people live beneath their potential, they live what we'll call the safe life.

But every once in a while you run into someone who heard Jesus say come and they went over the edge of the comfortable and predictable safe zone, and they're following Jesus in the Faith zone.

So many times we sit back in our comfortable safe places and talk about everything we would do for God (if) he ever called us.

.

Well my question is: What do you do when Jesus says Come?

You and I may never actually physically follow Peter out on the deep blue sea.

In other words: You and I may never literally get out of a boat and walk on top of water as Peter did.

We may never during the course of our lifetimes be in the situation or the circumstances that Peter was in when he literally and physically got out of his boat in the middle of a life threatening storm and physically in the presence of eye witnesses walked on top of the water.

Right there I can hear in my spirit a big sigh of relief; because as exciting as it is, and as encouraging as it is to read about Peter walking on top of the water, and Peter putting that which was over his head under his feet…

The truth is: most Christians have no desire to walk on the water when there is a perfectly good boat anywhere nearby.

But while we may never physically leave the safety of a perfectly good boat and leap out onto a raging sea. There will be times in our lives as we follow Christ, that we will be challenged to duplicate that same reckless faith and abandon that Peter had when he let go of everything, so he could hold onto a word.

There is going to be some point in your faith journey, when you will have to choose the high road or the low road.

If you choose the higher road, it means you will have to let go.

The higher road means higher in the realm of faith.

It takes a certain measure of faith just to ride out the storm. It takes a certain measure of faith to keep your sanity when all hell is breaking loose against your family, your finances, your health, and your ministry.

Some people are quick to criticize those other disciples as being fearful and faithless.

But I don't, because I know how it feels to be in a storm, and I know how much faith it took just to stay in the boat.

To keep praising, to keep trusting, to keep tithing, and keep sowing and keep confessing, when I couldn't see any relief in sight, and I couldn't feel any relief, and I couldn't see anything but storm clouds and rough waters.

No: I'm not condemning them; they made it thru the storm, they made it to the other side. Praise God they made it. That's something to shout about right there.

I made it: I didn't feel like I was going to make it, it didn't look like I was going to make it, people said I wouldn't make it, but here I am.

No I will not criticize them: I only have one thing to say about those other disciples. They missed the opportunity to take the high road. You see they were brought to a place where they could choose a greater glory.

They missed the testimony of a water walker:

Their testimony was: we made it, we survived. We rode out the storm.

But when Peter began to testify, his testimony was different.

Yes he was in the boat with all the rest, and yes he feared for his life like all the other disciples. But when Peter saw Jesus walking on the water something on the inside of Peter told him: You can do that. If Jesus can do it, you can too.

Something inside of Peter said: If the teacher can do it, so can the students.

(All I need is a Word from the Master)

All you need is a word from the Master.

All you need is a word: A can do word.

There may be a thousand voices telling you that you can't do it, and a thousand reasons why can't do it.

You're not educated enough. You're not old enough. You're too old. You're the wrong color. You're from the wrong side of town. You don't have enough money. You don't have any experience.

But if you have a can do word from God…

You can do the impossible: You can go where they said you could never go, and you can do what they said you can never do, and you can be what they said you could never be, and you can have what they said you could never have.

Say it out loud: I've got a can do word!

I can do all things through Christ who strengthens me… (Php 4:13).

If thou canst believe, all things are possible to him that believeth ... (Mt 9:23).

Ye are of God, little children, and have overcome them: because greater is he that is in you, than he that is in the world ... (1Jo 4:4).

Peter had a word: "Come."

That's all he had (but that's all he needed).

No doubt the disciples argued with him and told him, it was impossible, and begged him to stay in the boat, and stay on the same faith level that they were on. (But Peter had heard the call).

Everyone in the boat had the same opportunity Peter had to walk on the water. The circumstances were the same. Jesus was the same, and the word was the same.

They chose to hold on to the boat; Peter chose to step out on the Word.

When Peter stepped out on the word: He stepped into a brand new anointing.

He stepped into a supernatural water walking anointing. He began moving and walking and operating in the same realm and the same anointing that Jesus was functioning in.

Let me make a point here: Jesus didn't force Peter to get out of the boat, Jesus didn't threaten Peter.

Jesus didn't condemn the other disciples for not walking on the water.

Jesus simply came to them all in a way that presented an opportunity for them to move to another level in their faith.

He created an avenue for them to step from one realm of anointing to another; he called them to a higher experience, and a higher manifestation of his power in their lives.

But only one took that step: That step separated Peter from the rest of the disciples.

That step drew a line between the doers and the watchers, between the boat sitters and the water walkers.

Somebody said: I'm afraid, I'm afraid I might get wet.

Well you might get wet, in fact you probably will get wet.

But I made up my mind a long time ago, that I would rather be a wet water walker, than a dry boat sitter.

I'd rather fail trying to do something great for God, than to succeed at doing nothing.

I'd rather experience one day, one hour, one minute walking on the water, than a lifetime of sitting in the boat.

I prophesy and I declare to you that there is a new stirring in the spirit and many who have been comfortable and satisfied in the boat of mediocrity and religious expectation, and traditions of men, are getting uncomfortable.

The Spirit is calling, come up hither, come up higher.

And many of Gods people are realizing that they weren't created for the confines and the restrictions and the limitations of a barnyard religion.

In other words: we are discovering our destiny. We are discovering our purpose and we are discovering the power that resides in us.

And we are discovering that we are not chickens, we are eagles.

You can choose to live on the lower plane as a chicken, but your eagle spirit will never be satisfied.

Some of you reading these words right now can bear witness to what I'm saying: You can't figure it out, you're uncomfortable, you're uneasy and kind of edgy and irritable; nothing really satisfies you, you're not satisfied by what you eat or the job you have or the car you drive.

You leave church feeling like something's missing and you want to blame it on the Pastor, or the praise and worship team, or the teacher or the evangelist.

But the truth is: It's not their fault, a different job or different food, or a different church, or more money, isn't going to fix it.

The problem is: your spirit has heard the Eagle cry of the Spirit and your spirit wants to break free but your flesh is trying to hold you in captivity.

It's the anointing that is calling you; it's the anointing that is pulling at you.

It's that same anointing that pulled Peter out of that boat. It's that same word that called Peter to a life in the supernatural.

You can talk about the peter that started to sink.

But I prefer to talk about the Peter that walked on the water, cast out devils, healed the sick and raised the dead and preached the inauguration of the dispensation of the Holy Ghost and 3,000 souls were saved.

I want to talk about the man who let go of everything to take hold of one word from God.

As I said earlier, you and I may never jump out of a boat like Peter did and walk on water, but at some point in your faith journey, God is going to give you the opportunity to launch out into the supernatural: You're going to hear him say (Come).

And it's going to be just as crazy and just as reckless, and some people will criticize you and call you crazy, some people will make fun of you and forecast your failure and anticipate your demise.

But at some point you have to make a choice: Are you going to live by what man created (the job) (the position) (the reputation) or are you going to live by what created man?

Heb 11:3 Through faith we understand that (the worlds were framed by the word of God), so that things which are seen were not made of things which do appear.

Somebody is getting out of the boat. Somebody is making a decision today to go higher, to walk by faith and not by sight.

Somebody today is moving into what I call (Crazy Faith) it's the kind of faith that will let go of everything just to take hold of one word from God.

That one word from Jesus saved Peters life, and probably everyone on that boat: I want you to lift your hands right now and begin to praise God for some crazy people, people who are willing to risk everything on a word... People who will answer the call into the unknown. People who will say yes to God.

Abraham, Paul the apostle, Joseph, Daniel, the three Hebrew children, and Jesus himself are in that group.

That's a pretty good crowd to run with.

Somebody is hearing the voice of Jesus right now. He's saying Come, let's do this together ...

_Let's go to the mission field.

_Let's start that business.

_Let's build that church.

_Let's write that book.

_Let's go back to school and get your degree.

_Let's launch that ministry.

When Jesus says Come: He is inviting you to take hold of his power, his wisdom, and his ability.

I believe there is a call going out in the spirit right now, for men and women to let go of the safe life and step up to the faith life.

Peter did not sink and neither will you. Jesus would not have called you if he couldn't hold you up.

When Jesus says "Come" everything you need to accomplish the work is contained in that word.

55
Ugly Praise

Dear reader, I believe God is doing something fresh and new and powerful in your life right now.

I believe that God is using these words to breath life back into you, to renew, and restore and revitalize and re-fire your faith.

In 2011 the Devil tried to kill me; for over one year I went through a tremendous fiery trial that almost took my life.

I am not going to take the time to share my testimony here, If you would like to read it, it is in my other book "Keep On Walking".

In that book I share my testimony of walking through the fire and Gods delivering power in my life.

This book was born out of that fiery furnace.

On January 17th 2012 I posted this sermon; Ugly Praise, to Sermon Central; God really blessed it and it has went all over the world encouraging and blessing and helping people.

Recently God spoke to my heart that it was time to put the message into a book, because there are many wonderful people who have never been to sermon central. Well I humbly offer this book to you my dear reader, and I pray that it will be to you what it was to me when God spoke to my heart in the middle of my life and death battle. It was to me "A Life Line".

So we will start today by looking in the scriptures at a young man named Joseph. You'll find the story in Gen, Ch 37-47

When we read the story of Joseph there are some things that cannot be denied, because the scripture makes it clear that...

- Joseph was <u>chosen</u> by God.
- Joseph was <u>anointed</u> by God.
- Joseph had a <u>destiny</u> given by God.
- Joseph was <u>favored</u> by God.
- Joseph was <u>favored</u> by his earthly father.
- God was <u>with</u> Joseph.

That sounds like a winning combination doesn't it? Judging from that criteria it would look like Joseph had it made, it would seem as though he was living the life of riley. (You would expect to find his book and his picture under lifestyles of the rich and famous by Joseph).

But when we read the bible we find out that <u>this same Joseph</u> who had everything going for him, who was anointed by God, who was favored by his earthly father and had so many great advantages…

<u>One day this same Joseph found himself in a pit</u>!

I want to stop here for just a minute and tell you; if somebody told you when you became a Christian that all your problems would be over, and that you would never be hurt again, you would never cry again, you would never suffer again… (They Lied).

Ps 34:19 Many are the afflictions of the righteous, but the Lord delivereth him out of them all.

The point I'm trying to make is that Christians have problems too.

- Christians get sick.

- Christians get in debt.

- Christians get divorced.

- Christians get their hearts broken.

- Christians sometimes get in places they shouldn't be.

At some point in your life, whatever the reason; you will find yourself in a pit.

Sometimes you fall in, sometimes you jump in, and sometimes you're pushed in. (But regardless of how you got there or why you're there, a Pit is a Pit and if you stay there you will die).

Dreams die in the pit, ministries die in the pit, gifts, callings, marriages, die in the pit; Rueben was responsible for Josephs pit.

It was Rueben that suggested they throw Joseph in the pit. Now in all fairness we know from the scriptures that Rueben intended to come back later and take Joseph from the pit, but he wasn't going to go against the rest of his brothers, so he just went along with their plan. Now, we don't know what happened or where Rueben went but we know this... Rueben was there when Joseph was thrown into the pit, but he was not there when he was lifted out.

The point is, Rueben was surprised, he was shocked, because he saw Joseph go into the pit, he saw him struggling and begging to be delivered from the pit, but now he's looking into that same pit expecting to see pitiful Joseph full of fear and confusion, stressing and crying and begging to be delivered. But Joseph wasn't there. I'm going to prophesy to somebody reading these words right now; God is getting ready to do something that is going to blow some people away.

There are some people who saw you in the pit, there are some people that even helped put you in the pit, and they have watched you struggling, and pushing, and scratching and clawing trying to climb your way out. When they left, you were in the pit.

The last time they saw you, you were in the pit and you were a mess.

But I want to prophesy to you right now that you are coming out of the pit!

I'm not just saying these words, I'm prophesying, I am declaring to you with prophetic unction and authority that you are coming out.

I wish somebody would prophesy to yourself: I'm coming out. I don't know what that pit is for you today;

- It may be a pit of debt.
- It may be a pit of sickness.
- It may be a pit of bondage, or addiction.
- It may be a pit of despair, depression.

Or it may be a pit of marriage problems that looks so deep and so dark and impossible that you feel like giving up.

Or it may be a spiritual pit, and you just don't feel God like you used to, and you're dry and discouraged.

I don't know what your pit is: They come in all different shapes and sizes.

I don't know what that pit is for you, but what you need to do right now is open your mouth and prophesy. (I've spent my last night in the pit)!

Weeping may endure for a night but joy cometh in the morning...
Ps 30:5

Rueben came back to the pit <u>where he last saw Joseph</u>, and Joseph wasn't there.

There are some people that thought they knew you pretty good; they thought they knew where to look for you. They said, this is where they always go when they're down; and this is what they always do when they're down.

They even talked about your pitiful condition to other people.

But that was yesterday!

*Yesterday I was in the pit.

 *Yesterday it <u>looked like</u> I was going to die in the pit.\

*Yesterday I <u>felt like</u> I was going to die in the pit.

But I heard a word; I heard Joseph say, don't die in the Pit. I heard Joseph say… The fall doesn't have to be fatal).

If you could talk to Joseph he would tell you…

- Don't die in the pit.
- Don't quit dreaming.
- Don't quit believing.
- Don't quit trusting.
- Don't quit expecting.

The story is told of the two frogs that fell into a big giant vat of cream (one frog paddled around for awhile then gave up and sunk to the bottom and died,) but the other frog just kept paddling, until the cream turned into butter and then he just jumped out. My precious friend just keep paddling, just keep kicking, never quit, never say die.

It looked like Joseph was going to die in the pit, and it felt like Joseph was going to die in the pit, but through a turn of circumstances in a matter of minutes Joseph was up out of the pit on solid ground.

And this is my message to you today; God is going to turn it around.

- I don't know how he's going to do it.
- I don't know when he's going to do it.
- I don't know who he's going to use to do it.

I just need to tell you, if you'll keep the switch of faith on; (God will turn it around). If you learn anything from the bible it is that God is a God of the turn around.

 Here are some great examples... _Joseph, Jeremiah, Job, Daniel, the three Hebrew Children, Jonah, and of course the greatest example of all, Jesus.

From the lowest pit of hell he ascended to the right hand of the Father on high.

From Genesis to Revelation God is turning it around. And if you haven't been convinced yet, all you have to do is look in the mirror. We weren't all born with angel wings and a halo. Some of us use to be troublemakers. Some of us were thieves and liars. Some of us were fornicators. Some of us were alcoholics and drug addicts.

But that was the old man. That was B.C. that was before Christ.

2 Co 5:17 If any man be in Christ he is a new creature, old things are passed away behold all things become new.

 Dear reader, I want you to see something, it happened suddenly!

One minute he was in the pit. One minute he was in the dark. One minute it was terminal. One minute it looked like the end. Then suddenly everything changed.

<u>Suddenly</u>, he was standing in the sunshine. In an instant everything changed, in one minute what was terminal and staring him in the face was over and behind him.

I don't know who I'm talking to but God said to proph-esy to you and to tell you that you are standing on the verge of a suddenly that is going to change everything.

Peter fished all night and caught nothing, but in one act of obedience (suddenly) he went from nothing to too much.
He went from empty nets to breaking nets. He went from an empty boat to a sinking boat, from loss to profit, from weeping to rejoicing, from a loser to a winner, and it happened, (suddenly)!
Somebody snap your fingers, yeah just like that, suddenly!!
At the lowest point in Josephs life physically and spiritually, God stepped in.
<u>JUDAH GOT HIM OUT</u>

It wasn't his coat of many colors that got him out, it wasn't his anointing that got him out, it wasn't even his dreams that got him out.
(It was an ugly old Judah). JUDAH means PRAISE.
Rueben got him in, but <u>Judah</u> got him out, Hallelujah!

I don't care how you got in the pit; I don't care who it was or what it was.
(I am anointed to tell you, Judah will get you out).
The circumstances may not have been of Joseph's choosing; nevertheless Judah was responsible for getting him out of the pit.
Mean old ugly Judah got him out.
The point I'm trying to make is: Praise doesn't have to be pretty to be powerful!
Start right where you're at.
- Anybody can <u>put on a pretty praise</u> when the battles over.

- Anybody can give God a pretty praise when the sickness is healed.
- Anybody can praise God when the marriage is restored and the family is mended.
- Anybody can praise God when you've got a good retirement, money in your wallet and money in the bank.
- Anybody can praise God when the battles over and your holding the giants head in your hand standing on his back.

But I'm telling you my friend; it takes something to shout in the face of the devil. It takes something to praise in the face of the doctors bad report. It takes something to shout when you don't have two nickels to rub together. It takes something when you're going through the fire, to lift your hands and lift up your voice and say…

I will bless the lord at all times; his praise shall continually be in my mouth.

The point is; don't wait till the battles over; shout now!

Start where you are. Start in the dark with the walls closing in on you.

_Start where you are lying in that hospital bed.

_Start where you are at the bottom of that pit.

_Start where you are in the middle of your pain.

_Start where you are in the inner prison at midnight, with your hands and your feet bound and your back bloody, beaten black and blue.

It may not be pretty (In fact it may be ugly) but give God an Ugly Praise.

The dictionary defines ugly as;

"Very unattractive or unpleasant to look at, offensive to the sense of beauty, displeasing in appearance, messy, offensive, objectionable".

How many know that some people have a problem with real praisers?

Real praisers get loud, real praisers can get undignified, real praisers can get messy; they don't worry about their hair or their makeup. Real praisers can get offensive to pretty praisers.

Pretty praisers know how to control their praise. Pretty praisers, never mess up their hair and their makeup never runs, they don't get loud and they wouldn't think of running or jumping, or dancing.

But God said to tell you; "He wants your Ugly Praise".

He wants it through your tears and your groans. He wants it while your heart is breaking. He wants it through your bloodshot eyes.

- He wants it when it don't make no sense.
- He wants it loud and he wants it crazy.
- He wants it when you're going through hell.
- He wants it when you don't feel a thing.

Yes He does my friend…

I'm trying to get passed this; but I feel like I'm talking to somebody reading this book right now, you've been trying to get everything prim and proper, you're waiting till everything is just perfect, you want to give God a fancy praise, you want to dress it all up and make it pretty.

But God said to tell you, don't worry about trying to pretty it up, Just give it up.

Give him your Ugly Praise!

Because he's going to use your UGLY PRAISE to get you out.

Job lost everything that he had; But after he had lost everything, his heart was breaking into a million pieces, it was more tragedy than any human being should ever have to endure, but in the middle of it all, "Job gave God an Ugly Praise".

The bible says… He arose, he rent his mantle, he shaved his head and he fell down on the ground and he worshipped.

It wasn't a pretty sight.

- He worshipped through tears.
- He worshipped through groans.

- He worshipped with a broken heart.
- He worshipped through his pain, through his confusion.

He gave God an Ugly praise and God gave him
a Beautiful future.

His worship kept him connected to his destiny, and in the end God blessed him with more than he had ever had in his life. God restored him and gave him double for his trouble.

We don't have the benefit of choosing the problems and trials and afflictions that come our way in life; it may be divorce, sickness, the loss of a loved one, debt, false accusations, betrayal.

But I can choose my praise.

- My weapon of choice is Praise.
- Praise is a weapon.

  You've got to learn how to use your weapon of praise.

You see the devils purpose for the pit is to kill your praise.

The devil hates your praise.

The devil knows (if you ever get your praise on he's in trouble).

See I have learned; if I can get my praise on, I can get the devil off.

Joseph was not the only man of God who ever found himself in a pit.

David Said: *He brought me up also out of an horrible pit, out of the miry clay, and set my feet upon a rock and established my goings... (Ps 40:2).*

Jeremiah the Prophet found himself in a horrible pit. *And Ebed-melech the Ethiopian said to Jeremiah: put now these old cast clouts and rotten rags under thine armholes under the cords, and Jeremiah did so... (Jer 38:12).*

They offered Jeremiah: Gods man, the Prophet of God, the mighty man of faith and power, old thrown out filthy rotten stinking rags.

And he put them under his arms and they lifted him out.
Somebody ain't gonna like this, but the reason some of you haven't got out of your pit yet is you're too proud.
Yeah you want to praise God on your terms. You want to praise God when something big happens. You want to praise God when you feel like it. You want to praise God when it makes sense.
You want to praise God moderately, conveniently, quietly.
Your pride is keeping you bound, your pride is keeping you in the pit, and your pride is keeping you from your miracle.
Isaiah 61:13 Put on the garment of praise for the spirit of heaviness.
He didn't say it would be easy, he didn't say it would feel good, he didn't say it would be pretty.
As a matter of fact it's pretty easy to see that he's talking about something very difficult. He's talking about moving out of heaviness into praise. He's talking about getting something off and putting something better on.
Dear reader, my praise may look like old rags to you, it may be extravagant, it may be extreme, it may be emotional, it may be loud, it may even be offensive, and some may even go so far as to call it ugly, (but that's alright: it was an Ugly praise that brought Joseph out of the pit. (It was an Ugly praise that brought Jeremiah out of the Pit).
It was an Ugly praise that brought Paul and Silas out of their Prison.
And God said he would use Ugly Praise to get me and to get you out of the pit, and turn my situation and your situation around.
I hope I'm talking to someone today who still has some old rags hanging in your closet, and you're not too proud to put on an Ugly praise, like Jeremiah.
I know we're all dressed up today smelling good, looking good (but don't throw away those old rags).
Jeremiah would tell you; don't throw away those old rags, God will use them to get you out.

David would tell you; don't throw away those old rags (God will use them to get you out of your pit).

After many years of the ark of God being absent from Israel David the King finally brings it home.

The ark symbolizes, the presence, the guidance, the protection, and the favor of God to his people.

David was so excited about bringing the ark back that the bible says... *He danced before the lord with all his might.*

(He danced right out of his Kingly Apparel).

Michael David's wife saw him dancing and despised him in her heart: (His praise embarrassed her).

2 Sam 6:20 Then David returned to bless his household. And Michal the daughter of Saul came out to meet David, and said, How glorious was the king of Israel to day, who uncovered himself to day in the eyes of the handmaids of his servants, as one of the vain fellows shamelessly <u>uncovereth himself!</u>

What she was saying was this; that was shameful, that was embarrassing, that was ugly and that was humiliating.

David could have said, you're right honey, that was no way for a King to act, I should have composed myself, I should have behaved myself better, I'm sorry that I embarrassed you.

<u>But he didn't.</u>

I'm paraphrasing now; what David said was... If you thought that was embarrassing, and if you thought that was shameful, and if you thought that was Ugly, you haven't seen anything yet!

2 Sam 6:21-22 And David said unto Michal, It was before the LORD, which chose me before thy father, and before all his house, to appoint me ruler over the people of the LORD, over Israel: therefore will I play before the LORD. 22 And I will yet be more vile than thus, and will be base in mine own sight: and of the maidservants which thou hast spoken of, of them shall I be had in honour.

What David was saying was; if you didn't like my last praise, if you thought my last praise was over the top, if you thought my last praise was embarrassing, if you thought my last praise was Ugly.

You aint seen nothing yet!

I wish somebody today would quit worrying about what everybody else thinks and just give God the best praise you have. Don't dress it up, don't pretty it up, don't tidy it up, just give it up.

Give him your Ugly Praise. It may look Ugly to somebody else and it may sound Ugly to somebody else, it may even sound ugly to you, but by the time it reaches the ears of God it sounds like angels singing.

- Joseph was in a pit and they expected him to die there; but an Ugly Judah got him out.
- Jeremiah was in a pit and they expected him to die there, but some Ugly rags got him out.
- Paul and Silas were in the Inner prison embarrassed, humiliated, beaten black and blue, but in the middle of their pain they gave God an Ugly Praise and God shook the prison off its foundations, and every cell was opened and every prisoners bonds were broken.

There are some people that expected you to die in the pit, but you're going to disappoint them, there's an anointing in you that's bigger than the pit.

There's a palace anointing in you.

When Joseph was thrown into the Pit it was empty, but he filled it with praise.

If they would have filled it with dirt it would have been his grave but he filled it with praise and he came out.

I prophesy to you today that you are coming out. "If you're not too proud to put on some old rags." If you're not too proud to put on an Ugly Praise.

You can praise your way out.
*You can shout your way out.
*You can dance your way out.
*You can run your way out.

You can fill your pit with praise, and when that pit gets filled with praise, it will spit you out. Just like the whale spit out Jonah.

When Jonah praised God; God told the whale to spit him out.

When Jonah Came out of that whales belly he wasn't pretty, but he was free, he was out.

He came out Ugly, but he came out.

Somebody's coming out today: Gods going to use your Ugly praise to turn it around.

56
I Hear The Sound Of The Abundance Of Rain

1 Kings 18:15-45

That means my ear has picked up a signal in the airwaves.

Sound = vibrations, my ear has picked up the vibration of something that is coming.

I can't see it, I can't touch it, I don't feel it but it's on the way.

How do I know it's coming this way?

Because it's getting louder all the time, (the closer it gets the louder it gets).

When a train is coming your way, you feel the vibrations before it arrives.

When large hail is coming your way, you can hear it blocks away.

When 120 men and women had gathered in the upper room waiting for the promised power, the bible says: Suddenly there came a sound from heaven like a mighty rushing wind and it filled all the house where they were sitting.

There was a sound: The sound was an indication (Something is coming).

Suddenly cloven tongues as fire appeared on each of them and they were all filled with the Holy Ghost and began to speak with other tongues as the Spirit gave them utterance.

I hear the sound of an abundance of rain: Elijah spoke those words in a place and a time where there had not been one drop of water from the sky or due on the ground, in 3 1/2 years.

What did that mean ? (Rain)

It meant: life, recovery restoration, the rivers will run again, fish will be caught again, the crops will grow again,, there will be joy where there has been sorrow, there will be laughter where there has been weeping.

God said to prophesy to you and tell you it's getting ready to rain, the rain is on it's way, I hear the abundance of rain.

That may not mean anything to some of you, but for somebody listening to my voice it means everything.

It's on the way, it's on the way, it's on the way (tell your neighbor, it's on the way) Help is on the way, the answer is on the way, the breakthrough is on the way.

There's just something powerful about knowing that it's on the way that puts a fire back in your belly and a fight in your spirit, it gives you the strength to hold on.

I don't know who I'm talking to but you prayed and you fasted, and you've cried and you've confessed the word and from every natural evidence (nothing has changed, and if the truth be known for many of you it's gotten worse).

But I came to tell you: Change is in the atmosphere, the rain is coming, restoration is coming, healing is coming, peace is coming, joy is coming,

I hear the sound of the Abundance of rain: I don't see any evidence, I don't see any sign, but I hear it.

Say it with me… the sound is the sign.

Faith cometh by hearing and hearing by the word of God.

There is a sound: The word sound does not just mean noise or racket.

It means PROCLAMATION!

It's a decree in the spirit realm.

You have to pick this up in the spirit.

This is the victory that overcometh the world, even our faith.

Somebody's faith is going to another level right now. Somebody who has been struggling through the wilderness of just enough and barely getting by is getting ready to go into overflow.

Somebody is going to change addresses in the Spirit today. Some of the stuff that used to hinder you, and used to pull you down, won't bother you anymore because you won't be living in that same neighborhood anymore.

I hear the sound of the abundance of rain.

What is the rain to you?

The rain is Gods power visiting your life in whatever area or areas are in drought, or in lack, or broken or empty.

The rain is God taking every plan, every plot and every scheme and every weapon that the devil has launched at you and turning it around for your good.

The simplest definition of all, is just answered prayer.

I wish somebody would prophesy, Gods gonna turn it around, now prophesy... God's gonna make it rain. Come on say it again: God's gonna make it rain.

The rain was on the way but there was work to be done: Ahab went to play and Elijah went to pray.

E.M. Bounds, one of the greatest men of prayer that ever lived said: God does nothing except in answer to prayer.

So if things seem to be stagnate around you and nothing seems to be moving, you better check your prayer temperature.

For every miracle, every breakthrough, every prodigal who comes home, every son or daughter who is delivered from drugs and perversion, somebody has to pray.

Elijah got himself in the birth position (head between his knees) and began to labor in prayer for what he heard in the Spirit.

He sent his servant out to look toward the sea for an answer: The sea represents the word of God.

You have to get your eyes on the word.

His servant returns the answer: I'm looking but I don't see any evidence of an answer to your prayer.

But Elijah just keeps on praying, he sends his servant back to the sea and while the servant is running Elijah is praying.

You just have to keep on praying. When you have a word from God in your spirit, you just have to keep on praying.

Daniel prayed for 20 days with no evidence whatsoever that God had heard him, but on the 21rst day the breakthrough came. Michael the warring angel broke into the battle and Gabriel got the message through.

God will do whatever it takes to get it to you, if you don't quit!

Keep on praying, keep on praising, keep on confessing, keep on tithing, and sowing, and singing and dancing.

Don't let the devil see you sweat.

Delay is not denial, Abraham was delayed 25 years but not denied. Joseph was delayed 15 years but not denied.

Lazarus was delayed for 4 days but not denied.

Hab 2:3 For the vision is yet for an appointed time, but at the end it shall speak, and not lie: (though it tarry) wait for it because it will surely come , it will not tarry.

Num 23:19 God is not a man that he should lie, nor the son of man that he should repent: if he said it he will do it and if he hath spoken it, he will bring it to pass.

Every time you pray you are putting pressure on the spirit realm and you are filling with expectancy the clouds that are bringing your blessings.

We don't pray because we feel like it, we don't pray just because it's the Christian thing to do, or because it sounds like a good idea.

We pray because we have an objective that can only be reached and can only be won and conquered through prayer.

Elijah is still praying: (head between his knees) prayer is serious business and hard work.

Somebody said one time: Many Christians pray with such lukewarmness and indifference and uncertainty that they wouldn't even recognize the answer to their prayer when it came.

Elijah's servant has brought back another negative report: but Elijah keeps praying.

Go back to the sea look again (spend some more time in the word) then come tell me what you see.

On the 7th time the servant comes back with the report: Behold there ariseth a little cloud out of the sea.

In other word: There was a little word that came up to me.

(A word from the word)

A Rhema word: A specific word, for a specific purpose, for a specific time.

If you've got a word you can make it through the storm.

If you've got a word you can dance in the fiery furnace.

If you've got a word you can sleep like a baby in a den of lions.

If you've got a word you can beat the famine with a little meal and a little oil.

If you've got a word you can walk on water.

Now shout it out: I've got a word!

It was so small: Like a mans hand, it didn't look like much but Elijah's faith grabbed hold of it.

There's something about faith that lets you see the greatness in little things.

Faith can see: A weapon of mass destruction in the jawbone of an ass.

Faith can see: A meal for a multitude in a sack lunch.

Faith can see: An oil business in a room full of empty jars.

Faith can see: A king in a simple smelly shepherd boy.

The servant saw a little cloud but Elijah saw a river filling, ground soaking, drought busting rainstorm.

I don't care how big the problem may seem to you, or how long it has existed: The promises of God come in concentrated form and one little word from God will set you free, and will destroy that thing forever.

Jesus said: All it takes is faith like the size of a mustard seed and you can command mountains to jump into the sea and they will have to go.

I feel some mountains starting to shake in here right now.

I feel some mountains losing their hold.

I feel some real mountain moving faith rising up right now.

(I HEAR THE SOUND OF THE ABUNDANCE OF RAIN)

I feel something shifting in the atmosphere right now

I prophesy to you right now the drought is breaking and the rain is on the way: Somebody reading this book right now... that drought in your finances is breaking, that long dry spell is over in Jesus name.

Somebody else: Your spirit has been dry for so long, and you've felt so distant from the presence of God… that drought is breaking now, the wind is blowing and the rain of Gods supernatural presence is flooding your soul right now, Just open up and let it fall on you.

Somebody else: You've been fighting a long battle with your health, it's raining, there's healing in the rain, receive your healing, and receive your breakthrough.

Somebody: You've been going through a long dry place with your family, it seems like it just gets worse and worse, (you try to love them, you try to embrace them, but they just push you away and run harder.) It's time for that drought to break, it's time for it to rain on your family) Your husband, your wife, your children and even your grandchildren are going to get wet.

Come on and just lift your hands and tell God: Send the rain; tell him you want the rain.

Zec 10:1 Ask ye of the LORD rain in the time of the latter rain; so the LORD shall make bright clouds, and give them showers of rain.

It's the time of rain: The anointing is flowing right now, the rain is falling, yokes are being destroyed, burdens are being lifted.

Joy is being restored, peace is being restored.

Elijah got off his knees and told Ahab: It's here, The rain is here, If you don't get that chariot rolling you aren't getting off this mountain.

And while Elijah was prophesying the wind blew and the clouds turned black and the rain came.

Elijah heard it with his spirit.

He prophesied it with his mouth.

He saw it with his eyes.

I prophesy to you right now: Somebody is getting ready to see a manifestation of what you have heard God say in your spirit.

You've been confessing it and believing it and a lot of people thought you were crazy, but you're getting ready to see it, because the drought is over and the rain is here.

Is there anybody who knows how to enjoy the rain? Is there anybody who knows how to dance in the rain?

They used to sing a chorus all the time when I was growing up (Send down the rain Lord)

It said there's joy in the rain Lord

Healing in the rain Lord

Then it said: There's dancing in the rain Lord

There's freedom in the rain Lord

Somebody needs to lift your hands right now and begin to praise him for that rain.

Praise him like a man in the desert who was dying for water and stumbled into an Oasis.

Praise him because the drought is over.

About The Author

*The Author: Terry Sisney has been in
ministry for over thirty-five years, he has spoken
in conferences, camp meetings and revivals.
With a teaching and preaching ministry that focuses on the
maturing of the saints. He and his wife Pam
have been in ministry together for over 30 years,
they have ministered side by side
in full time evangelistic
and pastoral ministry.*

Terry Sisney

Other Books By Author

You're Supposed To Win
Fire From Heaven
Keep On Walking
A New Chapter
Taking It Back
The Indispensable Gift-Holy Spirit
Abundant Life Lessons
More Power To You
When You Pray
Armed And Dangerous
Ugly Praise
When The Tomb Becomes A Womb
A Winners Portrait
You Can Fly
Prosperity Road
You Have The Advantage Now
Anointed For The Battle
Positioned For Abundance
Secrets Of A Giant Killer
Trial By Fire
The Prophet In Your Valley
I Shall Not Be Moved

Sermons Forged In The Fire

For Busy Pastors

By

Terry Sisney

Books can be ordered from my website
"terrysisneyhigherlifebooks.com"
or Amazon.com

Author can be contacted by e-mail
twsisney@yahoo.com
Or
Terry Sisney
1120 Brighton Ave
Grover Beach Ca. 93433

Please Include Prayer Requests When You Write

For more information visit our website

terrysisneyhigherlifeministries.com

Made in the USA
Las Vegas, NV
29 November 2021

35598368R00226